ESSAYS
IN HONOR OF
JAMES EDWARD WALSH

ESSAYS
IN HONOR OF
JAMES EDWARD WALSH

On His Sixty-Fifth Birthday

CAMBRIDGE:

The Goethe Institute of Boston
and The Houghton Library

1983

Design and Typography by Susan Marsh, Cambridge, Massachusetts.
Composed in Sabon types on the Mergenthaler Linotron 202;
Printed on Mohawk Superfine;
Bound with Brillianta Cloth and Dresden Ingres Endpapers.

Contents

Illustrations

vii

Acknowledgments

QUITE APART from the necessity for secrecy — reminiscent of school-days, when the arrival of one or another companion might lead to valiant shifts in the topic of conversation — the production of a festschrift is surely an affair for amateurs; heaven forbid that there should ever be a professional editor of such collections! Thorough incompetents, we gratefully acknowledge the expert advice and assistance of those whose business is the production of books: of Susan Hayes of the Harvard University Press, who helped in the planning and costing, and showed us how these things begin; and of Susan Marsh, the designer, who "had never done a book with so many footnotes," but who imperturbably knew how it should handsomely look. DEKR Corporation of Woburn, Massachusetts composed it; Mercantile Printing Company of Worcester, Massachusetts printed it; and New Hampshire Bindery of Concord, New Hampshire bound it.

For the frontispiece, we were fortunate to secure the services of James Hodgson; one of the editors (not illustrated) stood to the hon-orand's left while he unconsciously posed for the picture. Rick Stafford of the Fogg Art Museum worked and reworked plates, producing one to order in a few hours, from books and manuscripts in our collections. William H. Bond laid even Thomas Hollis aside to produce the illustrations for Anne Anninger's essay. We are also grateful to the Special Collections of Indiana University Library and to the Boston Public Library for permission to reproduce books in their possession. John Lancaster and Ruth Mortimer, both former colleagues, prepared the index in idle moments spared from their avocations at Smith, Amherst, and the *Papers of the Bibliographical Society of America*.

None of this would have been possible without the astute imagination of Arthur Vershbow, an old and unfailing friend of Houghton, who first suggested the alliance with the Goethe Institute; still more, we thank its director, Dr. Gerhard Kirchoff, who sponsored our joint proposal, for his patient diplomacy, sure understanding, and warm support: *hoc juvat, et melli est, non mentiar.* As costs mounted with inflation and plans withered and bloomed, the anxiety of the editors was agreeably relieved by a generous subvention from the Harvard German Department, and by the munificence of William Bentinck-Smith, Mr. and Mrs.

ix

Arthur Vershbow, Mr. and Mrs. Philip J. McNiff, and of a donor who wishes to remain anonymous. A loan from the Publications Fund of the Department of Printing and Graphic Arts provided much-needed cash, as these negotiations were going forward; and we are happy to celebrate the birthday of our honored colleague not only with this festschrift, but also with a Symposium commemorating the 150th anniversary of Goethe's death, sponsored jointly with the Goethe Institute, at which Rodney Dennis and Robert Spaethling will read their essays, together with a fresh contribution by Eugene Weber.

Gladly would we claim to match this material aid with answerable spiritual gifts; but in truth, that side of our enterprise was already richly funded by the wide acquaintance and scholarly example of the dedicatee who, even as we industriously labored over our jots and tittles, was preparing with Eugene Weber yet another exhibition, on Goethe. It was not difficult to assemble contributions in such a cause:

> Des Menschen Tätigkeit kann allzuleicht erschlaffen,
> Er liebt sich bald die unbedingte Ruh;
> Drum geb' ich gern ihm den Gesellen zu,
> Der reizt und wirkt und muss als Teufel schaffen.

Die Gesellen: H. A.
R. G. D.

x

ESSAYS
IN HONOR OF
JAMES EDWARD WALSH

James Edward Walsh:
A Tribute

WILLIAM H. BOND

THE TRUE scholar-librarian is a very special breed, and in many ways James E. Walsh is the archetype of the species. The presence of such an expert on its staff lends distinction to the institution lucky enough to enjoy his services, and makes its collections more useful and more intelligible to the readers who consult them. A good bibliographer is trained to observe, to analyze, and to describe, and must have the inborn ability to carry out these exacting functions with more than ordinary acuteness. How to enumerate the requisite qualifications? Fortunately, in 1972 James Walsh himself summarized his work and his objectives in terms that could scarcely be bettered, revelatory of his own high standards of professionalism and scholarly service:

> To continue building, by discriminate book-selection, the great collections begun by our predecessors in the Harvard College Library; to make those collections more available than they have previously been to the international company of scholars by cataloguing of the highest quality; to be concerned for the physical maintenance of the printed book collections to ensure their preservation for posterity; and, as time and opportunity permit, to interpret individual items in the collections by solving particular bibliographical problems they may pose and publishing the results.

This statement is no idle boast. Bookmen of such calibre must be both born and made; innate talents must be developed by training, application, and circumstance. So they have been in the case of James Walsh.

He was born on January 8, 1918, and after secondary education he took the bachelor's degree at Northwestern University in Classics and English in 1943, earning the distinction of election to Phi Beta Kappa. He then came to Harvard University, part-time as a graduate student in Classics but primarily as skilled assistant to Professor Werner Jaeger in

I

the Institute for Classical Studies, working closely with Jaeger in the edition of Gregory of Nyssa as well as in Jaeger's other scholarly projects. In 1949, he joined the staff of the Houghton Library, becoming head cataloguer in the Department of Printed Books in 1951. In 1965, he took the more accurately descriptive title of Keeper of Printed Books, which better reflected the multifarious duties and responsibilities he had assumed. More learned than many a doctor, he could add to the old Harvard chestnut "Who would examine me?" a further and more daunting query, "And in which fields?"

For, although his principal work has been in Greek, Latin, and German, he is also thoroughly competent in French and Italian, and is no stranger to Spanish and Dutch: not only the languages, but also their history and literature. A Fulbright Fellowship in Vienna in 1958–59 led to a love of that city and a knowledge of its culture and history that culminated in a distinguished exhibition and catalogue, *Vienna 1888–1938* (1967), in collaboration with Professor Eugene M. Weber. A later product, fulfilling his ideal of service to international scholarship and resulting from the studies he pursued and the contacts he made during his Fulbright tenure, was the authoritative catalogue, *1848 Austrian Revolutionary Broadsides and Pamphlets . . . in the Houghton Library* (Boston, 1976).

No more critical audience exists than the scholarly antiquarian booksellers and librarians of the world, and he has been known and respected by them for many years — greatly to the profit of Harvard collections. His knowledge of the strengths and weaknesses of our collections has made his biennial sweep of the European bookstores immensely effective. Booksellers have been known to put by extraordinary volumes in anticipation of his visit, because they know he will recognize their importance, and they know, too, that their books will join distinguished company already placed on Harvard's shelves through his efforts. Others do not wait for his European trips, but write or cable when an unusual opportunity occurs, knowing from previous conversations that the significance of their finds will be fully appreciated. In a field where books emerge one at a time and the chance to acquire them may never recur during a lifetime, the value of such a person to a scholarly library cannot be overestimated.

In addition to such work, James Walsh has selected and trained several generations of cataloguers to his own high standards, and has monitored their work to ensure its quality and consistency. He has also found the time — "made" might be a juster word — to mount scholarly exhibitions and prepare catalogues of them with the status of reference works; to write and publish learned articles in several languages and on a wide variety of topics; and to review technical publications with easy authority.

All this sounds formidable to a degree, and conceals the humane qualities that underlie his thoroughgoing professionalism. Some of these emerge in the answer to another question to which he responded a decade ago: to state the personal qualifications and characteristics that should be present in a candidate for such a position as his:

> Meticulousness in attention to detail combined with an ability to grasp the totality of the purpose and aims of a rare book library; patience; persistence in pursuing information, even when it is elusive; willingness to work more than you are paid for; kindness in the face of human failings but firmness in the maintenance of high standards of human performance.

The reader will note that he also commands a muscular prose style. But there is a good deal more than this, and outside the library. He has a broadly based knowledge and love of the fine arts, and an expert's appreciation and delight in music, especially opera and *Lieder*; he is as meticulous in his appearance and in his home as he is in his scholarship; he is a gourmet cook, whose creations are fallen upon with cries of joy by those fortunate to share them; and he is a warm friend and the pleasantest of companions, with a wry wit that illuminates the occasions that call it forth. Such qualities make the character of the institution where they are brought to bear, and the Houghton Library has profited immeasurably from thirty-five years of association with James Edward Walsh.

Publications

ARTICLES

"The Chronology of the First Volumes of Herder's *Christliche Schriften*," *Harvard Library Bulletin*, 2 (1948), 403–405.

"The California and Oregon Trail: A Bibliographical Study," *The New Colophon*, 3 (1949), 279–285.

"William Penn Stops the Press," *Harvard Library Bulletin*, 5 (1951), 94–99.

"An Experiment in the Selection of Library Books for Storage," *Harvard Library Bulletin*, 8 (1954), 378–381.

'American Printings of Longfellow's "The Golden Legend", 1851–55,' *Papers of the Bibliographical Society of America*, 57 (1963), 81–88.

With Gedeon Borsa: "Eine gedruckte Selbstbibliographie von Johannes Sambucus," *Magyar Könyvszemle*, 1965, 2. számából, pp. [128]–133.

"Another Variant Page in the Gutenberg Bible," *Gutenberg Jahrbuch*, 1965, pp. 68–72.

"The Librarian's Library: The William A. Jackson Bibliographical Collection," *The Book Collector*, 14 (1965), 499–510, & 15 (1966), 35–45; also reprinted as a separate (23p.), 1966.

"Erasmus: *Von Walfart*, 1522," *Harvard Library Bulletin*, 16 (1968), 274–277.

"Contemporary Collectors XLV: Notes on the Philip Hofer Reference Collection," *The Book Collector*, 18 (1969), 159–169.

'The *Querela Pacis* of Erasmus: The "Lost" French Translation,' *Harvard Library Bulletin*, 17 (1969), 374–384.

With Philip Hofer: "A New Holbein Attribution," *Harvard Library Bulletin*, 23 (1975), 42–48.

"Contributions to the Bibliography of Heinrich Heine," *Philobiblon*, xxv/3 (1981), [181]–183.

"Variant Readings in the First Editions of Stefan George's *Algabal*," *Harvard Library Bulletin*, 29 (1981), 215–217.

EXHIBITION CATALOGUES

With Eugene M. Weber: *Vienna 1888–1938: An Exhibition* (Cambridge, Mass., 1967).

Erasmus on the 500th Anniversary of his Birth (Cambridge, Mass., 1969).

With Eugene M. Weber: *Goethe, 1749–1832: An Exhibition at the Houghton Library* (Cambridge, Mass., 1983).

HOUGHTON LIBRARY CATALOGUES

With Eugene M. Weber: *The Hofmannsthal Collection in the Houghton Library: A Descriptive Catalogue of Printed Books* (Heidelberg [1974]).

1848 Austrian Revolutionary Broadsides and Pamphlets: A Catalogue of the Collection in the Houghton Library (Boston [1976]).

Mazarinades: A Catalogue of the Collection of 17th-Century French Civil War Tracts in the Houghton Library (Boston [1976]).

REVIEWS

Letters of Eric Gill: *New York Times Book Review* (March 6, 1949), p. 3.

Oxford Classical Dictionary: *New York Times Book Review* (April 3, 1949), p. 5.

Max Radin, *Epicurus My Master: New York Times Book Review* (April 10, 1949), p. 7.

G. G. Sedgewick, *Of Irony, Especially in Drama: New York Times Book Review* (April 24, 1949), p. 15.

John Lempriere, *Lempriere's Classical Dictionary of Proper Names: New York Times Book Review* (July 17, 1949), p. 4.

Donald Gallup, *T. S. Eliot, A Bibliography: The Book Collector*, 1 (1952), 273–274.

Rudolf Hirsch, *Printing, Selling, and Reading, 1450–1550: Speculum*, 43 (1968), 344.

Adrian and J. L. Wilson, *The Making of the Nuremberg Chronicle: Papers of the Bibliographical Society of America*, 72 (1978), 147–149.

Martin Boghardt, *Analytische Druckforschung: Papers of the Bibliographical Society of America*, 73 (1979), 380–383.

Robert P. Bareikis, *The Transition to Modern Germany: The Eighteenth Century, An Exhibition, 1975: The Eighteenth Century: A Current Bibliography*, n.s. 2.

Johannes Gutenbergs zweiundvierzigzeilige Bibel, Faksimile-Ausgabe: *Papers of the Bibliographical Society of America,* 75 (1981), 107–110.

Gedeon Borsa, *Clavis typographorum librariorumque Italiae, 1465–1600: Papers of the Bibliographical Society of America* (forthcoming).

EDITIONS

Gustav Schwab, *Gods and Heroes,* tr. Olga Marx & Ernst Morwitz; introd. by Werner Jaeger (New York, 1947).

With William H. Bond: William A. Jackson, *An Annotated List of the Publications of the Rev. Thomas Frognall Dibdin* (Cambridge, Mass., 1965).

H . A .

Library History and the History of Books: Two Fields of Research for Librarians

PAUL RAABE

"BOOKS AND SOCIETY in History": the theme of a conference, Boston, July 1980, forms my contribution to James Walsh's festschrift. The subject is a challenge for librarians. It implies questions that those, particularly at libraries which contain historical holdings and source material, are well-placed to answer. I welcome the opportunity to take a thorough look at the present situation of the librarian's profession and to consider the possibilities open for the librarian today, to apply himself *ex officio* to questions pertaining to library and book history. As a librarian who, for more than thirty years, has regarded library history and the history of books unquestionably as an integral part of his professional work, I feel obliged to try to show whether, how, and with what degree of success the librarian's research in these fields can benefit academic learning and promote cultural projects.

I

In the European view, the librarian was originally in the truest sense of the word a scholar, a connoisseur of books who was fully familiar with the content and form of the books in his care, who knew every bit as much about how they came into being as he did about their authors and their authors' works. Numerous examples spring to mind dating from ancient times, from Callimachus in Alexandria on to the monks in the Middle Ages and the learned librarians of the early modern age: one only needs to think of Bernard de Montfaucon, the founder of paleography, or of Richard Bentley in Cambridge, the classical philologist, of the German philosopher Gottfried Wilhelm Leibniz, of the Italian historian, Ludovico Antonio Muratori, of the brothers Grimm and many others.

All of them were not only curators of books, but also well-known scholars of books in their time, learned men who, stimulated by their

7

libraries, increased the historical and philological knowledge of their age, furthered learning, and were thus instrumental in perpetuating tradition.

To recall such figures today would seem tantamount to reflecting on a profession whose situation has completely changed under the conditions imposed by industrialization and, more significantly, by technical and economic development. The reading of books has long since ceased to be the privilege of the upper classes; on the contrary, it is a skill taken for granted by most members of democratic and socialistic societies and states. Books are no longer solely means of communicating learned knowledge, but have become the media of instruction, education and entertainment. Consequently, libraries are no longer exclusively enclaves of scholarly work, but are institutions for the supplying of books to all classes and groups in the population. This has understandably enough led to a change in attitude towards what constitutes the librarian's profession and the librarian's image.

The more numerous libraries have become and the more diverse their duties, the more the situation of librarians today has changed. They are at work in university libraries, academic institutions, national, state and municipal research libraries, or in public libraries, of every conceivable dimension and specialized field. The library scene in the world is characterized by a vast variety of forms; they are not standardized institutions of scholarship and education; they bear the stamp of individuality. The two larger categories, research and public libraries, no longer stand opposed to each other, but are rather alternative manifestations of the same spirit, one more for an academically inclined public, the other more for a public seeking general education or entertainment.

In light of this, the librarian's relation to the sciences today should be obvious: in research libraries, where scholarship is promoted, his commitment to it must surely be deeper and taken more for granted than in public libraries, where knowledge is popularized. But in practice this is not the case. The predominance of administration, acquisition, cataloguing and making the holdings available, together with the services offered the user, lead, under the technocratic exigencies of the modern world, to activities and professional duties that no longer permit close academic involvement. The mastery of technical systems, the familiarization with computer science, presuppose aptitudes which are hardly compatible with the image of scholars devoted to books. The librarian regards himself more and more as a supplier of information, a bearer of data. The library, in modern society, is looked upon and run as an information and perhaps even as a communication center. One attempts, primarily, to supply the demand for information and assesses the book less for its own worth than as a part of a system or as only one medium among others. This, of course, leads to the librarian's alienation from the book and, by the same token, from academic work. The direct bond between the librarian and the scholars is often lost: the more manifold the divisions of work become in the running of the library, the more difficult it appears to be to establish a partnership between library science and scholarship.

Considering the conditions created by these developments, affecting all spheres of life, it is easy enough to understand how the librarian has become alienated and withdrawn from the historical world as a whole. The librarian, who, as a scholar, should be at home in the historical world, is in danger of becoming an outsider in a society geared to professional success, tolerated rather than respected, sometimes even ridiculed, a bookworm, who isn't easily integrated into the world of material achievement.

But our prime concern is the defense of this historically inclined, academically active librarian, the defense of his world, his work, his future, in the face of a professional image increasingly characterized and determined by administrative duties far removed from productive academic work. No librarian — wherever he may be — would deny that these daily chores have to be done. But one should also recognize the fact that the academically active librarian is honoring an indispensable commitment in libraries. It must repeatedly be made clear that libraries — as Goethe put it — were and have remained the memory of mankind. Without libraries there would ultimately be no history. The past— what has happened, what has been achieved, what has been thought, what has been experienced — is handed down through books. When one burns down libraries, one destroys the memory of man. The problem has to be looked at from this ideological point of view: librarians are not only suppliers of books; they are also preservers and guardians of tradition. Tradition, by the way, sets in early: each present becomes the past, and within a very few decades even newly founded libraries have a history.

The librarian is preserver and guardian: such an office requires training and an interest in history; it arouses the desire actively to promote historical research. This type of librarian still regards himself as a link in the long chain of scholarly tradition outlined at the beginning of my talk. The education of the librarian, about which a considerable amount was written in Germany at the beginning of the nineteenth century, must include an historical component: a knowledge of the history of books and of libraries, of scholars and of scholarship. On the basis of these prerequisites, the librarian should be a connoisseur of books, a representative of scholarly culture, a promoter of scholarship, a transmitter of what has been handed down in books.

This type of librarian is more akin in spirit to the archivist and the museum curator than to the administrator. Archives preserve and make available the unpublished historical material that has been handed down to us; museums house the works of art that mirror human life in its most sublime forms of expression. Libraries, archives and museums are places where our cultural legacy and the works that have been handed down through the ages are collected and preserved, cared for, and made accessible. These, then, are the areas of work in which one could expect the librarian to be involved.

My reflections are restricted to only the one sector: research *in* the library and, on the other hand, research *on* the library. Implied here are the two closely allied historical disciplines, library history and book history, for which the librarian no less than other scholars, might shape his career. But before going into the political consequences this would have for the profession in the future, let us take a closer look at each of these fields. Only when one realizes the extent of the area to be covered, will one see that there is nothing anachronistic about the plea for the academically active librarian — on the contrary, it is an extremely actual and burning question, which is becoming more and more pressing in many countries today.

2

Firstly, then: library history as a research area for the librarian. It is not necessary to describe the field *ex cathedra*, since any librarian can take the sphere of his own library as a starting point, and the information he gleans, spurred on by professional curiosity, will quickly lead to his being able to determine the historical position of his own institution, which, even if newly founded, will have built up a history within a few years. A library is not only a public service organization, such as a post office; it is also, and always has been, an intellectual and cultural center, whose immediate environment and the changes it has undergone can throw light on the forces of change generally. An interest in history then, is a prerequisite from the outset, and even the self-portrait of one library has a ·significance which reaches far beyond the bounds of that one institution. In other words, the librarian who investigates the history or phases of the history of "his" library is not pursuing an isolated line of research, but contributing in some way to the whole.

The whole: that is, to the interrelated library world, of which each institution is a part, whether the link be subject-specialization, or geographical, or political. What is meant, in the first place, is the contribution to the understanding of how a particular type of library, according to its specialization, has developed. The history of *one* public library contributes to the research of public libraries as a whole: the single study is a necessary means of gaining insight into the overall connections and common traits, and into historical changes of a general nature. At the same time, the history of *one* library provides material for the history of national interconnections. In this way one can gradually gain an overall view of the history of the libraries of any one country. It is clear, of course, that a generalization can only be made where justified. The history of the English college libraries, the German university libraries, the Danish or the American public libraries can be written. One will only be able to study particularities in specialization and ultimately even national particuliarities by examining processes of historical change.

The next step leads to international studies of library history on the basis of comparison, but also on the basis of common bonds. Library history is no more a national discipline than the history of knowledge itself. The aim, as in all historical research, is insight into universal relations. It is actually self-evident that the highest goal should be the international and universal aspect, for the national particularities can be regarded as variations of the general historical and human development. We all know that such demands are easier posed than met. Nevertheless one shouldn't neglect to emphasize the fact that this is the intention of historical research, and therefore also the intention of research into library history.

"Little by little the bird builds its nest," as the old proverb says. Research in library history, like any piece of historical work, proceeds from the investigation of the particular, the specific, the single case. The general presentation of interconnections can only be the result, the summary of a considerable number of individual studies and investigations.

One must realize at the outset that the development of libraries is determined by the tasks imposed upon them and therefore by the type of library they represent. Research and public libraries have differing areas of specialization and this applies, on the other hand, also to the various types of libraries, such as national libraries, university libraries, etc.

Within this framework, embracing all specific types of libraries, library history can be split up into individual subject areas.

HOLDINGS The history of holdings shows the development of the book-collection. It also affords insight into the history of private libraries, in as much as they initially formed the basis of public libraries. The history of holdings is the history of collections, a reflection of how the books housed in a library were brought together. The history of holdings is also the history of acquisition, and this mirrors the general development of a library.

CATALOGUES Catalogue history is the history of how the holdings collected in a library were made available to the user. This reveals to what extent the librarians were willing to make their collections accessible and usable. The history of catalogues, from the point of view of the history of knowledge, is also of considerable relevance. The study of specialized catalogues and means employed in making the holdings available, e.g. the compiling of manuscript catalogues, carries over into the field of the history of scholars.

LIBRARY USE The history of the using of a library implies the task of investigating and describing the use of a library in the course of its history: it is also historical reader-research and affords the opportunity of obtaining information about the reader and reading in early times. This aspect too is of general significance for the history of knowledge and learning.

LIBRARY BUILDINGS The history of library buildings should also be classified as a subject in its own right — library architecture has a long history. The analysis of innovative buildings of earlier times, as well as the study of the structural principles, can be very revealing in regard to the rôle of a library in the society in which it is located.

LIBRARY STAFF The history of library staff is the history of the librarians. In older accounts of library history, the phases of the library's development are always marked by the succession of librarians. Today we view the development in a less personal light. Nevertheless, a library's staff history, mostly in the form of biographical, individual studies, is an indispensable contribution to the understanding of the fate of a book-collection. On the other hand, such biographical studies are also the prerequisites for a history, still unwritten, of the librarian profession.

LIBRARY ADMINISTRATION To round off the systematization of the history of libraries, one ought actually to call one subject area the "history of library administration", for, in summarized presentations, aspects of the ever-changing administrative policies play an essential part. The investigation of the relationship between a library and its governing body alone provides valuable information on the status of a library in the social or state context. Even the analysis of the library's regulations within the legal situation of a library belong to the tasks involved in library-history research.

The basis of these single case studies of the history of individual libraries, of whatever type or specialization, is the perusal and examination of the historical sources. The greater the yields of handed-down source material, the more comprehensive the insight into the history of a library.

I should like to use one example, that of my own library, the Herzog August Library in Wolfenbüttel, to elucidate the different kinds of sources and their usefulness. In a library whose archives date back to the seventeenth century, various forms of source material are available.

For the history of holdings, there are, to begin with, the acquisition records, kept since the seventeenth century, which describe the course of the purchasing policy. In addition, there are the annual balance sheets, required by the governing body, and the collections of receipts for purchases made through booksellers or second-hand book-dealers. But the basic stock of the library, Duke August's collection of books, was not only supplemented by single purchases, but also by the acquisition of a number of complete private collections, mostly princely libraries. The catalogues of these libraries, mostly handwritten, are not only sources from which one can deduce the significance of a collection and how it was built up; they are, at the same time, invaluable sources for research on private libraries as a whole.

The old catalogues, which are no longer in use, have, of course, been preserved. They, together with the catalogue volumes still in use today, provide the reliable, basic material for research in catalogue history.

As the lending records since 1666 have been preserved in full, they too provide basic material for the detailed study of both the using and the use of an old ducal collection: the social strata of the users, the specialized subjects they were interested in, and their hobbies. Apart from the personal aspect, one can also ascertain the importance of particular frequently borrowed books and thus contribute to historical reader-research.

Furthermore, the visitors' books of the library, the destination of a great number of library tours since the seventeenth century, are excellent sources for the study of library history. From the entries one can gain insight into the renown and international standing of the library.

Of course the files and the correspondence between the librarians and the scholars, or the official bodies, are essential sources in library history, both for the history of the using of the library and for the general history of library administration. Such archival documentary materials is also necessary for the study of the acquisition policy. Lastly, it provides information on the librarians themselves, their activities, their interests, their successes, and their failures.

It is a great help that pictorial material has also been handed down in library archives: old prints, ground plans, photos of rooms and persons, the illustrated history of a library; objects used in past eras have also been handed down: typewriters from around 1900, official seals, library material, card files, book-trolleys etc.

Finally, the holdings that have been handed down are themselves an important source for library history. They are the most vital illustration of how a library has developed; particularly when the older sections — as is the case in the Herzog August Library in Wolfenbüttel — are complete and displayed *en bloc* to the public, a visual presentation of tradition. Besides, collections displayed in their entirety in a library enable one to gain particularly clear insight into the history of the holdings. Now, very few libraries house such a wealth of material for the study of library history as is to be found in Wolfenbüttel. Nevertheless, the kinds of sources I have just mentioned recur in general over and over again. The relevant material for university libraries can certainly be found in the university archives, just as material in the state and communal archives can supplement the archives of public libraries.

Younger libraries will be able to research and describe their history primarily by means of files, printed and handwritten annual reports and accession records. In addition, of course, the printed material on the subject, books about the libraries and articles in periodicals and newspapers, are useful source material.

The results of research work in library history, based on a broader study of the sources, provide contributions to one single library or to one type of library: in any case, such individual studies are the prerequisite for the comprehensive presentations of library history, the great works on library history, which are being and always have been written in all ages in all countries.

Such works are not only the finest testimony of the librarian's efforts in the field of library history, they contribute on the other hand, to the history of a country's academic and cultural institutions, i.e. to the history of scholarship in the case of research libraries and to the history of general education in the case of public libraries. Since libraries are also centers of intellectual communication, it is obvious that social history too can profit from such library-history studies.

To summarize briefly, it could be said that library history, regarded as the librarian's field of work, not only increases the knowledge about one's own library, but in addition can show the importance of libraries in the overall cultural development and thus secure them the place in history they deserve. It is clear that it must be in the interest of the librarian to work towards this goal. The preoccupation with library history is also regarded as an important task with respect to library politics, a subject which I shall discuss in detail at the conclusion of my paper.

3

It has been shown that the holdings of a library are excellent sources for library history. They are, of course, even more valuable with regard to the history of books. Libraries hand down certainly the most evident basic material for research in book history: the individual books are the starting-point for the researcher of book history; they are what he examines from various points of view, i.e. the printing or the publishing company, the illustration of the book or the binding.

As preserver and curator of books, the sources of book history, the librarian could have a more comprehensive knowledge of the subject than other scholars of book history, who have benefitted from the research done to date, and should continue to do so. One only needs to recall the fact that for centuries research on medieval manuscripts has been the domain of librarians, as has been the case with research on early prints and incunabula.

Our plea in this connection is for the recognition of libraries as the place where book history is handed down, and for the recognition of librarians as the historians of books. We shall have to raise the question at a later stage whether or not our plea is futile. In any case, it must first be decided what book history or "Geschichte des Buchwesens", as we call it in Germany, really implies.

Following the approach of the sciences of communication, one regards the book as a medium, proceeding from author to reader, between production and distribution. Book history no longer describes historical circumstances alone; on the contrary, the focus is on questions of historical change. Book history ought to be in the position to make a greater contribution to the history of economics and culture. In this aim, to integrate such a specialized historical discipline into a general context, we in Germany feel encouraged when we look at the results of English and American, French and Dutch research over the last few years. Admittedly, the librarian's strength will lie more in promoting detailed research in book history than in compiling summaries.

This detailed research applies to numerous specialized fields of book history. One can name eight fields based on the areas of production and distribution:

BOOK-MANUSCRIPTS The history of the writing of books: this discipline, today the prerogative of philologists, should be approached to a greater extent from points of view pertaining to book history. The question of book-manuscripts, the manner in which the manuscripts for the printer came into being, and also the relationship between the author and the publisher are aspects that can be examined by studying the source material which has been handed down. Precisely the posthumous, unpublished works preserved in libraries can be evaluated from these points of view.

BOOK PRODUCTION The history of book production is the classic field of book history. But it is not solely a question of the technical aspect: composing and proof-reading are also part of it, as are the questions of the letter-font and the typography. Besides, we still have only a very cursory knowledge of the history of book printing. A typical area of work for librarians in the field of the history of book production is provided by "descriptive bibliography", as it is termed in English, i.e. research into the questions of multiple copies of the same work, in order to classify their variations.

BOOK ILLUSTRATION The history of book illustration and decoration is closely connected with book production. However, the history of book illustration, ornamentation, initial letters, vignettes and publishers' marks in books are research areas in their own right, for which one is particularly dependent upon a thorough knowledge of the books themselves.

PRINTING BASES The history of the material used for the printing base applies particularly to the history of paper, an independent discipline, often studied without reference to book history. But research in this field, as in the other fields already mentioned, belongs to our domain. For example, without a knowledge of the subject of watermarks, historical printing research is impossible.

BOOK BINDINGS The history of bookbindings is also a classic field for librarians, whose preoccupation with the works that have been handed down enables them to study certain bindings and bookbinders. The field involves questions relating to the craftsmanship of old bindings, aesthetic problems, and also questions relating to the binder's trade, what tasks he undertook and what he accomplished, in a word, the activity of the artisan and salesman in times of change over the centuries.

BOOK-TRADE The history of the book-trade: this has long been one of the main research fields of book history. According to the methods of economic and social history, individual firms are studied, or, on the other hand, the trading transactions of a town or a country over a limited period of time are analyzed. The history of the book-trade is an extensive research field. It includes the history of publishing companies, the history of bookshops, of the retail book-trade, or second-hand bookshops, as well as the history of book-clubs and book-trade organizations.

CRITICISM The history of book criticism should also be included in a systematic listing, even if it is a research area for literary and journalistic scholars on the one hand, and for economic historians on the other.

READING Lastly, the history of reading, i.e. research into the historical evolution of reading, is a more recent branch of studies in book history. Its purpose is to research the reading habits and social classes of readers in earlier times as well as to establish the extent to which books were used for cultural and academic learning, or for general education and entertainment.

Apart from these systematic aspects, one can also apply formal criteria to the study of book history: not only production and distribution in general in its various contexts has to be researched, but one must remember that the scholar of book history has to do with all manner of types of books and their historical development, with periodicals and almanacs, newspapers and broadsheets. Moreover, the word "book" is a general term covering numerous varying kinds of content: there are scientific and instructive books, literary works and publications for pure entertainment. Each type has its own history. To name but a few examples: dictionaries and commentaries, Bibles and prayer books, books for daily use, namely school texts, cookery books, children's books, readers, poetry books and so on. Each type of book has undergone changes in the course of the centuries: to investigate these changes is one of the tasks of book history.

A large number of research projects has been cited: one should balance this list against a list of completed projects, but this would be too extensive a task to undertake here. Broadly speaking, however, it should be emphasized that comprehensive research literature, general and specific studies and analyses on questions pertaining to book history, are available in countries which have a long-standing book tradition. To become familiar with these main works should be one of the first requirements for those who have books in their charge today.

The librarian should not only know the elementary facts in the various fields of book history, but he should also be able to familiarize himself with the most important results of recent research in these areas. Without this knowledge, a librarian is blind to the way in which he approaches the wealth of tradition handed down and entrusted to him. Only when he has attained to a specialist's knowledge of book history, can he assess the significance of the books among which he works. A knowledge of books ought to be the distinguishing mark of the librarian in the historical sector too.

It should not be difficult, then, for the librarian to take the step from specialized knowledge in book history to participation in research in the field, if he is interested in his subject. As in library history, he will take his own milieu as a starting point. The books of his library are the most accessible sources for manifold questions relating to book history. He can use the library's copies to follow up the history of individual types of books, or he can follow up the reader records, or establish the significance of any particularly rare book. In any case, the books in one's own library provide the incentive for the involvement with history. At the same time it is clear that mediaeval manuscripts and incunabula have long since ceased to be the only center of interest: the librarian's interest will be aroused by the books of all centuries, right up to the most recent past. Particularly the latter deserves the special attention of librarians: the twentieth-century history of printing and publishing, of the book-trade and of the reading public are especially comprehensive projects, that still lie before us.

Book history, regarded as a librarian's task, has as little to do with library-political narcissism as has library history. It is not a form of *l'art pour l'art* but a contribution to the research of our historical world in its cultural context. Particularly book history provides exemplary contributions for many other historical disciplines. Books are objects of trade: book history, then, illustrates a segment of the history of commerce, and its study affords insight into general developments in economic history. With regard to the technical history, studies on those involved with the production and distribution of books, the typesetter and printer, the salesman and publisher, can enrich our view of socio-historical relations. But above all, book history has its share in the history of literature and art, and ultimately, in the history of knowledge and of cultural education.

Evidently, however indispensable the knowledge of book history, as one of the tools of the trade, might be to the librarian in his dealings with borrowers engaged in historical study, the part it plays in historical research in the broader context is equally indispensable.

Libraries, then, can prove their worth as research centers for book-history. One would be hard put to write book history without them: their historical holdings, together with other forms of source material of course, constitute the solid basis of research. Book history is therefore regarded as an area of work in which particularly librarians should participate.

4

Let us summarize our argument briefly: library history and book history have been described as two research fields for the librarian. Such postulations infer consequences. Do these claims not disregard the pragmatic realities? Is it really the case that the librarian today is adequately equipped and capable of carrying out such historical projects? or is it even reasonable to commission him to do so? Is the type of librarian to whom these words are addressed not long since a forgotten figure of the past? Should the librarian today not concentrate solely on the daily duties prescribed for him by the technocratic and administrative structure of his work? Are such scholarly projects not romantic illusions that have little to do with the reality of a professional existence? When such academic demands are made upon them, won't the majority of librarians echo the sentiments expressed in Goethe's words:

> I can see the advantage of it,
> But I haven't any faith in it.

As one has no illusions either about the place given to history in the present world or about the situation of the librarian's profession, one can be even more vehement in voicing the demands that are not only my concern, but the concern of the present-day world.

The librarian carries a particularly high degree of responsibility today, as does the archivist and the museum curator. It cannot be denied that the use of historical research is being given less and less recognition, that in a materialistically oriented world, all values which do not directly bring in economic profit are endangered. However much one is still prepared to recognize moral values, one is less and less capable of placing them in their historical context, and without the knowledge and experience of the historical development, present-day man, in a world of economic superfluity, is in danger of reverting to an archaic condition. When one looks at the worldwide political situation, one can no longer entertain any illusions.

All the more is one called upon, particularly as a librarian, to resist the general trend of material and economic thinking. The librarian will have to realize, that his efforts primarily serve human culture, the preservation and defense of human values and traditions. He should grasp the fact that he cannot get out of facing up to these demands made upon him. It would certainly be more comfortable for him to regard himself as nothing but an instrument of general needs, a servant of the wishes of those using the library. But one must remind him that he is not only obliged to do his own work, but, as one in charge or on the staff of a library, which is rooted in history, he has a responsibility, whether he likes it or not, towards the future. I know that such lofty sentiments will bring a smile to the lips of most of my colleagues. But one has to see the situation as it is: even the librarian, as curator of books, can, in his own little corner, most certainly make his small contribution to the building up of a humane future. One of the prime concerns in this respect is the preservation of our cultural tradition. The librarian is employed in this service, and it is his duty to uphold the continuity of intellectual traditions.

He can make his contribution to this cultural political cause in various ways, by arranging cultural events in his library, or — the contention here — by promoting historical research, and, specifically in his own subject, by contributing to the studies in library and book history. To place such a demand upon the librarian has consequences, as far as staff is concerned: it will most certainly only be rarely possible today to promote library-history and book-history research in the library to the greatest possible extent. Routine work will hold the librarian back from taking advantage of the possibilities to which he feels inclined. It is therefore all the more necessary to ensure through long-term planning that historical research is firmly entrenched in the library. What is required is a greater number of permanent positions for librarians who would be able to apportion a part of their working day to research projects. Library history and book history would then no longer play a subordinate role in the library, but would be included in the daily routine. Only if such demands are met can one ultimately hope to succeed in creating within the humanities the scope the two historical disciplines require.

Not every librarian can and should be an historian, but in the technical, industrialized world today, one should consider it one's duty to make sure that at least some librarians look upon their work in this light. These particular tasks help to present book-collections as a stabilizing factor (more than is really the case today) in a changing world. Libraries are not only book supply-depots for day-to-day consumption, but are also institutes which present, in the form of the written word, the archives of history.

In this light, the plea to consider library history and book history as two tasks for the librarian is actually an obvious claim on a present-day world which is all too ready to abandon its historical dimension.

The claims raised here are in no way purely academic: as director of one of the old European libraries, I feel under the present circumstances obliged to plead emphatically for library history and book history. For us in Wolfenbüttel, with our 350,000 imprints of the early modern age between the Renaissance and the Enlightenment, this task is self-evident. Concern for the present-day difficulties has convinced us of the need to put all our weight into supporting history by deed and by word. The more historical consciousness today is in danger of disappearing, the stronger the appeal to those scholars who preserve in their collections the sources relating to historical change.

Libraries are the memory of man: in conclusion, let Goethe's maxim be once more emphasized. Library and book history, promoted by libraries in many countries, could contribute to the preservation of the continuity of history. In this spirit, we, as librarians, voice the demand, despite all contrary trends, to be allowed to be active in the research of our history, not as men of yesterday, but as men of tomorrow. We know that we cannot live as human beings without history; therefore we shall give it our support, whenever the opportunity arises. This cry of warning is the only means we have. The clearer and more distinctly we express it, the more chance we have of being heard. We, the librarians, still live in the consciousness expressed in the words of a writer in ancient times: *Bibliotheca docet* — the library is our teacher.

Gifts

Richard Beer-Hofmann:
A *Stammbuchblatt* and the *Schlaflied*

MIRIAM BEER-HOFMANN LENS

T HE INHERITANCE of the Jewish dramatist and poet Richard Beer-Hofmann — or at least its material expression — is now divided between Harvard, which holds his literary manuscripts and correspondence, and the Leo Baeck Institute, New York, which holds his family papers; even in these poststructuralist days, the partition seems peculiarly artificial for so passionate a writer — where does the *Schlaflied für Mirjam* belong, one might ask? Fortunately for us, Mirjam herself has decided for Harvard: in honor of Jim Walsh's 65th birthday, Mrs. Lens has presented us with correspondence by Karl Darmstaedter relating to his translation of the *Schlaflied* into English, when he was librarian at the Jewish Community Center in Washington, D.C., together with a typescript of his version. Still more generously, she has sent Beer-Hofmann's autograph manuscript of a poem (see plate, p. 24) written in the album (a two-ring loose-leaf binder) of Hilla Fischer, daughter of the publisher S. Fischer, in June 1937.

> Wie gut ein solches Stammbuch es doch hat:
> Kein Autor will in ihm mehr, als ein einziges Blatt —
> Oh, liessen manche es auch *sonst* bewenden
> Bei *einem Blatt*, statt bei sehr vielen Bänden!
> Trost: dass es doch — seit je — ein strenges Stammbuch
>   giebt,
> Drin, kaum zu *einem* Blatt, die Zeit oft *Bände* siebt!

In the *Schlaflied*, Beer-Hofmann wrote how he could give the baby only the sound, not the meaning, of his poetry; so that

> Was ich gewonnen gräbt mit mir man ein,
> Keiner kann Keinem ein Erbe hier sein.

To be sure, he here also alludes to their bitter disinheritance as Jews,

23

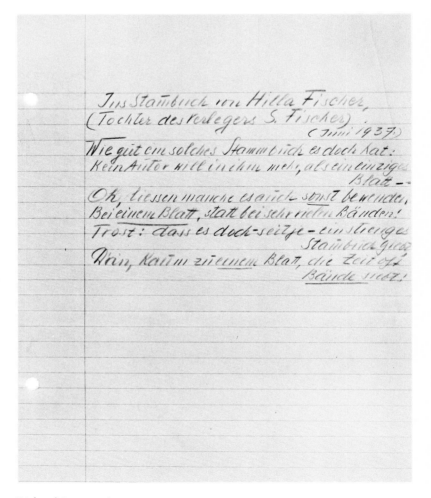

Richard Beer-Hofmann, "Ins Stammbuch von Hilla Fischer". Autograph, June, 1937; 265×223mm. *Houghton Library.*

refugees, and sojourners in an alien land. Like Karl Darmstaedter, who tried to make the *Schlaflied* available to those who (like the sleepy Mirjam) spoke no German, we at Harvard are enriched with his sense of loss, heirs by election who (like all librarians) own nothing yet have everything to pass on to our readers.

THE EDITORS

The Melk *Modus scribendi*

PHILIP HOFER

NOTHING COULD BE more difficult for an amateur bibliographer than to write for a Festschrift honoring the Houghton Library's Keeper of Printed Books, yet the task is agreeable, since he is a close friend as well as a most loyal, helpful colleague. James E. Walsh has devoted his spare time to visiting Austria for vacations, for purchasing books, and for study, during the many years I have known him. Therefore it seemed fitting to choose a Middle European topic, and a manuscript *Modus scribendi* from the Benedictine monastery of Melk on the Austrian Danube came to mind (see plate, p. 27). I had acquired it in 1947 from John Carter of Scribner's. Its recent history was quite brief: E. P. Goldschmidt had brought it back from Melk in 1937 to his shop in Bond Street, where Stanley Morison, the leading English authority on letterforms, "quickly" bought it.[1] It had already been the subject of a study by the paleographer Bernhard Bischoff, before leaving Austria. Morison celebrated his purchase by translating Bischoff's study, with additions and corrections by the refugee scholar Saul Steinberg. Despite wartime conditions, the Cambridge university press printed the translation in 1940, in a type specially designed by Morison and cut by the Monotype Corporation. One observes that Morison had influence whenever he chose to exert it! In his working copy of the translation (now in my possession), Morison noted that "This is the only time this fount was ever used." By this time, a year and a half after Austria became the new Reich's reluctant Ostmark, Britain was at war with Germany; and Morison told me, after I had bought the manuscript, that his labor gave him psychological relief during the Battle of Britain. Much of Morison's library, indeed, as well as many notes and photostats of Steinberg, were destroyed by bombing, so that it is fortunate that the Melk manuscript escaped.

Even these publications, however, have not made the text as accessible as it deserves to be: Bischoff's original study, written for a Festschrift in honor of Dr. Karl Klingspor's seventieth birthday, is uncom-

[1] According to a note in his copy of the translation of Bischoff.

mon, and Morison and Steinberg's translation was printed in only 50 copies.[2] My manuscript is an early example of an unusual text: a treatise on calligraphy written around 1440. It was not intended to be used by novices to copy, but as a compendium from which a competent master of the art might teach the subject. It is "by no means the product of an individual talent aiming at an ideal of an aesthetically immaculate script," Bischoff observed (p. xxii); on the contrary, the writer's aim was severely practical — in this contrasting strongly with Renaissance treatises — and his product is accordingly unassuming. Written on eight small quarto (8⅝ × 5⅝″) leaves, numbered medieval-fashion 3–10, my manuscript served to teach young scribes the different forms of *Notula* or, as Morison terms it, the Bastard secretary hand. Letters addressed to the Holy Roman Emperor Sigismund (1368–1437) in a specimen of the *Notula liberalis*, and to his successor Frederick III (elected 1440) in the *Notula antiqua* suggest a date around 1440. Beneath the first specimen, a later but still contemporary gloss irreverently comments, "Anno domini milessimo quadragenario nullus [versiculus umquam] scribebatur per pedes" — i.e. (in Morison's interpretation) "1440. No [verse] was [ever] written by feet."

There is no solid evidence of the place of writing, though it was probably written at Melk, and Father Martin Kropff in his *Bibliotheca mellicensis* (Vienna, 1747) declares that it is in the autograph of Melk's learned Prior, Martin Senging, who died about 1485. What may be Kropff's own note to this effect appears at the beginning of the text, below the reference mark "Monasterij Mellicensis 115".[3] We may doubt, with Bischoff, that the excellent prior would have committed the many grammatical howlers that fill the text, but he may have authorized the production.

In 1943, Steinberg could record only four similar medieval texts, attested in six surviving manuscripts. Most of these are single sheets, moreover: the scope of my manuscript, Bischoff notes, is "perhaps unique" (p. [ix]). My own research has been limited both by lack of time and by want of opportunity to explore the libraries of Central Europe, but to the best of my knowledge no new manuscripts have turned up

[2] The National Union Catalogue records only 3 copies of the offprint in the U.S.A., and 3 copies of the translation; the British Library Catalogue lists only the translation. I have not been able to locate a copy of the Festschrift.

[3] This reference apparently conflicts with the Melk shelf mark (4.G.16) recorded in Kropff, p. 459.

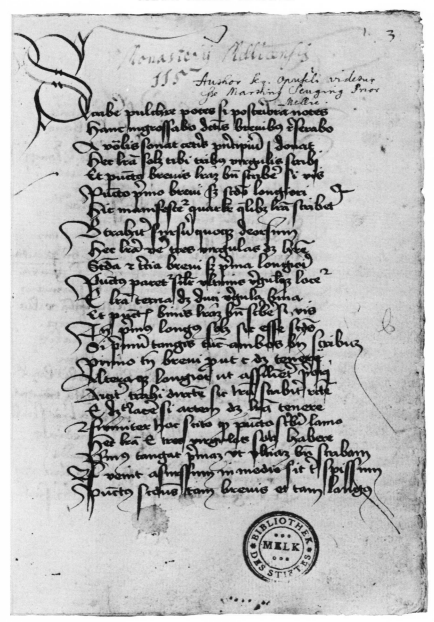

The Melk *Modus scribendi*, f. 3ʳ. Manuscript, ca. 1440; 220×143mm.
Houghton Library.

since Steinberg's hand-list.[4] For those who care to read further on the subject, I append a bibliography, which should satisfy all but the most fastidious student. In honor of James Walsh, I intend to present the manuscript to the Department of Printing and Graphic Arts, at Houghton Library, where it may readily be consulted.

PHILIP HOFER

BIBLIOGRAPHY

Bernhard Bischoff (ed.) *Ein neuentdeckter Modus scribendi des XV. Jahrhunderts aus der Abtei Melk* (Berlin, 1939); English trans. by Stanley Morison and S. H. Steinberg, *A Fifteenth Century Modus scribendi from the Abbey of Melk* (Cambridge, 1940). Morison's working copy of the translation accompanies the original manuscript.

Portland Art Association. *Calligraphy: The Golden Age & its Modern Revival . . .* (Portland, Ore., 1958). A catalogue of the exhibition, in which my manuscript appears as no. 6 (plate 4).

S. H. Steinberg, "The *Forma scribendi* of Hugo Spechtshart," *The Library*, 4th ser., 21 (1940), 264–78.

———, "A Hand-list of Specimens of Medieval Writing Masters," *The Library*, 4th ser., 23 (1943), [191]–194.

———, "Instructions in Writing by Members of the Congregation of Melk," *Speculum*, 16 (1941), 210–15 (with facsimile).

Walters Art Gallery. *Illuminated Books of the Middle Ages and Renaissance* (Baltimore, 1949). A catalogue of the exhibition, in which my manuscript appears as no. 229.

———. *2,000 Years of Calligraphy* [London, repr. 1972]. A catalogue of the 1965 exhibition, in which my manuscript appears as no. 36 (with facsimile).

[4] I am confirmed in this opinion by letters from my friend James M. Wells, dated June 13, 1980, and from Bernard M. Rosenthal, dated June 15, 1980; both very competent judges.

The Provenance and Date
of the Houghton Chessbook Manuscript
and Its Miniatures

ECKEHARD SIMON

WHEN W. H. Bond and Philip Hofer, in 1955, mounted the first of a number of exhibitions of illuminated manuscripts in Houghton Library, a prominent piece on display was an illustrated chessbook (MS Typ 45) that had been acquired by the library in 1938. What the catalogue does not mention[1] is that this vellum manuscript with its twelve splendid miniatures had been placed on exhibition once before — and in the context of the kind of cultural grandeur that only the Victorian Age could muster.

After the codex containing the chessbook was first described, albeit sketchily, in 1868 by the Benedictine historian Beda Dudík as part of his inventory of the manuscript library of Fürst Dietrichstein at Nikolsburg (now Mikulov, Czechoslovakia),[2] the manuscript was taken in 1873 from this Moravian castle to Vienna. There its miniatures were put on display in the Österreichisches Museum in honor of the gilded World Exposition being held at Vienna in the summer of 1873.

While on exhibit, the chessbook codex — which had attestedly belonged to the Dietrichstein library at Nikolsburg castle since the seventeenth century — caught the eye of the Viennese art historian Albert Ilg. It was Ilg who, in an article published that year in the *Mittheilungen der k.k. Central-Commission*,[3] was first to recognize the artistic merit of the

---

[1] Houghton Library, *Illuminated and Calligraphic Manuscripts. An Exhibition Held at the Fogg Art Museum and Houghton Library, February 14–April 1 1955*, comp. W. H. Bond & Philip Hofer (Cambridge, Mass., 1955). Plate 46 shows miniatures 7 (fol. 54^r) and 12 (75^v).

[2] Beda Dudík, "Handschriften der Fürstlich Dietrichstein'schen Bibliothek zu Nikolsburg in Mähren," *Archiv für österreichische Geschichte*, 39 (1868), 419–534, at pp. 497f.

[3] Albert Ilg, "Ein deutsches Schachzabelbuch des XIV. Jahrhunderts," *Mittheilungen der k.k. Central-Commission zur Erforschung und Erhaltung der Baudenkmale*, 18 (1873), 323–28.

twelve miniatures and to give the first (and until now, only) description of them. Ilg's article remains of some value today for the information it provides on clothes and equipment worn by the personified chess figures, although his costumological dating — shortly after 1350 — needs to be reconsidered.

Offered for sale by the Dietrichstein family through Sotheby, London, as early as 1928,[4] but apparently withdrawn, the codex was eventually sold in 1933 at Lucerne[5] to an American collector of chessbooks, Silas Howland, who bequeathed it to Harvard College Library in 1938.

The scribal idiom in all three fascicles comprising our codex is Middle Bavarian, and the first fascicle, containing the chessbook, was most likely written in the region to the southwest of Nikolsburg, in Lower Austria, with some indicators (see below) pointing to Vienna. The chess tract itself belongs to what Gerard F. Schmidt has designated the second redaction of the German *Prosa-Schachzabelbücher*.[6] Like all vernacular chessbooks, it is ultimately based on the famed chess treatise of the Dominican Friar Jacobus de Cessolis, which was probably written around 1275 and is known, variously, as *Liber* or *Libellus de moribus hominum et officiis nobilium ac popularium super ludo scaccorum* or, more succinctly, as *Solatium ludi scaccorum*. In his unpublished Harvard thesis of 1953, Gerard Schmidt presented a composite edition of this second prose redaction, basing his text mainly on the Houghton codex.[7] In his 1961 edition in the series "Texte des späten Mittelalters" (see n.6), however, Schmidt brought out instead the oldest and most faithful German prose rendition of Friar Jacob's *Solatium* (hence called the first prose version), transmitted to us in two Munich manuscripts, from which derives the shortened (by almost one-third) second redaction, preserved in the Houghton codex. It was, to be sure, this less tedious

---

[4] According to a note identifying a reproduction of miniature 12 (fol. 75ᵛ) in Adolph Goldschmidt, "Die Luzerner illustrierten Handschriften des Schachzabelbuches des Schweizer Dichters Konrad von Ammenhausen. Ein Beitrag zur Geschichte der Buchmalerei im 14. und 15. Jahrhundert," *Innerschweizerisches Jahrbuch für Heimatkunde*, 8/10 (1944/46), 9–33, at p. 15 (Tafel 8, Abb. 37).

[5] Gilhofer & Ranschburg, Lucerne, *Versteigerung XI: Bibliothek Alexander Fürst Dietrichstein, Schloss Nikolsburg* (November 21, 1933), no. 508.

[6] Gerard F. Schmidt, ed., *Das Schachzabelbuch des Jacobus de Cessolis, O.P. in mittelhochdeutscher Prosa-Übersetzung*, Texte des späten Mittelalters, 13 [Berlin, 1961], pp. 9–11.

[7] Gerard F. Schmidt, ed., *Das deutsche Prosa-Schachzabelbuch (Kritische Ausgabe)*, Diss. Harvard University, 1953.

version, which still awaits a modern edition, that turned out to be the most popular German chessbook of all, still surviving in thirty-nine manuscripts and four incunables.

Being an astute preacher by the calling of his order, Jacobus de Cessolis, who probably hailed from the village of Céssole, near Alessandria, in the Asti province of northwestern Italy, had hit upon the idea of employing the game of chess — which had attained great popularity since returning crusaders brought it to Europe — as an allegorical and didactic device within a cycle of homilies. What Friar Jacob actually did was to lend each chess piece a human shape and assign to the powerful first row the offices of the ruling estates, from king to governor (rook), and to the lowly but hardworking pawns the whole bevy of human trades and professions, from peasant to vagabond message carrier. He also attached didactic meaning to the way the chessmen were grouped in relation to each other, to the different moves each one was permitted to make, and to the layout of the chessboard itself.

Jacobus de Cessolis was, to be sure, not the first to discover the allegorical potential of chess, the idea that the game could be viewed as a microcosm of man in society. As early as the ninth century, a Persian poet known by the slightly prosaic if practical name of Omar the Tent-Maker first struck the allegorical vein of chess in a quatrain invoking the *vanitas*-theme:

> The world is a chessboard, day and night in sequel,
> Where Fate moves men back and forth,
> Intersperses them, cries checkmate and defeats them,
> And puts them in the end, one by one, into the box.[8]

The systematic personification of the chess pieces, however, was essentially a product of the Dominican friar's imagination and — in medieval times at least — was never transposed to chessmen carved for actual use. As both surviving chess sets and depictions of chess games reveal, all pieces — with the exception of King, Queen, and Knight in semblances still familiar to us — were given the block-like and faceless shapes taken over from Arabic usage.

As an indication of how popular Friar Jacob's "Solace of Chess" was to become throughout Europe in the waning Middle Ages, suffice

---

[8] Quoted from Waldemar Weigand, *Das königliche Spiel. Eine kulturgeschichtliche Studie* (Berlin, 1959), p. 48 (English translation mine).

it to point out that one of the first books the famous prototypographer William Caxton published, after settling in England in 1476, was *The Game and Playe of the Chesse* (1478), a Middle English rendition of our tract. What made the *Solatium* so popular, mainly as a primer for preachers, was not so much the chess allegory, but rather the 140 or so stories appended thereto, which richly "exemplify" the guidelines to human conduct central to the tract.

Before we examine the miniatures of the Houghton chessbook, we need to determine when and where it was written. The date of 1408 that Gerard Schmidt cites as *terminus ante quem* in his 1961 edition (also given in the Houghton catalogue) is taken from the scribal *Explicit* of an "eternal calendar" or Computus, applicable to the fourteenth century, that makes up the third and last fascicle of the codex containing, as its first fascicle, our chess tract. But the two texts are, in fact, by different hands and there is no evidence that fascicle 3 (the Computus) and fascicle 1 (our chessbook) were necessarily written at the same time. In the absence of other clues, dating the chessbook will have to proceed from the miniatures and their iconographical style. Here I was fortunate to secure the advice of the Manchester art historian J. J. Alexander, a specialist on manuscript illumination, who was kind enough to examine the miniatures with me during a 1977 visit to Houghton. Dr. Alexander drew my attention to a splendidly illustrated study of the "Wenzelhandschriften" — the eight illuminated codices of Wenceslas IV, King of Bohemia (including the famed "Wenzelbibel" and a "Willehalm") — published in 1971 by the Czech art historian Josef Krása.[9] Closer inspection revealed that the miniatures in the Houghton chessbook show a distinct similarity to the magnificently illuminated "Wenzelhandschriften," which were produced by a school of major artists, working in Prague, between 1387 and 1402. The discrepancy in provenance (the dialect of our text is the Middle Bavarian spoken in Lower Austria) does not vitiate this observation. For one thing, Krása posits that the Master illuminator of the Wenceslas court atelier at Prague received his training in the South German/Austrian school that produced the major illustrated Universal Chronicles *(Weltchroniken)* of the fourteenth century and that he may, in fact, have been Austrian himself.[10] More important, the

[9] Josef Krása, *Rukopisy Václava IV.*, Odp. red. Milena Freimanová, Vyd. 1, Edice České dějiny, svazek 44 [Praha, 1971]. German edition: *Die Handschriften König Wenzels IV.*, tr. Herta Sowinski (Wien, 1971).

[10] Krása (see n.9), p. 288 (Czech edition).

Bohemian school exerted a rapid and profound influence on manuscript illumination in Austria. It appears to have prompted Duke Albrecht III to establish— at Vienna, about 1385 — a court atelier of his own that was, in turn, to remain the center of book illumination in Austria until the middle of the fifteenth century.[11] The Bohemian features of the style of our miniatures would seem to permit us to associate them with this Austrian school and to posit that the chessbook was produced at Vienna. It would also seem to corroborate the dating of the miniatures— to about 1390 — first proposed to me by Dr. Alexander.

A piece of evidence from MS Typ 45 itself might be marshalled in support of both the date and provenance proposed. The front flyleaf consists of half of a vellum charter (last will and testament) issued at Vienna and making reference (in its truncated witness and date section) to an "Albrecht of Austria."[12] One is tempted to identify this Albrecht with Duke Albrecht III of Austria, the founder of the above-mentioned court atelier, and to posit that all three fascicles of MS Typ 45 were written at Vienna and then bound there after 1408 (date on fascicle 3). Yet while the charter does make the provenance case for Vienna quite certain, it is possible that the Albrecht it refers to might be a later one, such as Duke Albrecht V (ca. 1430–1450).

Still, as far as our chessbook is concerned, dating it and its minia-tures to ca. 1390 would now seem warranted. The script is in line with this date. Our scribe writes a clearly executed Austro-Bavarian *Bastarda* hand that can be attested in dated southeast German manuscripts as early as 1377 and, judging from Unterkircher's Vienna catalogue,[13] was by 1390 in fairly common use in the Austrian regions.

If this dating withstands future expert scrutiny by others, we would have to consider the Houghton manuscript the oldest German prose chessbook to come adorned with miniatures. What is more, since the oldest illustrated *Solatium* manuscript known is a Florentine text dated

[11] See Otto Mazal, *Buchkunst der Gotik*, Buchkunst im Wandel der Zeiten, 1 (Graz, 1975), pp. 83, 86, 87.

[12] "Vnd das das gescheft . . . ainem warn vrchund der sach versiegelten mit meiner . . . [Alb]rechts ze Oesterreich etc. Chamerer vnd Ulrichs des . . . [i]nsigeln. Der brief ist geben zu wienn nach kristi . . . der zwelifpotten." On this charter, see Albert Ilg, "Mittelalterliche Heil- und Segenssprüche," *Anzeiger für Kunde der deutschen Vorzeit*, n.s., 20(1873), cols. 226–229, at col. 227.

[13] Franz Unterkircher, *Die datierten Handschriften der Österreichischen Nationalbibliothek bis zum Jahre 1400*, Katalog der datierten Handschriften in lateinischer Schrift in Österreich, 1 (Wien, 1969).

to *ca.* 1390,[14] the Houghton codex may have some claim to be ranked as the first illuminated manuscript among those containing a direct rendition of Friar Jacob's chèss tract. As such, it would rival the earliest illustrated manuscript of any of the four German verse adaptations of the *Solatium*. This is held to be a Berne codex of Konrad von Ammenhausen's *Schachzabelbuch*, produced around 1380 by the Lucerne scribe and illuminator Hans zum Bach.[15]

But chronological oneupmanship aside, our Houghton codex can assuredly claim to be the oldest chessbook to contain miniatures, all fullpage, of substantial artistic merit. For most of the other illustrated chessbooks from the early period that I have been able to examine, notably the Ammenhausen manuscripts, offer no more than small colored drawings whose crude execution reveals the amateur illuminator, often none other than the text scribe himself.

As we now proceed to take a closer look at the twelve miniatures (only four of which had hitherto been published, mainly in small catalogues), let us briefly make note of the technique used by our illuminator. After sketching them out in lead point, the artist drew his figures with the quill and brownish-black ink. Then, with the brush, he added the colors: mainly water colors, often applied in the layered (and hence opaque) form known as gouache *(Deckfarbe)*, but also silver paint (now tarnished) and gold. For shaping and shadowing (following gouache procedure), he took up the quill again, putting in numerous fine strokes with black ink and highlighting with white. Finally, the legends were inserted into the banderoles with red ink, using the formal Gothic bookhand known as *Textura*. This was most likely not done by the miniaturist, but by the text scribe, since he served as his own rubricator (mainly red and blue pen-work initials).

Missing from our chessbook are the first leaf — which (judging from other manuscripts) contained a picture of Friar Jacob preaching to the flock — and two others of the first quire with miniatures of King and Queen. Because they were in likelihood heavily gilded and silvered, they made tempting targets for the kind of pilferers that have remained the bane of curators to our day.

The first miniature (fol. 17ᵛ, fig. 1) depicts the Alphyns or Judges, known today as Bishops. In line with Friar Jacob's instructions, our text

---

[14] According to Goldschmidt (cf. n.4), p. 15.
[15] Goldschmidt, p. 18.

Fig. 1. The Alphyns (Judges).
218×145mm. *Houghton Library.*

Fig. 2. The Knight. 218×145mm.
Houghton Library.

Fig. 3. The Rook. 218×145mm.
Houghton Library.

Fig. 4. 1st Pawn (Peasant).
218×145mm. *Houghton Library.*

specifies that *dẏ alten*, as they are called here, are to signify judges *(richter)* and assistant judges or assessors *(anweyser)*. Because the text states that two judges are needed, one (black square) for criminal cases, the other (white square) to adjudicate breaches of civil law, our illuminator (like others) drew in two figures. What Friar Jacob meant to say, however, was that the Alphyn — like Knight and Rook (never doubled) — appears twice in the line of principals. Since judges carry out the king's laws, it is fitting that they flank the royal couple. The legend in the banderole reads: *Von der gestalt der alten vnd von irn ampten.*

Next to the Judges stands the Knight *(ritter)* in full armor (fol. 22ᵛ, fig. 2), including an open-faced helmet known as *Hundskogel* that the *Limburger Chronik* — a famed source book for late medieval garb and fashion — first mentions around 1380. Examining the Knight we first notice the most striking feature of the clothes worn by many of our personified chess pieces: the long fall-away sleeves which — as town clerk Tilemann of Limburg reports — first hit the German fashion scene in 1349.[16] This particular variety, lavishly edge-cut, is called *Zattelärmel*. The legend in banderole reads: *Das vierd Capitel von Rittern vnd von irn sẏten.*

Manning the flanks is the Rook or *Turm*, to which the chessbook refers as *das roch* (fol. 30ᵛ, fig. 3). Decked out in a furlined hood *(gugel)*, connoting nobility, the Rook personifies governors *(vitztum)*, ministers *(legatum)*, and viceroys *(verwĕsĕr)* of the King. As sign of his royal office he carries a leafed staff *(ein reyss)*, a symbol that Friar Jacob also associates with the agricultural activities supervised by him. The legend is simple: *von der gestalt des Rochs.*

The pawns of the exposed front line personify the working people, craftsmen and professionals, whom our text calls *gemain lewt vnd arbaiter*. In Persian usage, the pawn was known as *"baidaq"* or *"footsoldier,"* which was rendered accurately into Latin as *"pedes"* or *"pedo"*, from which derives, in turn, the English term "pawn." The German equivalent *vende*, used both in the chessbooks and when playing chess at that time, basically means "youth, young man." Setting aside this tradition (pawns as infantry) in its entirety, Friar Jacob's signal contribution was to have the *pedites* personify a whole array of different trades of the "commons." Since he had only eight *populares* to work with, however, he was forced to bestow on each pawn at least three,

---

[16] See Ilg (cf. n.3), p. 327.

often more, different occupations. In addition, the resourceful Dominican did his best to forge *significatio* links between the working "commons" and the various figures of the ruling estate in front of which they
stand. Hence the blacksmith pawn is placed forward of the Knight
because he manufactures armor and weapons for him and the innkeeper
fronts the Judge (Bishop), because judges are needed, one reads, to settle
the many legal hassles in which his profession gets involved. But since
each pawn, as noted, embodies several different trades and because
Judge, Knight, and Rook— appearing twice— had to be linked with
two different composite pawns each, Friar Jacob was not averse to using
strong-arm tactics in order to keep the allegorical fabric in line.

The first *vende* in front of the Rook to the King's right stands for
the peasant *(pawman)* (fol. 40ᵛ, fig. 4). The hoe *(hawe)* in his left hand,
the switch *(gᵃrten)* for driving animals in his right, and the sickel or
knife *(besneit messer)* under his belt for pruning trees and grapevines,
are meant to signify the three major tasks incumbent upon the husband-
man. The term *"Bauer,"* used in modern German for all pawns (not just
the first), appears to be the sole living inheritance from Friar Jacob's
chess allegory.[17] The enscrolled legend reads: *von der gestalt des ersten
vᵃnden.*

The second *vende* (fol. 44ʳ, fig. 5) embodies the three major artisan
and building trades: the blacksmith, figured by the hammer and, perhaps,
the belted sword; the carpenter, represented by the axe *(zymmerparte)*;
and the mason or bricklayer, signaled by the trowel *(chol, "trulla")*
under the belt. As figure five reveals, however, our illuminator mistook
the term *chol*, more commonly spelled *kell*, for the familiar word *kol*
("Kohle"). Thus, instead of a trowel, he drew a lump of coal that
liberally blackens the white apron of our pawn. Reading "trowel" as
"coal," then, this artist must have associated the mason's emblem with
the blacksmith and his furnace. In the banderole: *von der gestalt des
andern venden vnd auch von seim gevᵃrt.*

The only denominator that appears to link the motley trades personified by the third pawn (fol. 47ʳ, fig. 6) is that in all of them either
scissors or knives figure as tools. The pair of scissors is to signify tailors
(sneyder), clothshearers *(tᵘchperaiter)*, and weavers *(wᵃber)*. The large

---

[17] See Heinz-Jürgen Kliewer, *Die mittelalterliche Schachallegorie und die
deutschen Schachzabelbücher in der Nachfolge des Jacobus de Cessolis*, Diss.
Heidelberg, 1966.

knife is a basic tool to butchers *(fleschhakcher)*, tanners *(ledrer)*, tawers *(jrcher)*, cobblers *(schuster)*, and furriers *(chŭrssner)*. Yet the most important profession personified here is that of scribe, the clerk. While his trade may not be at the cutting edge, as it were, the scribe is associated with the knife because he sharpens his quill with one. As clerk *(notarius)*, he is assistant to the Judge (Bishop), in front of whom he stands. To indicate his importance (chessbooks are, after all, the stuff of clerks), the scribe is given three additional emblems: ink horn and quill quiver *(schreibzeug)* on his belt and an everready quill sticking out above his right ear. The *schreibveder*, specified by the text, was in fact sketched in dimly with lead point, but the miniaturist overlooked it in the final drawing. The banderole text reads: *Der dritt vềnd wie sein gestalt sein sol vnd sein gevềrt.*

The fourth pawn (fol. 54ʳ, fig. 7), on whose mercantile skills the King he is fronting greatly depends, carries a gilded balance with weight, betokening money changers *(wềchslềr)* and money lenders *(leyher)*. In addition, he holds an ell *(ellen)* in his left, standing for the draper's trade *(tŭchperaiter)* and, on his belt, wears a large buckled purse *(pewtel, taschen)*, signalling the office of tax collector *(herren phennig jnnềmer vnd trager)*. Our motto scribe, for once curiously shaken, waxed moralistic at this figure and let fly with a curse on human greed: *O verfluchtew geitichaid Dir ist nahet all welt berait.*

The fifth pawn (fol. 59ᵛ, fig. 8) personifies the healing trades: physicians *(ềrtzt)*, surgeons *(wunt ertzt, wunten sneyder)*, and apothecaries *(Apotekềr)*. The book signifies the Seven Liberal Arts which, marvelous to contemplate, a true physician was to master before plying his trade in medieval times. The surgeon's specialty is indicated by the probe *(wunteysen)* tucked under the belt, a slender and flexible instrument used to explore a wound. The ointment jar *(zŭberl, pŭchsen)* signals the druggist. The physician is the only pawn accorded the dignity of being depicted in seated position *(auf ains maysters stŭl)*. The text banderole is omitted in this and the next miniature.

By waving his right hand, the sixth *vende* (fol. 64ʳ, fig. 9) is inviting imbibers and guests to his tavern, a toylike Gothic stone and tile house wherein a man and a woman are seen carousing at the wine barrel. He stands for the trade of tavernkeeper or tapster *(leikhgebin)*, signalled by wheat loaf *(sềmel)* and glass *(glềslein)* in his left, as well as for the innkeeper *(gastgebin)*, indicated by the large key hanging from the belt.

Fig. 5. 2d Pawn (Builders).
218×145mm. *Houghton Library.*

Fig. 6. 3d Pawn (Clothiers, etc.).
218×145mm. *Houghton Library.*

Fig. 7. 4th Pawn (Money changers).
218×145mm. *Houghton Library.*

Fig. 8. 5th Pawn (Healers).
218×145mm. *Houghton Library.*

The seventh pawn, cutting an elegant figure (fol. 67ᵛ, fig. 10), personifies the major administrative officers charged with running a medieval town. The gilded key *(slussel)* and the ell *(stab als ein ellen)* signify senior administrators *(amptlewt)* and town managers *(phlëger der stët)*, one of whose major tasks was checking on the weights *(gewicht)* and measures *(masz)* used by tradesmen. Toll collectors *(zolner)* and merchants *(chramer)* are connoted by the money purse *(pëwtel mit phennigen)* dangling low from the belt. The enscrolled legend makes note of the need for clever wits to get the host of supervisory duties done quickly: *wer vil sache ausrichten sol Der pedarf guter witz wol.* The tightfitting frock and hose, the most extravagant *Zattelärmel*, the fiercely pointed shoes, and the low-slung belt — comparable with today's hip-huggers — make this young gent appear terribly mod and very much with it.

To the eighth and last pawn (fol. 72ʳ, fig. 11) is assigned a motley combination of callings, most of them unattractive. He embodies, first off, the gamblers *(spilër)*, calumniators *(schelter)*, and vagabond rogues *(ribalden)*, shady customers all, signalled by the three dice in his left hand. In representing professional *schelter* (a kind of public gadfly akin to today's columnists), he is charged with denouncing corruption among the governing officials of the King who are, as one recalls, personified by the Rook in front of whom he stands. The luxurious shock of tousled hair and, graphically, the coins in his right hand are supposed to brand him as a wastrel and braggart *(gufter)*. From the gambler, our chessbook makes a remarkable transition to the message carrier: after losing their shirts at dice, the *spilër* are allegedly ready and eager to recoup their losses by ferrying messages across the land. Thus the gambler assumes the calling of courier *(lauffer)*, herald (note the diagonal, so-called heraldic striping) and missive carrier *(priefftrager)*, in emblem of which he carries the letter drum *(priffass)* at his belt. To the illuminator, this occupation — which to our mind would perhaps call for a more solid citizen — was the major one, as the banderole would have us know: *wer sich mit priefen macht auf ain strasz Der sol sich nichts auf halten lasz.*

The last miniature (fol. 75ᵛ, fig. 12), depicting a young lady and gent at chess, marks the beginning of the closing chapter that deals with the chessmen's moves on the squared board. This is announced by the legend that is less a banderole text than a chapter rubric: *Von dem schachzabel spil wie is sein fürgang hat mit seim gestain.* The gentleman, seated, is about to complete a successful move and collar one of the

Fig. 9. 6th Pawn (Innkeeper).
218×145mm. *Houghton Library.*

Fig. 10. 7th Pawn (Townsmen).
218×145mm. *Houghton Library.*

Fig. 11. 8th Pawn (Crooks).
218×145mm. *Houghton Library.*

Fig. 12. Chess players.
218×145mm. *Houghton Library.*

lady's chessmen, while the young woman, who is standing, has placed her right hand on his arm in an intimate gesture of protest.

In appreciation of Gerard Schmidt's work on the *Prosa-Schachzabelbuch* and his generosity in making available to me microfilms of all twenty-three illustrated prose chessbooks, I should like, in closing, to ride a little joust in defense of his dating of the first prose version. In his 1961 edition,[18] Schmidt had assigned it to the first half of the fourteenth century. Hermann Menhardt, in a 1962 review,[19] took issue with the younger scholar's dating and argued, with the pugnaciousness of a Nestor, that the first prose translation did not come into being until the end of the fourteenth century. Our new dating of the Houghton codex and its miniatures to about 1390 would seem to invalidate Menhardt's view. Since the second prose rendering preserved in the Houghton codex — which, it should be noted, is already laced with textual corruptions — constitutes a shortened redaction made directly from the first prose version, this first text, edited by Schmidt, must have existed by 1360–70, and probably earlier than that. Thus while Schmidt's dating — proceeding from Ilg's view (see n.3), now untenable, that the Houghton illustrations originated shortly after 1350 — may still be a bit optimistic, it is likely not too far off the mark.

Because Jacobus de Cessolis prescribed, specifically, at the outset of each chapter how a given chess piece should look as emblem of man's estates in society, most scribes felt compelled to add illustrations to their chessbooks. One senses that chessbook manuscripts were considered incomplete without the graphics, and that in omitting miniatures a scribe risked offending his patron or selling at loss. It is perhaps fitting tribute to the honorand of this miscellany — who has devoted decades of his life to enriching its holdings — that Houghton Library can now be said to possess in its MS Typ 45 one of the earliest illustrated chessbooks of medieval Europe (ca. 1390), and one reflecting in its cycle of miniatures (originally fifteen) a measure of the achievement attained by the Prague school of illuminators under Wenceslas IV.[20]

[18] See n.6. [19] Hermann Menhardt, in *Deutsche Literaturzeitung*, 83 (1962), cols. 503–505.

[20] For the latest study of this school in its European context, see Josef Krása *et al.*, "Prag und Böhmen, Die Buchmalerei," in: *Die Parler und der schöne Stil 1350–1400, Europäische Kunst unter den Luxemburgern*, ed. Anton Legner, Ein Handbuch zur Ausstellung des Schnütgen-Museums in der Kunsthalle Köln, (Köln, 1978), II, 731–57.

Goethe and Mozart:
The Abduction in Weimar

ROBERT SPAETHLING

I N AN ATTEMPT to strengthen the sporadic and faltering efforts of the local amateur theater, Karl August, Duke of Sachsen-Weimar, Goethe's friend and benefactor, invited the acting troupe of Giuseppe Bellomo to his capital city of Weimar. Bellomo, who had been performing in and around Dresden,[1] came with his company and moved into the "Redoutensaal," an old building opposite the Ducal palace which had been refurbished in 1780 to house the new Court Theater.[2] Bellomo opened on January 1, 1784 with Friedrich Gotter's *Marianne*, a bourgeois tragedy in three acts, and, in general, surprised the staid and sleepy community of six thousand with a brisk pace of new performances. Comedies, light operas, *Singspiele*, a modest number of tragedies were staged in rapid succession; even Shakespeare made his first Weimar appearance under Bellomo's direction: *Hamlet*, *King Lear*, *Macbeth* were all performed in 1785 and apparently with success.[3] Goethe reported later (in a speech intended for the "Freitagsgesellschaft," a weekly science colloquium) that between 1784 and 1795 over four hundred new works had been launched at the Weimar theater.[4] Yet, in spite of these commendable efforts, Bellomo did not find favor with the Weimar court and theater public, and when he received an invitation in 1790 to move his company to Graz, Austria, no one in Weimar strenuously objected. A new company was founded and Goethe himself was appointed the

[1] According to Julius Wahle, *Das Weimarer Hoftheater unter Goethes Leitung*, Goethe-Gesellschaft, v.6 (Weimar, 1892), p. 16, Bellomo's troupe had played last "im Linkeschen Bad zu Dresden."

[2] Marvin A. Carlson, *Goethe and the Weimar Theatre* (Ithaca, [1978]), pp. 38 and 39.

[3] For a detailed account of Bellomo's repertoire see Carlson, pp. 48–50.

[4] "Über die verschiedenen Zweige der hiesigen Tätigkeit," *Goethes Werke*, Sophienausgabe, 143v. (Weimar, 1887–1912) (hereafter cited as "Sophienausgabe," by division: volume/part, and page) 1:53, 182. This is a speech concerning the cultural activities in Weimar during the preceding decade.

general director of the new Ducal Court Theater, a post he held for twenty-six years. He opened on April 5, 1791 with Iffland's *Die Jäger* and concluded his tenure on April 7, 1817 with Beethoven's *Fidelio*.[5]

Giuseppe Bellomo may not have satisfied the taste and expectations of Weimar high society, but wittingly or unwittingly he played an important part in the musical life and development of Johann Wolfgang von Goethe: in September 1785 Bellomo staged a performance of Mozart's *Die Entführung aus dem Serail*, an event that proved to have a significant effect on Goethe's relationship to Mozart and probably to music in general. For over twenty years Goethe had not given much thought to Mozart and his music. Not that he had neglected music altogether: he had gone to the French *opéra comique* in Frankfurt, and he had been inspired by the German *Singspiel* in Leipzig; as a young student in Leipzig he had even discussed music with Johann Adam Hiller, the most prominent German *Singspiel* composer at that time.[6] But Mozart, whom he had seen and heard as a *Wunderkind* in Frankfurt in August 1763 — Mozart had been seven years of age, Goethe fourteen — Mozart seems to have been far from his mind. But now, after Bellomo's performance of *Die Entführung*, Mozart's name began to appear in Goethe's letters and diaries with some frequency and regularity. In fact, the event kindled Goethe's conscious awareness of Mozart and his music; it was the beginning of Goethe's recognition of the composer's greatness.

The recognition did not develop, however, without some struggle. On December 22, 1785, Goethe wrote to Philipp Christoph Kayser, a young musician he had met ten years earlier in Frankfurt: "Not long ago *Die Entführung aus dem Serail* was performed here. Everybody was in favor of the music. The first time I saw it, it turned out to be a mediocre performance; the text is very poor and the music, too, didn't really impress me. The second performance I saw was so bad that I walked out. But the play remained in the repertoire and everybody praised the music. When it was given for the fifth time I went to see it once more. They acted and sang better than before; I distanced myself

---

[5] The opening date and work are mentioned by Johannes Höffner, *Goethe und das Weimarer Hoftheater* (Weimar, 1913), p. 26. Apparently the regular "Spielplan" did not start until May 19th and featured *Lilla* (*Una rosa rara*) by Martin y Solar. Cf. also Alfred Orel, *Goethe als Operndirektor* (Bregenz, 1949), pp. 115 and 162.

[6] Johann Wolfgang Goethe, *Gedenkausgabe der Werke, Briefe und Gespräche*, ed. Ernst Beutler, 24v. (Zürich, [1948–54]), XIV, 337 ("Für Freunde der Tonkunst").

from the text and understood now why I had come to such a different judgment from the rest of the audience."[7]

What are we to make of such coolness towards Mozart's *Entführung?* Obviously Goethe encountered difficulties with the piece. What were these difficulties, we might ask? Were they based entirely on aesthetic criteria, as he seems to indicate, or were there other, more personal reasons as well? Let us examine briefly this fascinating chapter of Goethe biography.

First of all there was, as Goethe says, the poor quality of the text, and even though the libretto appears to be no worse than the average German theater text of the time, one finds it hard to disagree with him on this point. The play, published in Leipzig in 1781 under the title of *Belmont und Constanze, oder die Entführung aus dem Serail,* "Eine Operette in drey Akten,"[8] had been adapted from various French and English sources by Christoph Friedrich Bretzner to serve as a libretto for an operetta by the well-known *Singspiel* composer Johann André. Bretzner's play was set in Turkey, a favored eighteenth-century stage locale, and featured the popular enlightenment theme of divided lovers and generous (i.e., "noble savage") despots. Mozart and his librettist, Gottlieb Stephanie,[9] had made some changes in the text, increasing, for instance, Osmin's role (and singing part) and, in general, tightening the structure of the play by correlating action, dramatis personae and music to form a coherent musical drama. "The whole story is being altered," wrote Mozart to his father on September 26, 1781 in a detailed account of his work on *Die Entführung.*[10] (The alterations in the piece were actually not as drastic or substantial as Mozart's letter indicates. The most important addition in the first scene is Osmin's major aria: "Drum,

---

[7] Sophienausgabe, IV:7, 143.

[8] (Leipzig: bey Carl Friedrich Schneider, 1781). For a detailed discussion of Bretzner's text in relation to Mozart's libretto consult: Otto Jahn, *W. A. Mozart,* 5th ed., rev. Hermann Abert (Leipzig, 1919–21), I, 931–973. For an account of the English predecessors of the play check: Edward J. Dent, *Mozart's Operas* (London, 1947), p. 71. For the "Turkish" tradition on the eighteenth-century stage check: William Mann, "Mozart alla Turca," *Opera News* XLIV/19 (April 12, 1980), 14–16.

[9] Stephanie der Jüngere also wrote the libretto for Mozart's *Der Schauspieldirektor* as well as the popular comic opera *Der Apotheker und der Doktor* (apparently a Goethe favorite) with music by Karl Ditters von Dittersdorf.

[10] *The Letters of Mozart and his Family,* ed. Emily Anderson (London, 1938), III, 1146.

beim Barte des Propheten," which shifts the emphasis in that scene from Belmont to Osmin. The other major change comes in the conclusion of the *Singspiel*. In Bretzner's version Belmont turns out to be Selim Pasha's own son, in the Mozart-Stephanie version, Belmonte is the son of Selim's arch-enemy, the Commander of Oran. Generally speaking, it is almost surprising that Mozart and Stephanie did not make more substantial changes in the text.[11]

Christoph Friedrich Bretzner did not like any of this. He wrote an indignant letter to a Leipzig newspaper in which he protested vigorously against such mistreatment of his operetta: "A certain person by the name of Mozart, in Vienna, has had the audacity to misuse my drama *Belmont and Constanze* as an opera text. I hereby protest most solemnly against this infringement of my rights and reserve the right to take further measures. Christoph Friedrich Bretzner, author of *Das Räuschchen*."[12] There is no evidence that any "further measures" were taken, but even so, Stephanie's rewriting of the piece did not substantially improve its literary quality. It was and remained a somewhat flat and uninspired text, "the very worst" that Mozart "ever set to music," as the unflinchingly candid Mozart scholar Edward Dent contends — with some exaggeration, I think.[13]

A second reason for Goethe's initial discomfort with Mozart's *Singspiel* was, as he himself admits, the music. Goethe was used to chamber music and small ensembles; his taste in music was simple and straightforward; he liked cheerful, "optimistic" songs and musical comedy. During his stay in Italy he developed a taste for choral singing and sacred music, but heavy sounds with large dynamics (as introduced at the time by the Mannheim school of music) overwhelmed him, and they were most certainly one of the reasons why, later on, he shied away

[11] Bretzner's play contains many of the songs and arias which we identify with Mozart's *Die Entführung*, e.g. "Wer ein Liebchen hat gefunden" (Act I), "O wie ängstlich, o wie feurig" (Act I), "Marsch! Marsch! Marsch!" (Act I), "Durch Zärtlichkeit und Schmeicheln" (Act II), "Traurigkeit ward mir zum Lose" (Act II), "Vivat Bachus!" (Act II), "Im Mohrenland gefangen war" (Act III), "Ach, mit freudigem Entzücken" (Act III). There is a copy of Bretzner's *Belmont und Constanze* in the Austrian National Library in Vienna.

[12] Quoted by Alfred Einstein in *Mozart, His Character, His Work*. (New York, 1945), pp. 455–56. Otto Erich Deutsch, *Mozart. Die Dokumente seines Lebens* (Kassel: 1961), p. 187, lists this quotation as from 1782 and adds: "Das Datum dieses Protestes ist noch unbekannt. Er fand sich in den *Leipziger Zeitungen*."

[13] Dent, p. 87.

from Beethoven. We have no evidence that Mozart's music ever affected him adversely, yet the relatively large sound and rich orchestration of *Die Entführung*, an orchestration that includes bass drum, cymbals, triangle and piccolo to produce exotic — i.e. "Turkish" — coloration, was something new and unfamiliar. (*Die Entführung* is scored for fifteen instruments as is *Die Zauberflöte*. By comparison Joseph Haydn's comic opera *L'infedeltà delusa* is scored for seven, his *Il mondo della luna* for eight instruments. Haydn's scoring is much more typical of what Goethe was accustomed to and enjoyed).

Nor was Goethe alone with his preference for simple sound. One of the reviews of *Die Entführung* which appeared (after a performance in Hannover) in Baron von Knigge's *Dramaturgische Blätter* of 1788, contained points of criticism that might well have come from Goethe himself: "The composer is too loquacious with the wind instruments. Instead of using them to underline a special part of a melody, and to support the harmonic whole, they often darkly color the whole orchestral palette and confuse it; they swallow up a beautiful, simple song and disturb the singer in performance."[14] And Joseph II, the Austrian monarch, is supposed to have remarked to maestro Mozart after the first performance of *Die Entführung* on July 16, 1782 in Vienna: "Too beautiful for our ears, and far too many notes, my dear Mozart," to which Mozart allegedly replied: "Exactly as many, Your Majesty, as are needed."[15] Even if such exchanges reside entirely within the realm of fantasy and anecdote, they always contain a kernel of truth. In this case it is certainly true that, in contrast to our sensibilities today, Mozart's contemporaries often perceived his music as "heavy" and difficult. Mozart's quartets, writes one reviewer in *Cramers Magazin der Musik*, "are, after all, too sharply spiced — and what palate can endure that for any length of time."[16]

Die Entführung, in particular, contains a variety of musical innovations which make Goethe's uneasiness quite understandable. As Alfred Einstein observed: "This orchestra speaks a new language, new also as regards dynamics which are here of infinitely fine gradations. The whole work marks the complete emergence of Mozart's personality as a dra-

[14] Quoted by H. C. Robbins Landon in "Mozart on the Eighteenth Century Stage," *High Fidelity*, XV/11 (Nov. 1965), 64. The complete review can be found in Deutsch, *Dokumente*, p. 287.

[15] Einstein, p. 458.

[16] Wolfgang Hildesheimer, *Mozart* (Frankfurt, 1977), p. 212.

matic composer."[17] In fact, Mozart was fully aware of creating new and special effects in his music, effects designed not only to create an oriental atmosphere, but also to convey a broad range of human emotions, such as anger, fear, humor, wit, and the palpitations of a loving heart. In the famous letter of September 26, 1781 to his father he writes: "Let me now turn to Belmonte's aria in A major, 'O wie ängstlich, o wie feurig.' Would you like to know how I have expressed it — and even indicated his throbbing heart? By the two violins playing octaves. This is the favourite aria of all those who have heard it, and it is mine also. I wrote it expressly to suit Adamberger's voice. You feel the trembling — the faltering — you see how his throbbing breast begins to swell; this I have expressed by a crescendo. You hear the whispering and the sighing — which I have indicated by the first violin with mutes and a flute playing in unison."[18] The "throbbing heart," the "whispering and sighing," the rendering of human feelings in musical language — for Mozart this was an exciting artistic challenge and venture; for Goethe, however, such individualization of musical sound was a new experience — only gradually did he get used to these rich tonalities. Ironically it was he who, just a decade earlier, had introduced a similar enlivening process into German poetry.

In all fairness to Goethe, let it be said that *Die Entführung* is a difficult and uneven work. It is a fascinating and enormously colorful creation, rich in musical ideas, alive with wit, humor and individual expression, all brilliantly rendered by an exciting orchestration. But Mozart had not yet found the precise style of his later years; the placement of arias is, as Conrad Osborne says, "at points unbelievably bad."[19] Several of the arias suffer from excessive length and technical difficulties. For instance, Osmin's aria "Solche hergelaufne Laffen," Belmonte's "O wie ängstlich, o wie feurig," Constanze's "Traurigkeit ward mir zum Lose" as well as "Martern aller Art," each one of these arias is long and repetitive; in fact, the last aria, in particular, has been characterized as more suitable for the concert stage than for theater.[20] These arias can be a challenge, indeed, even for first-rate singers. Vienna was blessed with good voices, and Mozart, when composing, did not

---

[17] Einstein, p. 459.   [18] *Letters*, ed. Anderson, III, 1141–1145.

[19] "The Operas of Mozart on Microgroove," *High Fidelity*, XV/11 (Nov. 1965), 65.

[20] Dent, p. 77.

have to be overly concerned with the technical limitations of his singers; in fact, the most difficult singing parts in *Die Entführung* were written expressly for specific artists: Osmin for the bass Ludwig Fischer (probably a basso profundo), Belmonte for the tenor Valentin Joseph Adamberger, Constanze for the soprano Caterina Cavalieri. But Weimar was quite another story. Marvin Carlson describes it in his book *Goethe and the Weimar Theater:* "The actors were hired according to traditional specialties and performed, as was the custom, in both spoken and musical theatre. Thus one actress played leading romantic roles and sang first and second operatic roles, another played lovers and bravura roles in operettas, a third played heroines and mothers and danced, a fourth played confidantes and comic mothers in operettas, and so on."[21] Goethe, in other words, most likely witnessed a performance of *Die Entführung* that was not exactly a model of perfection. And when we read his later reminiscences of these early days of the Weimar theater, we realize that such a supposition is not entirely off the mark. In a small essay (a sort of memorandum for the Duke) entitled "On the Separation of Stageplays and Operas," written in 1808, Goethe reflects: "We will all remember the wife of Director Bellomo who for years presented leading romantic roles ("die ersten Liebhaberinnen") with a barely tolerable voice, an unmistakable South German accent and an inconspicuous appearance."[22]

The poor libretto, the novelty of the musical language, the lengthy arias, a questionable performance, given these odds it would have required a very patient and favorably disposed listener to have an enjoyable first night at the opera. It is doubtful, however, that Goethe was in any mood to be either patient or favorably disposed. Indeed he may well have been deliberately critical and captious. For it is no secret that he had his own ambitions for writing *Singspiele*. He had written five such pieces between 1775 and 1785: *Erwin und Elmire* ("Ein Schauspiel mit Gesang," changed to a *Singspiel* during Goethe's stay in Rome), *Claudine von Villa Bella* ("Ein Schauspiel mit Gesang," also changed to a *Singspiel*), *Die Fischerin* ("Ein Singspiel"), *Lila* ("Ein Singspiel"), *Jery und Bätely* ("Ein Singspiel").[23]

During his stay in Italy, Goethe not only reworked some of his older pieces, but gave serious thought to a general reform of the entire genre.

---

[21] Carlson, p. 48. [22] Sophienausgabe, I:53, 268. [23] Hans-Albrecht Koch, *Das deutsche Singspiel* (Stuttgart, 1974), pp. 87–94.

The older *Singspiele*, his own and Bretzner's *Belmont und Constanze* included, were by and large loosely structured plays with intermittent songs— "Schauspiele mit Gesang." The new format Goethe aspired to was much closer to the *opera buffa;*[24] there was to be greater unity between text and music, greater integration of all constituent elements. Still, Goethe's taste remained, for the most part, within the limits of neo-classical music-theater; he continued to favor simple plots, simple music, simple orchestration, the type of *Singspiel* espoused by Christoph Martin Wieland, who prescribes in his "Versuch über das deutsche *Singspiel*" that the "plot be as simple as possible . . . and confined to as few characters as possible."[25]

Just prior to Bellomo's performance of Mozart's *Die Entführung* in Weimar, Goethe had begun to write yet another such *Singspiel*, entitled *Scherz, List und Rache*,[26] for which Philipp Christoph Kayser, the young musician who had won Goethe's favor, was composing the music. This *Singspiel*, a fast-paced enlightenment farce about greed and deception, was doomed from the beginning: in fact, it is usually assumed that Kayser never finished the music for the piece,[27] and it appears that none other than Mozart helped carry it to an early grave. Goethe himself freely admitted the devastating effect *Die Entführung* had wrought on his and Kayser's delicate work. "All our efforts to keep within the bounds of the simple and limited were lost when Mozart appeared," he wrote two years later in Rome with remarkable objectivity, and perhaps a bit of chagrin. "*Die Entführung* overthrew all our plans and hopes, and our carefully prepared *Scherz, List und Rache* was heard of no more."[28] It may have taken two years to gain the necessary distance so that he could comment on the situation soberly, but his first reaction to

[24] Goethe, *Gedenkausgabe*, ed. Beutler, VI, 1243.

[25] *Wielands Gesammelte Schriften*, ed. Deutsche Kommission der k. Preussichen Akademie der Wissenschaften (Berlin, 1909–), I:14, 91.

[26] First published in Johann Wolfgang Goethe, *Schriften*, v.7 (Leipzig: Göschen, 1790), [225]–320.

[27] While it is commonly held that Kayser did not finish the composition, Goethe, in a letter to K. F. Zelter, May 4, 1814, makes a reference that could indicate that Kayser did complete the score: "Was ich senden werde, ist die Ouvertüre und der erste Akt von 'Scherz, List und Rache' das er [Kayser] ganz komponiert hat. Ich gedenke sein jetzt, da ich meine italienische Reise bearbeite. . . ." *Der Briefwechsel zwischen Goethe und Zelter*, ed. Max Hecker (Leipzig, 1913), I, 390.

[28] *Sophienausgabe*, I:32, 145.

Die Entführung in Weimar was probably anything but objective. He may well have perceived instinctively that Mozart's *Singspiel* was superior to his own effort, and this recognition may well have disturbed, perhaps even prejudiced him, when he saw the work for the first time.

Ultimately, however, Goethe could not resist the charm and power of Mozart's *Singspiel*. After he became Director of the Weimar Court Theater, he opened the Fall season with none other than *Die Entführung aus dem Serail*, and, in the end, the work was performed forty-nine times under his stewardship, ranking third among his all-time favorites: *Die Zauberflöte* came first, with eighty-two, and *Don Giovanni* second, with sixty-eight performances. (*Das rote Käppchen* by Karl Ditters von Dittersdorf was fourth, with thirty-nine performances).[29] In 1808 Goethe noted that *Die Entführung* had made a real impact on the theatrical and musical world, an impact "im höheren Sinne" as he put it, meaning not as simple entertainment, but as an artistic experience of cultural significance.[30]

Indeed, once he had overcome his initial scepticism and reluctance, there was so much for Goethe to enjoy and admire in this *Singspiel*. Blondchen's arias, for instance, "Durch Zärtlichkeit und Schmeicheln" and "Welche Wonne, welche Lust," are exactly what Goethe normally liked in operatic music: cheerful melodies with a folksong-like quality and a crisp strophic setting (strophic here as the opposite of "durchkomponiert").[31] And then, who can resist for long Osmin's "poison and dagger" shenanigans, communicated as they are by a music of wit, mockery and infectious humor? Yet, in the end, it may well have been the serious element in the play which received Goethe's closest attention: the theme of self-restraint and forgiveness. Pasha Selim, the barbarian king, reveals himself as a noble and magnanimous ruler: he controls his emotions and defeats his desire for revenge by allowing the four captives, Constanze, Belmonte, Blonde and Pedrillo, to return to their homeland, even though he desires the beautiful Constanze and Belmonte, her lover,

---

[29] Alfred Orel, *Goethe als Operndirektor*, p. 190. *Das rote Käppchen*, incidentally, has nothing to do with the fairy tale "Rotkäppchen." It is a Singspiel based on an opera buffa by Filippo Livignis called *Giannini e Bernadone* (music by Cimarosa); the original theme came from Boccaccio's *Decamerone*.

[30] Sophienausgabe, 1:53, 268.

[31] Goethe talks about "Durchkomponieren" in a letter to Zelter (March 14, 1803). He rejected this technique of "Lieder"-composition and along with it Schubert's settings of his poems.

turns out to be the son of his worst enemy. When the freed and happy lovers join their voices in a concluding quartet, "Nichts ist hässlicher als die Rache," they intone not only a favorite theme of the Enlightenment, one that Mozart splendidly recreated in Sarastro's aria "In diesen heil'gen Hallen, kennt man die Rache nicht," but they touch on something very close to Goethe's heart: self-control and individual restraint. He himself had begun to dramatize this very theme in his play *Iphigenie auf Tauris*, begun in 1779 and published in 1787; Goethe had written at least two versions of the play when he saw *Die Entführung* in 1785.[32] Thoas, the barbarian king in Goethe's play, much like Pasha Selim in *Die Entführung*, overcomes his personal desires, his feelings of anger and revenge, to spare the lives of the captive Greeks. He allows them to leave his island and bids them farewell, even Iphigenia, whom he had hoped to win as his queen. The similarities between the play and the *Singspiel* are striking: both depict generous and humane despots; both depict heroines, Iphigenia and Constanze (Pamina, too, belongs here) who possess the same personal characteristics: strength, steadfastness and incorruptibility. And while Thoas and Iphigenia are cut from much finer poetic cloth than either Pasha Selim or Constanze, the theme and the dramatic configurations are too much alike for Goethe not to have noticed their essential relationship.

Whatever the objective and subjective reasons for Goethe's initial difficulties with *Die Entführung*, he overcame them. He overcame the effects of technical shortcomings and, what is more, he overcame his own prejudice. He recognized that Mozart had composed a *Singspiel* more powerful and effective than what he and Kayser had created. So he did something not altogether characteristic: he bowed before the younger artist, he accepted his work and, in the course of time, became his complete admirer. As director of the Court Theater he promoted Mozart's operatic works in Weimar, and later, when Mozart was long dead, he again and again returned to Mozart in thought and artistic association. "Mozart ought to have composed the music for Faust," he mused on one occasion, when discussing with Eckermann, his secretary, some possible musical settings for his great drama. "The music would have to be in the character of *Don Giovanni*."[33] (There are several

---

[32] Cf. *Iphigenie*, Prosafassung von 1778 und *Iphigenie*, Zweite Prosafassung, in: *Gedenkausgabe*, ed. Beutler, VI, 102–147 and 148–212.

[33] Johann Peter Eckermann, *Gespräche mit Goethe* (München, 1976), p. 313 (Conversation of Feb. 12, 1829).

examples of Mozart-inspired works by Goethe. The most obvious, of course, is *Der Zauberflöte, zweiter Theil*, which remained a fragment. But we also find Mozartean themes and forms in *Faust, Novelle, Das Märchen*, and perhaps even in *Die Wahlverwandtschaften).*[34]

Goethe's artistic relationship to Mozart is based, however, on more than enjoyment and inspiration; it is based on a genuine understanding of Mozart's music, of its power and its vitality. The works of Mozart, he observed to Eckermann, belong to those creations in the world which are of "consequence" and "permanence"; they possess a "procreative power ('eine zeugende Kraft') that carries them from generation to generation," and their effect will not easily diminish in the course of time.[35] The observation is remarkable. It reveals unusual sensitivity to music, particularly to Mozart's music, which was perceived at that time all too frequently as either too difficult or too light and playful, as either demonic and mystical or as the rococo products of a sunny "Olympian." Goethe's judgment was as correct as it was uncommon: in fact, he seems to have had an understanding not only of Mozart's art, but of the entire phenomenon called Mozart. Of all the great artists to whom Goethe offered the full measure of his reverence (e.g. Homer, Shakespeare, Raphael), it is Mozart of whom he speaks with special fondness and to whom he shows a special affinity. And when, toward the end of his life, he said of the composer that he was "ein Wunder, das nicht weiter zu erklären ist," he stated succinctly a deep insight which twentieth-century Mozarteans are just beginning to perceive:[36] "But, of course," Goethe said, "a phenomenon like Mozart will always remain a miracle. But how

[34] The subject of direct and indirect influences or associations between Mozart and Goethe can only be mentioned here. There are beginnings of such inquiries in: Oskar Seidlin, "Goethe's Magic Flute," (1943) repr. in his *Essays in German and Comparative Literature* (Chapel Hill, N.C., 1961), pp. [45]–59: Hans-Albrecht Koch, "Goethes Fortsetzung der Schikanederschen 'Zauberflöte'," in *Jahrbuch des Freien Deutschen Hochstifts 1969* (Tübingen, 1969), p. 121 ff.; Robert Spaethling, "The Unwritten Masterpiece of German Classicism: Mozart's Music for Goethe's *Faust*," *Forum* (Houston), XIV:2/3 (1976), 25–31.

[35] Eckermann, *Gespräche*, p. 673 (Conversation of March 11, 1828).

[36] I am thinking in particular here of Wolfgang Hildesheimer's recent book on Mozart, which presents some fascinating new aspects of Mozart's life and art, but in essence maintains: all our efforts will not bring us closer to the real Mozart — Mozart's "Gestalt . . . entzieht [sich uns,] indem sie sich hinter ihrer Musik verbirgt, und auch sie ist uns, in ihrer tiefsten Bedeutung, unzugänglich." *Mozart* (Frankfurt, 1977), p. 17.

else would the Divinity find opportunity to do miracles if not at times through extraordinary individuals whom we behold in awe and cannot grasp whence they come."[37]

Goethe spoke these words in 1831, a year before his death; but it was forty-five years earlier, in 1785, and through *Die Entführung* in Weimar, that he first opened himself to the ineffable experience of Mozart.

[37] Eckermann, *Gespräche*, p. 450. (Conversation of February 14, 1831).

The Golden Shoes of Frau von Spiegel: An Incident from Goethe's Last Years

RODNEY G. DENNIS

"DEAREST FRIEND, I am having the very same trouble with your leaf and books that I once had with Frau von Spiegel's album." Goethe, writing to Julie von Egloffstein in 1827, recalled the time six years before when he had returned a young woman's album uninscribed because nothing had occurred to him.[1] The event, made prominent by his customary fluency, was apparently hard to excuse. Goethe could not put it out of his mind, took pains to make repairs, and wrote at last a beautiful poem for Frau von Spiegel's album. The album itself disappeared at the owner's death and completely eluded scholarship until in due course it found its way to the Houghton Library laden with matters of interest.[2] I shall recount here something of Frau von Spiegel's brief acquaintance with fame and then describe those parts of her album that bear on Goethe.

On January 30th, 1810, the birthday of Luise, Grand Duchess of Sachse-Weimar was celebrated with more than usual enthusiasm because of the Princess Caroline's impending engagement, and Goethe wrote and produced an elaborate *Maskenzug*, "Die romantische Poesie," for the occasion. Thirty members of the court, richly costumed and representing figures in the history of Germanic literature, processed and declaimed

[1] *Goethes Werke*, Sophienausgabe, 143v. (Weimar: H. Böhlau, 1887–1912) (hereafter cited as "Sophienausgabe," by division: volume/part, and page) IV:42, 239: Goethe to Gräfin Julie v. Egloffstein [end of June 1827].

[2] Houghton Library MS Ger 203. The album was purchased by the Library in June, 1950 from Dietrich Hoffmann of Jamaica Plain, Massachusetts with funds bequeathed by Henry Saltonstall Howe. My thanks to Patrick Miehe for bringing it to my attention.

[3] Sophienausgabe I:16, [215]–227; H. Düntzer, *Goethes Maskenzüge* (Leipzig, 1886), pp. 74ff. and 87ff.; W. Hecht, "Goethes Maskenzüge," in *Studien zur Goethezeit. Festschrift für Lieselotte Blumenthal* (Weimar, 1968), pp. 137–138.

verses in the great hall of the *Stadthaus*.[3] The particular success of the evening, by all reports, was Emilie Freifrau von Spiegel von und zu Pickelsheim, the twenty-three year old wife of Karl Emil Freiherr von Spiegel, Hofmarschall at Weimar. She played the part of the Princess of Byzantium, courted and abducted by the German King Rother, according to a twelfth-century poem that had recently been discovered by Ludwig Tieck.[4] Goethe's lavishness in questions of production was such that Voigt, the minister responsible for finance, refused to attend these celebrations,[5] and Emilie von Spiegel's costume was reported at length in the *Journal des Luxus and der Moden:* "The lower garment of white satin with a great train and long sleeves with gold fringe. The first tunic of muslin was very richly embroidered, double trimmed with lace with a rich border of silver. The second tunic was *drap d'argent* richly embroidered with gold; the short sleeves trimmed with fur. . . . The head piece was a turban of *drap d'or* wound with muslin with two long pearl-ended tassels. In front a pearl diadem with colored precious stones. . . . The shoes were sandals with gold laces."[6]

Thus attired, Frau von Spiegel recited her stanza beginning

> Nun geht es auf das Licht der Morgenländer,
> Die Tochter von Byzanz; Ihr seht sie hier!

The effect was memorable (see plate, p. 57). Riemer said she was "himmlisch schön!"[7] Chancellor von Müller spoke of an "unforgettable impression."[8] Goethe himself, many years later, recalled the Princess and King Rother in "the brilliance of beauty and majesty" and added "It is a shame that one cannot hold such sights fast, nor even repeat them as one can good plays."[9] The *Maskenzug* was, to be sure, repeated on the 16th of February at a birthday party for the Princess Maria Paulowna, along with a group of Russian folksongs and dances, which required

---

[4] First published in F. H. von der Hagen and J. G. Busching (eds.), *Deutsche Gedichte des Mittelalters* (Berlin, 1808), I, 1–64.

[5] Düntzer, p. 88.

[6] *Journal des Luxus und der Moden*, VII (March, 1810), p. 198.

[7] Robert Kiel, "Aus den Tagebüchern Riemers, des vertrauten Freundes von Goethe," *Deutsche Revue*, XII/3 (July, 1887), 57.

[8] Friedrich v. Müller, *Unterhaltungen mit Goethe*, ed. E. Grumach (Weimar, 1956), p. 275.

[9] *Goethes Werke*, Ausgabe letzter Hand, 55 v. (Stuttgart & Tübingen: J. G. Cotta, 1828–33) (hereafter cited as "*Werke*, Ausgabe letzter Hand") IV, 183.

Maskenzug in Weimar am 30 Januar 1810.

Prinzessin.   Rother.   Brunehild.   Siegfried.

Journal des Luxus und der Moden, VII (1810). 175×190mm.
Boston Public Library.

new costumes.[10] Riemer, still under an impression, wrote hurriedly to a friend in Bern for a Swiss *Tracht* for Frau von Spiegel, who didn't like to dance in heavy Russian clothes. "Think," he said, "what beautiful lips will give you thanks!"[11]

Frau von Spiegel was born Emilie von Rotberg-Rheinweiler in the Black Forest town of Rheinweiler on January 26th, 1787. She married the Hofmarschall on April 18th, 1805, had four children and died in Weimar in 1870 after a life quiet, uneventful, and long. Her husband, according to the not disinterested Riemer, was not attentive,[12] but despite her beauty and her continuing interest in the theater, there was never any serious gossip. Her daughters married well. We remember her now because on January 26th, 1821, her thirty-fourth birthday, she received

[10] Kiel, p. 57.

[11] F. W. Reimer, *Aus dem Goethehause* (Stuttgart, 1892), p. 156: Riemer to K. F. E. Frommann, February, 1810.

[12] *Ibid.*, p. 209.

a red morocco album with her name in gilt on the front cover, the date of the gift on the back, and 46 leaves measuring 23½ by 20 centimeters, all blank except for page one, which bore a poem "Das Vergissmeinnicht unter Felstrümmern," perhaps in Herr von Spiegel's hand.

> Sei mir gegrüsst der Liebe Bild.
> In Felsenschütte, graus und wild,
> Wo jede Blume sich verlohr
> Dringst freundlich dennoch du hervor.
> Ach! wahre Liebe hat bald Raum,
> Und fragt nach vielem Gute kaum.
> Sollt' alles um sie her vergehn,
> *So bleibt doch wahre Liebe stehn.*

The first entry in the hand of the album's new owner was on folio 2[r], a poem to an unnamed person:

> Zum 26ten Januar 1821
>
> Wem gedenket die Freundin heut zu bringen
> Einen würdigen Kranz zur Tagesfeier?
> Welcher nehme beglückt so sehr die Herzen,
> Dass sich Freundinnen ihm und Freunde nahen? —
> Nennen will ich ihn nicht; doch immer sollen
> Diese Blättchen sein Lob den Freunden sagen,
> Und die Wünsche des Herzens, die ihm folgen:
> "Lange möge den Tag mit Bluhmenkränzen
> "Die frohlockende Schaar der Lieben feiern! . . ."[13]

The next page she saved for Goethe, to whom she took the album that same week.

In due course the album was returned. Across the top of folios 2[v] and 3[r] were the words "Ein Freund bittet ihm diese beyden Seiten offen zu halten. G." Frau von Spiegel's reaction to the disappointment is not recorded, but Chancellor von Müller reports that after this "a thousand accidental occurrences" kept her away from Goethe, and the affair must have become uncomfortable. At last, three years later, Goethe had her informed that he had heard that her album contained work by a young poet which he wished to read and that she was in a position to oblige

---

[13] Possibly to the Erbgrossherzog, Karl Friedrich, whose birthday, always an important event, came a week later on February 2d.

him. On Sunday, February 22, 1824, Frau von Spiegel and Müller paid Goethe a visit, which, according to Müller, was a success. Frau von Spiegel departed leaving her album behind.[14] Goethe's diary gives the essential information: 22 February 1824: "at 12 o'clock Frau von Spiegel and Chancellor von Müller . . . . [E]vening Frau von Spiegel's *Erinnerungsbuch.* Poem for same." 23 February: "Frau von Spiegel's *Gedächtnissbuch.*" 24 February: "I worked on the poem for Frau von Spiegel . . . ." 25 February: "copied over the poem for Frau von Spiegel."[15]

Frédéric Soret, a young Swiss geologist who was a tutor in the ducal household, saw Goethe on Monday evening February the 23rd: "I had chosen a Bulgarian costume for the birthday Masquerade for the Erbgrossherzog,[16] and I thought it quite becoming. Goethe wanted to see it and invited me to drop by during the course of the evening and show myself in masquerade. I found him all alone in his big hall, which was illuminated by a multitude of candles. Without saying a word he inspected me carefully; finally he pronounced the costume extremely pleasing, had punch brought to me and asked me to stay with him for a while. We strolled together up and down the hall without saying very much; I was becoming bored and burned with impatience to be off because people were waiting for me, but Goethe seemed completely lost in thought. Perhaps he was brooding over a new poem . . . ."[17]

Two evenings later the brooding was at an end. Eckermann reports "At dinner Goethe was in the best of moods. He showed me Frau von Spiegel's album in which he had written very beautiful verses. A space had been left for him for two years, and now he was happy finally to have succeeded in fulfilling his promise. After I had read the poem for Frau von Spiegel, I leafed through the book and encountered some significant names. Right on the next page was a poem by Tiedge written in the very same mood and tone as his *Urania.* 'In a fit of mischief,' said Goethe, 'I was just about to write some verses beneath it. I am glad I did not, for it would not have been the first time that by careless

---

[14] Müller, p. 275. The album itself does not definitively reveal who the young poet might have been.

[15] Sophienausgabe, III:9, 182–184.

[16] Three weeks before, on February 2d. Goethe had not attended the ball.

[17] F. Soret, *Zehn Jahre bei Goethe* (Leipzig, 1929), p. 106 has a German translation by H. H. Houben; the original French may be found in *Goethes Gespräche,* ed. W. Herwig (Zürich & Stuttgart [1965–72]), III/1, 657–658.

statements I had offended good people and spoiled the effect of my own best things.'"[18] These sentiments notwithstanding, we shall presently observe him failing to resist an almost identical temptation.

As for the text of Goethe's poem for Frau von Spiegel, the following may be conjectured. When Frau von Spiegel handed Goethe her album on Sunday the 22nd, he put it aside without opening it and did not return to it until Wednesday, when he copied his new poem into it. To replace the sentence that he had written into the album in 1821 he composed a new couplet:

> Der Dichtung Faden lässt sich heut nicht fassen;
> Ich bitte mir die Blätter weiss zu lassen![19]

The poem itself follows. It has four stanzas, the second and third of which were those stanzas spoken by the Princess and by Rother in the *Maskenzug* of 1810. Of these two stanzas, Rother's needed some rewriting for the new occasion. On the 25th Goethe copied the poem into the album, leaving out the new couplet, either for lack of space or because it duplicated the words already written, and rewrote the first half of the third stanza once again. He gave the date not of the composition of the poem but of Frau von Spiegel's visit. On the same day Eckermann copied Goethe's draft. The couplet was retained, preceded by the date "Januar 1821", when the album had first been offered. Goethe oversaw the copy and added the date "25 Febr 1824" at the end. Eckermann deleted this and placed it after the couplet at the head of the poem. Goethe's draft was not saved.[20] Müller, however, saw the album and copied its version almost exactly, but of course, in the absence of the album itself his copy lacked authority.[21] Folios 2ᵛ and 3ʳ of Frau von Spiegel's album are as follows:

> Ein Freund bittet ihm diese beyden Seiten offen zu halten.
> G.
>
> Seit jener Zeile bis zum heutigen Tage
> Sind fast zweyhundert Wochen fortgeschritten,

---

[18] J. P. Eckermann, *Gespräche mit Goethe in den letzten Jahren seines Lebens* [Wiesbaden, 1955], p. 83. Note that the lapse in time was three years, not two.

[19] *Werke*, Ausgabe letzter Hand, IV, 121.

[20] Sophienausgabe, 1:5/2, 22.   [21] Müller, p. 275.

Und immer ist es noch die alte Klage
Als lasse sich die Muse nicht erbitten;
Doch wenn ich sie im Stillen erns[t]lich frage
Versetzt sie mich mit Adlerflug in mitten
Von jener Feyer einzigen Augenblicken
Wie es erscholl im freudigsten Entzücken:

"Nun geht es auf das Licht der Morgenländer,
Die Tochter von Byzanz; Ihr seht sie hier!
Als Kaiserskind traegt sie die Goldgewänder,
Und doch ist sie des Schmuckes hoechste Zier.
Die goldnen Schuhe, jene theuren Pfänder,
Die Liebesboten zwischen ihm und ihr,
Sie bringt der Zwerg, die frohste Morgengabe:
Ein Liebespfand ist mehr als Gut und Habe."

"Die Dichtung rühmte, heiter wie bedächtig,
Dann König Rothers unbezwungne Kraft;
Und wie er schon in Waffen gros und mächtig,
Hat Liebe nun ihm solches Glück verschafft.
Als Pilger klug, als Gast freygebig, prächtig,
Hat er als Held zuletzt sie weggerafft,
Zum schönsten Glück, zum höchsten Mutterloose:
Von ihnen stammt Pipin und Carl der Grosse."

Wie denn das Gute, Schoene nimmer schwindet
Und, immer wirckend, immer sich erhält,
Sich ungesäumt zum höchsten Wahren findet,
Als lebend zu Lebendigem gesellt;
Und glücklich ist wer ihnen sich verbindet,
Beständig bleibt ihm die bewegte Welt;
So wars auch mir, im Augenblick dem Süssen,
Nach langer Zeit die Freundin zu begrüssen.

Zur frohen Erinnerung der Schönen Morgenstunde,
Weimar. d. 22 Febr. 1824
Goethe

The three versions of the first half of the third stanza, according to the conjectured order of their composition are as follows:

from "Die romantische Poesie" (*Werke*, Ausgabe letzter Hand, XIII, 215)

Rother

Ich spreche nun so heiter als bedächtig
Von König Rother's unbezwungner Kraft;
Und ob er gleich in Waffen gross und mächtig,
Hat Liebe doch ihm solches Glück verschafft.

from "In das Stammbuch der Frau Hofmarschall v. Spiegel" (*Werke*, Ausgabe letzter Hand, IV, 122)

Das sprach das Lied, so heiter als bedächtig
Von König Rothers unbezwungner Kraft,
Dem, wie er schon in Waffen gross und mächtig,
Auch Liebe nun das höchste Glück verschafft.

from Frau von Spiegel's album

Die Dichtung rühmte, heiter wie bedächtig,
Dann König Rothers unbezwungne Kraft;
Und wie er schon in Waffen gros und mächtig,
Hat Liebe nun ihm solches Glück verschafft.

Notwithstanding this somewhat complicated order of events, the Eckermann copy, the version that Goethe himself saw into print, must be regarded as the definitive one. And yet the version of the album, a little less formal in tone, might seem the more appropriate one for the occasion. In either version the poem was a success, and Frau von Spiegel must have been pleased.

The album, 46 leaves in all, extends in time from January 21st 1821, to December 14th 1825. When Goethe and Eckermann looked through it, it was complete up to folio 33. Besides Tiedge, the "significant names" included Shakespeare, J. J. Rousseau, Schiller, and F. L. Graf Stolberg. The only literary autograph was an entry in Allemanec by J. P. Hebel acquired during a trip to Carlsruhe in October 1822.[22]

f. 23^r   Ne Wörtli us der Heimeth her
möcht, edli Frau, gern mittich goh.
wo's ane goht, enander no,
mit gutem Wunsch, mit guter Bitt.
Uf Euere Wege gleitich Gott,
und was uf Erde liebs und guets

---

[22] Apparently an uncollected dedication.

für frummi zarti Gmuethen spriest,
wo Erd und Himmel z'seme fliest,
das gunnich Gott, das gebich Gott.

Carlsruhe d. 31 Octob 1822. J. P. Hebel

Confirmation sermons for Frau von Spiegel's daughters Pauline and Melanie and their confessions of faith written out by their mother and confirming minister take up a good deal of space, as do many entries, poetry and prose, in French and German made during a trip home to Rheinweiler in 1822. There are anonymous poems and quotations mostly moral or religious and birthday poems for Emilie von Spiegel, two of which may be quoted here. The first, in an unidentified hand, is apparently by one of the sons:

f. 6ʳ

Zum Geburtstag meiner lieben Mutter
den 26ten Januar 1820

Du hast mich stets zu dem, was fromm und gut geleitet,
Dies fühlend und mit Dank erkennend weihe,
Ich heute Dir, was Herrliches, Erhabnes mir bereitet
Der gütigen Mutter Liebe, Huld und Treue!
Und wenn mich einst, erwachsen Durst nach Thaten
Hinaustreibt in den wilden Sturm der Welt,
Dann soll Dein Wort, Dein himmlisch Bild, mich noch einladen.
Was *böss zu hassen* für TUGEND RECHT zu stehen wie ein Held.

Weimar, den 8ten April 1822.

The second is in Frau von Spiegel's hand:

f. 14ʳ   bei überreichen eines Engel Köpfchens als Ring den ich
zum Geburtstag am 26 Januar 1822 erhielt lagen folgende
Worte anbei

Es Schweben Engel um dein frommes Leben
und schützen es mit unsichtbarer Macht.
Drum sei der Engel den ich dir gegeben
dir nur als Liebes-Zeichen dargebracht.

The volume is a family album without literary pretension. Still, considering the prominence that Frau von Spiegel gave to Goethe's entry, it is noticeable that he is neither named nor cited on the other pages written before he finally kept his promise. Afterwards this changed, and folios 39^v to 41^r all contain matters relating directly to him. First the poem "Erwählter Fels" appears in Frau von Spiegel's hand with the words "in Goethe's Berggarten" beneath the title and at the end "Zum Andenken an den Morgen des 7 Juli 1825." We know from Müller of a breakfast in Goethe's garden on that day attended by Goethe, Müller, Frau von Spiegel and her sister Albertine, Gräfin von Rapp who at that point was everyone's favorite and who received her own album poem that very day. Müller had eyes only for the sister wearing a hat of white and a dress of cherry-brown: "Mild air and a pleasant stroll . . . a sudden rain drove us indoors. How quiet and amiable is the view onto the park through the little window. 'It is just,' said the darling, 'as if we had been enchanted away, far, far, from the noise and confusion of city life!'"[23] Frau von Spiegel apparently felt this too and chose her poem accordingly.

Folio 40^r begins with a quotation from Jean Paul in Frau von Spiegel's hand:

> Der Mensch hat dritthalb Minuten; eine zu lächeln, eine
> zu seufzen, und eine halbe zu lieben; denn mitten in dieser
> Minute stirbt er. — den 1 October 25

In the middle of f. 40^v, also in Frau von Spiegel's hand:

> Räthsel
>
> Nicht sterblich, noch unsterblich aber von Natur
> Gebildet also dass es nicht nach Menschen Art,
> Noch Götterweise lebt, sondern stets aufs neue
> Gebohren wird, wechselsweise zum Untergang;
> Gesehen von keinem, allen aber wohlbekannt
> Vorzüglich Kindern, die er sich besonders liebt.
>
> Seinem 7. Jährigen Enkel ins Stammbuch geschrieben vom
> *grossen*, Grossvater den 9. October 1825.

Both of these quotations are from the album of Goethe's grandson Walter. The first was written there by Emilie von Spiegel herself, and it is known that Goethe, objecting to its sentimentality, dealt with Jean Paul as he had threatened to deal with Tiedge. He instantly composed and inscribed in Walter's album the following lines (understandably omitted from Frau von Spiegel's album):

---

[23] Müller, p. 140.

> Ihrer sechzig hat die Stunde,
> Über tausend hat der Tag.
> Söhnchen! werde dir die Kunde
> Was man alles leisten mag.

According to Goethe, these words and the *Räthsel*, his own rendition of a puzzle by Alexis Athenaios, were entered into Walter's album on April 9th 1825 at a party for his seventh birthday. The reason Frau von Spiegel wrote them into her own album six months later is not known.[24]

Between these two inscriptions, beginning on f. 40^r is a poem, also in Frau von Spiegel's hand:

> Dem G. H. v. S. W. zu seiner goldenen Hochzeit
> überreichte goldene Schuhe von S. M. Schiede [Schmiede?]

> Zum goldnen Feste bring ich goldne Schuh'
> Die Du mit gnädgen Augen wollest sehen
> Wer solchen Weg, o Herr! genoss wie du
> Hat recht verdient in goldnen jetzt zu gehen.

> Sie sind geschmeidig, immer reich fournirt
> Und werden sanft sich *deinem* Fuss bequemen
> Dass reich und künstlich aussen sie verziert
> Wird Dich o bester Herr nicht Wunder nehmen

> Denn da die Kunst Dein ganzes Leben Du
> Zu schutzen, zu beford ern nie verfehlet
> Was Wunder also? wenn sie bis zum Schuh
> Dem Handwerk sich in Deinem Reich vermählet

Grand Duke Karl August's fiftieth wedding anniversary was celebrated on October 3rd 1825, one month after the great *Jubelfest* commemorating the fiftieth year of his reign. Frau von Spiegel was close to his family.

The entry on folio 41^r, the last one to be cited here, concerns Goethe's "feierlichster Tag", the 7th of November 1825, the fiftieth anniversary of his residence in Weimar. It had occurred more than once to Goethe's friends to awaken him with music. Sulpiz Boisserée tells how on Goethe's 66th birthday, while he was staying in Gerbermühle, his hosts had him serenaded from a boat on the Main while he was

---

[24] Müller, p. 166; Sophienausgabe, I:4, 267 & 334, I:5/2, 161 & 210–211.

awakening. Goethe, somewhat frightened, cried out "Ei, ei, musicians are coming!" and spoiled the moment.[25] This story was apparently not known in Weimar, for on the stated morning in 1825 the ladies of the court, standing outside his window, awakened their genius with soft chorales and then, entering his reception room, no less than forty in number, greeted his descent from his bedroom with an entire "Morning Cantata," text by Riemer, music by Eberwein.[26]

Frau von Spiegel was, of course, among those present. She had composed her own poem to let him know she was there, and to tell him again what he had done for her. Her gift of golden shoes to the Grand Duke on his anniversary and the similar gift to Goethe reveal expressively that her own identity had been permanently established in the *Maskenzug* in 1810. The entry in her album is not in her own hand, but I have not been able to identify the writer.

An Goethe
zum frühen Morgen
des 7. Nov. 1825
die Tochter von Byzanz

Die Freundin, die durch Dich in goldnen Schuhe
Das heitre Reich der Dichtung einst betrat,
Sie ist's, die heut' nach sanfter Morgenruhe
Zuerst mit frohem Jubelgruss dir naht.
O könnte sie Dir frische Rosen streuen!
Doch solch' ein Tag leiht jedem Streben Muth;
So lass das alte Traumspiel sich erneuen,
Gönn' ihr den Stolz, dass *sie* DICH
heut BESCHUHT."

---

[25] S. Boisserée, *Briefwechsel, Tagebücher*, Faksimiledruck (Stuttgart, 1862, repr. Göttingen, 1970), I, 271–272.

[26] W. Bode, *Goethe in vertraulichen Briefen siener Zeitgenossen*, neu verlegt (Berne, 1969), III, 245–247: H. F. K. Peucer to K. A. Böttiger, 8 Nov. 1825; F. W. Riemer, *Morgengruss an Goethe zum Siebenten November 1825* (Weimar, [1825]).

Fontane's Craft of Fiction:
Art or Artifice?

KARL S. GUTHKE

I

ONE AFTERNOON during a New England heat-wave two summers
ago I was looking for excuses to linger in the cool comfort of
Houghton Library. I leafed through a catalogue of autograph acquisi-
tions and almost immediately felt a heat-wave from within. One item I
found was an unknown and most interesting Novalis letter which eventually sent ripples of excitement all the way down under to Melbourne,
Australia. The other item was a batch of four Fontane letters which
eventually became an object of polite attention in my Fontane seminar
in the building next door to Houghton Library. At least one of these
was remarkable because it revealed a most surprising side of Fontane,
namely the fact that he could be a dull letter-writer. One of the other
letters sheds less new light but caught my eye nonetheless. It is dated
August 15, 1890, and addressed to an anonymous gentleman who is still
defying all detective efforts to determine his identity, even though he
was clearly a critic — one of those "lice on the locks of literature," as
Lord Tennyson said, who don't usually hide on contact. This one took
tender loving care of literary locks, though, for Fontane thanks him as
profusely as a Berliner can for "diese neue Liebesthat." He must be
referring to a favorable review, and no doubt a review of his novel *Stine*,
published in April that year. "Es ist so vieles darin," says Fontaine about
the critic's comments, "was mir wohlgethan hat, unter anderm auch das,
dass ich den Adel selbst über den Adel sprechen lasse und auf Abgabe
persönlicher Meinungen verzichte. Freilich," he continues, "wer auf
Adelsseite will, kann dies Verfahren auch doppelt perfide finden. Ich
selber bin beruhigt."

What Fontane the citizen here calls the sophistication or even per-
fidiousness of his criticism of the class he loved and hated, Fontane the
craftsman would have called the subtlety or refinement of art: "Finesse,"
to use his preferred term, which critics have taken up since. What is a

"Finesse?" One that Fontane readers will most readily think of is the words "Effi, komm," in *Effi Briest*. These words are used twice. First, in the opening scene, when Effi, playing tag with her friends Bertha, Hertha and Hulda around the rhubarb patch, is called inside by her mother who tells her that Baron Innstetten has just asked for her hand in marriage; as Effi — "Ich bin gleich wieder da" [1] — catches sight of Innstetten she trembles nervously, "aber nicht auf lange, denn im selben Augenblicke fast, wo sich Innstetten unter freundlicher Verneigung ihr näherte, wurden an dem mittleren der weit offenstehenden und von wildem Wein halb überwachsenen Fenster die rotblonden Köpfe der Zwillinge sichtbar, und Hertha, die Ausgelassenste, rief in den Saal hinein: 'Effi, komm'" (VII, 19). Then, near the end of the novel, after marriage, adultery, divorce and years of ostracism by family and society, Effi is called back to Hohen-Cremmen, the family estate, by her parents, who have finally come around to the view that their only child means more to them than society. "Ich werde," says her father, "ganz einfach telegraphieren: 'Effi, komm'" (VII, 291).

Fontane was very proud of his "Finessen," and of this one in particular.[2] Critics have generally agreed, and as a result, it is such "Finessen" — I shall introduce several others presently — that have been responsible, more than anything else, for elevating Fontane's novels to the rank of world literature. This elevation (which puts *Effi Briest* in the company of *Madame Bovary* and *Anna Karenina*) is a fairly recent development, dating from the 1950's, and culminating, perhaps, in Walther Killy's *Romane des 19. Jahrhunderts* of 1963. This is a study of a number of European and American novels in which natural and social reality has been successfully transformed into poetic reality by means of "Kunst" — the art of "narration, its technique and form"; [3] and it includes, along with chapters on Goethe, Stendhal, Dickens, Poe and Henry James, a discussion of the compositional art of *Irrungen, Wirrungen* — the novel into which, Fontane flattered himself, he had incorporated "tausend Finessen," no less (*DD*, 363).

---

[1] Theodor Fontane, *Romane und Erzählungen*, ed. Peter Goldammer et al. (Berlin, 1969), VII, 17. All references appearing after quotations from Fontane's novels are to this edition.

[2] Richard Brinkmann ed., *Theodor Fontane*, in the series Dichter über ihre Dichtungen (München, 1973), II, 449, 460. Quotations from this volume are identified as *DD*, followed by the page number.

[3] Göttingen, 1967, p. 15.

Fontane was right, of course, and so was Killy in tracing a few of the thousand; and yet we may have our doubts, even about the exemplary "Effi, komm" "Finesse," which the author himself was so pleased with, claiming in fact that it represented the very germ or inspiration of the entire novel (*DD*, 449, 460). We ourselves, trained as we are to raise our eyebrows compulsively at the slightest provocation, may not be quite so sure about the quality of this subtle echo ("Effi, komm"), which supposedly ties the whole novel together so artistically.[4] Doesn't it seem more contrived than subtle, especially when we recall that there is a third time that Fontane refers to it in *Effi Briest*, three pages after the first mention? Innstetten, we hear there, pays only perfunctory attention to Major von Briest's conversation: he is

> wenig bei der Sache, sah vielmehr, wie gebannt, immer aufs neue nach dem drüben am Fenster rankenden wilden Wein hinüber, von dem Briest eben gesprochen, und während er dem nachhing, war es ihm, als säh er wieder die rotblonden Mädchenköpfe zwischen den Weinranken und höre dabei den übermütigen Zuruf: "Effi, komm."
>
> Er glaubte nicht an Zeichen und ähnliches, im Gegenteil, wies alles Abergläubische weit zurück. Aber er konnte trotzdem von den zwei Worten nicht los, und während Briest immer weiter perorierte, war es ihm beständig, als wäre der kleine Hergang doch mehr als ein blosser Zufall gewesen (VII, 22).

A suggestion of ominous, even fateful foreboding, obviously — and that seems to be "rubbing it in" rather than subtlety, contrivance or artifice rather than art. "Man spürt die Absicht, und man ist verstimmt." Or is one? There are critics, of course, who are not,[5] and there are even

---

[4] Cf. Walter Müller-Seidel, *Theodor Fontane. Soziale Romankunst in Deutschland* (Stuttgart, 1975), p. 373: "höchst kunstvoll — allzu kunstvoll vielleicht."

[5] See e.g. Mary E. Gilbert, "Fontanes *Effi Briest*," *Der Deutschunterricht*, XI:4 (1959), 67; Dietrich Weber, "*Effi Briest* — 'Auch wie ein Schicksal'. Über den Andeutungsstil bei Fontane," *Jahrbuch des Freien Deutschen Hochstifts* (1966), 468. Weber concludes from the "Effi, komm" passages that Fontane "die Geschichte Effis als Schicksalsgeschehen verstanden wissen will," as "mehr als Zufall" (ibid.). He sees the same "Tendenz zur Irrationalisierung des Geschehens" ("Schicksalsroman") as does Riechel (p. 473; see below, note 18 and my criticism of this view in the text).

those who feel that there is an additional and very esoteric subtlety here in that the voice of the playmate comes from a window framed by luxuriating wild vines — for wild vines, we are told, regularly point to the sphere of unrestraint and freedom from convention in Fontane's novels.[6] But we may well wonder if this is not a subtlety that exists only in the eye of the beholder. For after all, who is to appreciate this elusive symbolism, especially as it occurs so early in the novel — before the author has established any such frame of symbolic reference within the novel itself (assuming that he does establish it, which in fact he does not). Doesn't it take a rare case of professional malformation to see this subtlety, or else training in the safari method of literary criticism, which stalks any and all possible symbols and guns them down on sight without the slightest concern for the textual environment and without stopping to think that they might be optical illusions? And how does such (supposed) subtlety go with the heavy-handed *avis-au-lecteur* given by Innstetten when he is made to think, for our benefit, that "Effi, komm" was more than just coincidence?

To sum up, is it not possible that the latter-day critical apotheosis of Fontane[7] — his canonization by the College of Comparative Literature as St. Theodore of Berlin (Potsdamer Str. 134c) — is based, in part, on refinements so fine that ordinary mortals cannot perceive them and, on the other hand, on a charitable effort to look the other way on encountering the heavy-handed "Finessen" which smack more of artifice than art, as Flaubert's or Jane Austen's clearly do not? This is not to deny, of course, that there are "Finessen" in between these extremes, subtleties which *do* deserve the name, as "Effi, komm" would, if Innstetten were not allowed to meditate upon it so obtrusively. It would seem, therefore, that there is no harm in discriminating and evaluating Fontane's "Finessen" rather than using them wholesale as evidence of his art: what might emerge from an effort to discriminate in this matter is a more critical and differentiated assessment of the artist, who was, after all, the first to put the German novel on the European map.

[6] Max Tau, *Der assoziative Faktor in der Landschafts- und Ortsdarstellung Theodor Fontanes* (Oldenburg, 1928), p. 18; Peter Demetz, *Formen des Realismus: Theodor Fontane. Kritische Untersuchungen*, 2nd ed. (München, 1966), p. 204; Weber, p. 468.

[7] There is some criticism of this apotheosis in the preface to the second edition of Brinkmann's *Theodor Fontane. Über die Verbindlichkeit des Unverbindlichen* (Tübingen, 1977), but Brinkmann aims at the canonization of Fontane's "Menschlichkeit" rather than his artistic achievement.

2

Fontane himself was very much aware that his stature as a novelist depended largely or even exclusively on the *quality* of his artistic subtlety, on his "Finessen," for short. It may, therefore, be pardonable to go into his own view of the matter a bit, by way of introduction, in order to throw the problem into relief as a worthwhile topic of investigation rather than as matter of what Fontane called "quacklige Wichtigtuerei."[8] Discussing "Finessen" was, for him, emphatically no "Quackelei."

Let us have a look then, at Fontane's philosophy of "Finessen," as he articulates it not only as a commentator on his own works, but also as a professional critic of others (which he was to a much greater extent than his own assessment of literary criticism — unhealthier than splitting firewood (*DD*, 679) — would lead you to suspect). What develops is nothing less than his theory of art.

Art ("Kunst"), according to Fontane's scattered remarks, is always precariously perched between "reality," "life," "nature," and "truth," on the one hand, and artifice ("Künstelei") on the other. It touches both extremes, sometimes becoming indistinguishable from one or the other, and yet it is to maintain its own identity — which is defined as the opposite of either extreme.

One criterion of art is that it is life-like: that a novel or a play gives us the impression of real life, reality, "das Natürliche"[9]: "Kunst [soll] einfach das Leben widerspiegeln" (*DD*, 273). "*Was soll ein Roman?* . . . [E]r soll uns eine Welt der Fiktion . . . als eine Welt der Wirklichkeit erscheinen . . . lassen" (*DD*, 639). Fontane made no bones about the fact that the material of a good many of his novels was taken from real occurrences in contemporaneous Prussian society — *Effi Briest, L'Adultera, Unwiederbringlich* — "alles Tatsache," as he writes about the case of *Schach von Wuthenow* (*DD*, 296): "Ein Stück Leben," then, "das wirkliche Leben," the more accurately lifted from reality, the better (*DD*, 271, 372). To be sure, Fontane knew that, strictly speaking, this is impossible to achieve: when you walk from the Anhalt station in Berlin to the Zoo, he says in a letter about *Irrungen, Wirrungen*, you do not in fact pass a certain tobacconist's shop — contrary to the novel;

[8] *Sämtliche Werke* [München: Nymphenburger Verlagshandlung, 1959–1975], XXI:1, 339. References of this type are always to the Nymphenburger Ausgabe.

[9] XXII:1, 839; cf. *DD*, 461.

nor can you see Charlottenburg Palace from a balcony in Land-grafenstrasse; the circus would be closed in summer, his wife had com-plained, and meteorologists might point out that at such and such a time of the year a half-moon could not have been seen over the elephant house, etc. Still, Fontane says, granting all this and more, such as inac-curacies about the military, gardening and fishing, "Man muss schon zufrieden sein, wenn wenigstens der Totaleindruck der ist: 'Ja, das ist Leben'" (*DD*, 372).

This may sound like Naturalism and indeed we seem to hear Arno Holz when Fontane states in a theater review that the art of a certain actress has unfortunately not quite found its way back to nature (XXII:1, 903). Nonetheless, lifelikeness for Fontane is not what it was for some Naturalists: He rejected the muse of Naturalists such as Zola and Tur-genev because it was a "Muse in Sack und Asche, Apollo mit Zahn-weh."[10] What their novels practice is "das nackte Wiedergeben alltäglichen Lebens"; they present mere "Griffe ins Leben" (XXII:1, 743), reality in the raw as it were — the crude ore rather than the metal, the rough chunks of marble as they come from the quarry; "die Läuterung fehlt" (XXI:1, 12). "Daguerreotyp des Lebens" will not do; it is not art (XXII:3, 113).

The paradox of Fontane's aesthetics, then, is that it is to achieve the impression of nature, "die Wirkung des Natürlichen" (XXII:1, 839), but can succeed in this endeavor only if it somehow transforms the "natural" raw material. Accordingly, Fontane says about Hauptmann's *Vor Sonnenaufgang*: "Dabei . . . spricht sich in *dem*, was dem Laien einfach als abgeschriebnes Leben erscheint, ein Mass von Kunst aus, wie's nicht grösser gedacht werden kann" (*DD*, 694). The appearance of nature is the triumph of art, *not* of nature. In real life, Lieschen Selicke, wasting away in a working-class apartment in the North End of Berlin, would not have affected him, Fontane says; in the play by Holz and Schlaf, surely the most lifelike of the slice-of-life dramas of the time, she moves him to tears. Why? Because, after all is said and done, even in these slices of life ("'Ausschnitten' aus dem Leben") there remains a difference between life and art, "zwischen dem Bilde, das das Leben stellt, und dem Bilde, das die Kunst stellt" (XXII:2, 734). What sort of difference? A "mysterious shaping" ("rätselvolle Modelung") occurs as

---

[10] To Emilie Fontane, 9. Juli 1881, in *Briefe I*, ed. Kurt Schreinert and Charlotte Jolles (Berlin, 1968), p. 164; cf. XXI:1, 473; XXII:3, 113.

life is transposed into literature, and this is the very essence of its artistic quality, the very "law" of art (XXI:1, 300). It is, in fact, all that matters in literature and criticism: "ob nach dem Leben oder nicht, die Kunst hat eben ihre eignen Gesetze" (*DD*, 423).

But, more specifically, what is this law of art? For one thing, it is a matter of what Fontane calls "Verklärung," that is, of letting human substance and significance shine through mere reality.[11] For another, the law of art involves the shaping of material into those aesthetic proportions, constellations, correspondences, configurations which constitute the well-rounded and well-articulated whole or entity of the literary work: it is a matter of "composition, skillful preparations and solutions, . . . treatment of details, pointed dialogue" (XXII:1, 671), die "Kunst des Anknüpfens, des Inbeziehungbringens, des Brückenschlagens" (XXI:2, 109). The hand that snatches a chunk of life must be an "artistic hand" — a hand that is capable of creating artistic subtleties, in short, those "Finessen" which, Fontane implies, are the hallmark of art.[12] His own hand, Fontane thought, was such a hand. He liked to point out that he was a "stylist" first and foremost (*DD*, 281). The first draft of a novel, he often remarked, the fixation of the material in its rough shape and outline, never caused him any problems: it was "eigentlich ein Vergnügen" (*DD*, 280) — much like taking dictation from a spirit appearing at an occultist séance, he liked to say (*DD*, 384). It was the "correcting," the "revision" ("Durcharbeitung," "Durchsicht," "Fertigmachen") that was "a hell of a job" (*DD*, 280), requiring him to "account for every word" (XXII:2, 114), a task that took much longer and extended well into the proof-reading stage, to the polite distress of his publishers. Fontane suffered, as he diagnosed the case himself, from the "'immer-besser Machungs-wollen'-Krankheit" (*DD*, 615); he was afflicted with a compulsion for "grenzenlose Düftelei" (*DD*, 384), for tinkering endlessly with the smallest details, with "Nebensachen," as he says (*DD*, 391). Of course, such "Nebensachen" were in fact "immer die Hauptsache; *das*, wodurch man sich vom Riffraff unterscheidet" (*DD*, 280) — namely that which turns reality into "art" or "style."[13] Art or style, then, is a result of highly conscious, highly self-critical

---

[11] Cf. Hugo Aust, *Theodor Fontane: "Verklärung". Eine Untersuchung zum Ideengehalt seiner Werke* (Bonn, 1974), esp. p. 20: "Sinnorientierte 'Modelung' der erfassten Wirklichkeit." See also Richard Brinkmann (above, note 7), p. 40.

[12] *DD*, 405; XXI:1, 12–14.

[13] See also *DD*, 262, 277, 360, 379, 453.

remodeling of the raw material (*DD*, 671, 701); it is *produced* with a high degree of awareness and deliberateness.

To formulate the paradox of Fontane's aesthetics the other way round, we could say, then, that literature is to distinguish itself from reality through its style or art — which in turn, however, should give the impression of reality; which is to say that the triumph of art is its own vanishing act. "Die Kunst soll da sein, aber man soll sie nicht als solche fühlen," if the "effect of naturalness" is to be achieved, Fontane says.[14] Unwittingly, he highlights the crux of this aesthetic credo when he quotes a Berlin architect as saying: "Der Stil wird angeputzt": style, art, is a matter of stucco or plaster trimmings added on for decoration (*DD*, 397). Among architects, Fontane continues when he quotes this memorable phrase a second time, this is the ultimate in bad taste, but "bei uns ist es schliesslich alles" (*DD*, 444). Is it really? If it were (if "style" were indeed a matter of adding on decorative detail arbitrarily, regardless of whether or not it fitted the nature or structure of the object so decorated), then Gottfried Keller would be a great stylist. This, however, Fontane denies, precisely because, as he noted in 1881, Keller fails to portray "real life" and "real people," subjecting them instead to his own arbitrariness ("Willkür"); he has no "style" because he does not let the objects speak for themselves, but instead adds his own conspicuous idiosyncrasies of diction: "Ein Werk ist um so stilvoller, je *objektiver* es ist," Fontane generalizes — clearly echoing Goethe's "Einfache Nachahmung, Manier, Stil" — "d. h. je mehr nur der Gegenstand selbst spricht, je freier es ist von zufälligen oder wohl gar der darzustellenden Idee widersprechenden Eigenheiten und Angewöhnungen des Künstlers" (XXI:1, 260, 264–265). This obtrusiveness of the artist, this obviousness of the art, of the "shaping" of the material is for Fontane the opposite of art — it is artifice: "Künstelei." "Und vor dieser hat man sich in der Kunst zu hüten" (XXI:1, 261).

This is the crux: the material must be consciously shaped; but "in dem 'Komponieren' liegt immer etwas Künstliches" (XXI:2, 224). So, if the shaping becomes obvious or too obvious, art turns into artifice. What is lost is the impression of "Organisch-Gewachsensein," of an "innerhalb der Kunst sich vollziehender Naturprozess," of a "Kunstwerk [das] organisch erwächst . . . nach den Gesetzen eines Naturprozesses" (XXI:2, 223–224). As examples of Fontane's practical criticism will show,

---

[14] XXII:1, 839, cf. 903.

these laws do not permit chance or the strikingly implausible (just as they did not in the classical aesthetics of Lessing and Goethe which Fontane's statements regularly hark back to): a "Kunstwerk" is to be "ein blühender Busch," not "ein Bukett" (ibid.).

A telltale adjective, from this point of view, in Fontane's criticism of Keller is "gezwungen" (XXI:1, 260), or "willkürlich." "Willkür" is the opposite of "Kunst" (XXI:1, 300). And just as Fontane distinguishes art from nature on the one hand, he distinguishes it from artifice on the other, in fact more so. "Corriger la nature" by touches of contrivance is to the detriment of art, says the theater critic (XXII:1, 505).

For what results is "gezwungen" (XXII:1, 671), "forciert" (XXI:1, 13), "geschraubt" (XXII:2, 735), "gekünstelt" (XXII:1, 671), "raffiniert" (XXI:2, 97), "konstruiert" (XXI:2, 334). The value of an authentic work of art, on the contrary, is for Fontane its natural and truthful "Ungezwungenheit"; we are even to be spared the impression of difficulties overcome (XXII:1, 671). If we are not, we become aware of unnatural, improbable "caprice" (XXII:1, 701) or the "erkältend wirkende Element des Erstudierten" (XXII:1, 839). One such case he finds, perhaps not surprisingly, in Lessing's *Emilia Galotti*, in the Freudian slip of Countess Orsina: "Des Morgens sprach der Prinz Ihre Tochter in der Messe, des Nachmittags hat er sie auf seinem Lust — Lustschlosse." Lessing, Fontane thinks, has gone to the outer limit of the artistically permissible here, a simple "auf seinem Lustschlosse" would have been preferable, i.e. less obvious, less "bedeutungsvoll" (XXII:2, 317). A cardinal sinner in this respect is Ibsen with his "Bestreben, das Zugespitzte noch immer spitzer zu machen, bis dann die Spitze zuletzt abbricht" (XXII:2, 713). This is, as Fontane puts it in a critique of an actor, a case of "Finessen, die versagen, weil sie noch feiner als fein sind" (contrived and therefore, in effect, crude). This actor, Fontane suggests, "müsste Jäger oder Schachspieler oder Mitglied des Seglerclubs werden, alle Donnerstag ein Erbsendiner haben und am Sonnabend flott darauf losspielen. Dann hätt' er's leichter, und wir auch" (XXII:2, 110).

This, then, is the logical risk of the artist who creates by that critical revision which turns "real life" into "art." On the one hand, "das 'Wie'," "die Mache" as Fontane calls it, is all-important (*DD*, 469, 474). On the other, Fontane tells the story of Sir Joshua Reynolds, who took the paint off some paintings of Titian in order to grasp the secret of his technique, and ended up painting less successfully than Titian and than he himself had before his attempt to grasp and imitate Titian's technique

(DD, 652–653) — ended up painting "gezwungen" or "gekünstelt", no doubt.

Fontane was very much in this quandary himself. Take the case of the love letters in *Effi Briest*, which lead to the discovery of the adultery and the tragic conclusion of the novel simply because Effi did not burn them. Fontane admits, in a letter, that this is a blemish: too trivial, he says; yet all the other possible solutions he had pondered did not seem "natural" or "probable" enough to him, he continues, "und das gesucht Wirkende ist noch schlimmer als das Triviale" (DD, 461). Here, then, he steered clear of "Künstelei," or thought he did. At other times he wondered whether, with his habitual love of detail, he was not treating "Nebensachen . . . zu liebevoll," so carefully that they resulted in shortcomings, "Mängel" (DD, 391–392). In *Effi Briest*, for example, he regretted "so billige Namenswitze, wie beispielsweise mit dem Namen 'Grasenapp'" (DD, 450) and with the name of the hotel in Sassnitz, which was "in reality" Fahrenberg, but is Fahrenheit in *Effi Briest*, suggesting a "kleiner Wortwitz" ("die Preise hoffentlich nach Réaumur"). "Ja, man wird mich in Verdacht haben, dass ich die Umtaufe, um mein Witzelchen anzubringen, absichtlich vollführt habe. Und das ist das Unangenehmste von der Sache" (DD, 447). In other words, he is worried about a "Finesse" that was too crude in retrospect and since "Finessen," for him, are tantamount to art, as he suggests at least once (DD, 405), he is worried about the quality of his novelistic art.

3

This, then, brings us back to our main inquiry: did Fontane need to worry about his "Finessen" — about intended "Finessen" that possibly weren't so fine? Yes and no — and it is this "and" between the two answers that will be the most intriguing question (which I shall come back to at the end).

The No first, however: he shouldn't have worried. This is what critics have been saying, of course, ever since Fontane's own days: when Otto Pniower, for instance, pointed out "Finessen" such as the art of symbolic anticipation in *Effi Briest*, Fontane was particularly pleased,[15]

---

[15] The review is reprinted in Reclam's Erläuterungen und Dokumente series, *Effi Briest*, ed. Walter Schafarschik (Stuttgart, 1975), pp. 121–123 ("Decenz . . . eine überaus fein ausgebildete Kunst des Vor- und Andeutens"). Fontane's reply: DD, 459.

and rightly so, for the most part. *Der Stechlin*, Fontane's undisputed masterpiece, is full of superbly realized "Finessen." The use of Lake Stechlin itself as symbol and leitmotif is perhaps not the prime example of this unobtrusive but unmistakable art, but think of the deftly and ironically manipulated political symbolism of the color red — on the roofs of the workers' village, on the necktie of the substitute doctor with his newfangled ideas (and black bugs on his tie), on the stockings of the working-class girl who keeps the old baron company as he dies, not to mention the lake's "der rote Hahn." Or think of the century-old "false aloe" growing in a planter in front of Castle Stechlin like an emblem of the family that is on its way out or down: its blossom is not its own but that of a garden-variety flower planted in the same planter. Or think of the name Melusine and the nice touch that it is she, the water sprite, who elucidates the symbolic meaning of Lake Stechlin, even if she nearly reduces the symbol to simple allegory. "Sich abschliessen heisst sich einmauern," she says, referring to the social attitudes of the nobility, "und sich einmauern ist Tod" (VIII, 288). Adelheid (the choice of this name for the representative of what the nobility used to be may be unfortunate — too cute or "obvious"), Adelheid, the baron's bizarrely fossilized sister, who, in her perversely charming innocence, hopes that the word "petrefakt" is not unforgivably obscene, lives, literally *in the wall* of her dilapidated secular convent — surviving, *there*, her brother, who is rather more liberal, and surely more alive even as he lies dying.

There are a good many such "Finessen" in *Effi Briest*, too, of course, Fontane's major claim to international fame, yet, paradoxically, it is in this novel that we may begin to have our doubts and reservations. First the good news, as brought to you by critics like Peter Demetz, M. C. Devine, Mary Gilbert, Reinhard Thum and others. There is, for example, the unobtrusively skillful, repeated use of the motif of Effi's passion for swinging on the swing, of her yearning to fly freely through the air like a "daughter of the air," as her mother calls her.[16] Rather than enjoy the jewelry her fiancé wants to give her, she would swing — "ich schaukle mich lieber, und am liebsten immer in der Furcht, dass es irgendwo reissen oder brechen und ich niederstürzen könnte"; and, "am liebsten aber hatte sie . . . auf dem durch die Luft fliegenden Schaukelbrett gestanden, und in dem Gefühle: 'Jetzt stürz ich', etwas eigentümlich Prickelndes,

---

[16] Cf. Demetz, pp. 211–215; Gilbert, 66–67; Reinhard H. Thum, "Symbol, Motif, and Leitmotif in Fontane's *Effi Briest*," *Germanic Review*, 54 (1979), 118.

einen Schauer süsser Gefahr empfunden"; and finally, "sie flog durch die Luft, und bloss mit einer Hand sich haltend, . . . schwenkte [sie ihr Halstuch] wie in Glück und Übermut. . . . 'Mir war, als flög ich in den Himmel'" (VII, 35, 124, 295–296). It is clear in these three widely scattered passages (and Fontane does not rub it in in the least beyond what I have quoted) that this motif—Effi's love of free and airy flight and flying, her dangerous penchant for the adventure of anti-gravity, for which there are other indications such as her love of swift sleigh-rides— points to a dominant trait in Effi's character: her uncontrollable urge, in her desire for happiness, to test and to go beyond the stifling limits and laws of social convention—her adultery will occur as the sleigh glides over the snow "im Fluge" (p. 169). Her destiny fulfills itself as a *natural* destiny, we sense, in which the symbolic motifs of "flying" suggest that Effi, acting compulsively, self-destructively, is more pardonable than guilty, possibly even innocent, swinging eventually into Heaven, as the pastor assures her at the end (p. 296). Significantly also, the swing in the garden of the Briest estate is invariably associated with the special spot that will be Effi's grave-site. The motif, then, almost unnoticeably but no less deftly, mirrors the theme of the novel and its distinctive articulation.

Another such highly successful "Finesse' in *Effi Briest* is the motif of the Chinaman, which Fontane claimed was "ein Drehpunkt für die ganze Geschichte" (*DD*, 454). Actually, it amounts to a whole string of "Finessen"— so many thematic associations radiate forth from this mysterious figure, whose ghost is frequently alluded to in the novel. This Chinaman apparently had an illicit affair with a captain's granddaughter or niece in Kessin, was seen dancing with her at her wedding to another man just before she disappeared into the night, never to be seen again— while he, the Chinaman, died soon thereafter and was buried in the dunes just outside the churchyard wall. Without ever dropping a real hint, Fontane manages to let us sense the atmospheric connections between the affair of the Chinaman—the outsider and stranger and epitome of everything unconventional and out-of-the-ordinary—and Crampas' illicit affair with Effi: for in this affair, too, the lure of the exotically anti-social and unconventional (to which the "swinging" Effi is subject all along) is irresistible and disastrous; and the references to the Chinaman and his ghost do not merely establish a neat parallel (it isn't neat in fact and, therefore, isn't "contrived") but also an elusive and fascinating atmospheric presence throughout the novel, with a variety of psychological, moral and social ramifications, all of them of thematic and structural import. I'll point out just one such subtlety, one which was not discovered until 1979, by M. C. Devine:[17] the site of the grave of the Chinaman, in the dunes outside the Kessin churchyard wall, is also the site of Effi's clandestine and adulterous rendezvous with Crampas. Effi, too, will be buried just outside the churchyard wall in a grave identical in appearance to that of the Chinaman.

One could go on, and critics did and still do, but as they do, especially in the last few years when the treasure hunt seemed to be all but over, they now tend to discover "Finessen" so fine that those of us with 20/20 vision cannot perceive them. This has nothing to do with what Fontane had in mind when he wrote about his ideal of artistic naturalness: "Die Kunst soll da sein, aber man soll sie nicht als solche fühlen." The "Finessen" I will now turn to for a brief moment are, to my mind, not really "da," except in the mind of the beholder (to whom I am, of course, quite willing to concede ingeniousness surpassing common sense). One such supposed "Finesse" that was recently made much of is the latent dominance of the magic number three. Not only is the novel believed to be arranged in 6 groups of 6 chapters each — or, alternatively, in 4 groups of 9 chapters, a structure which allegedly points to the arithmetic integer 3 — but also the real ghost haunting the Effi Briest story is discovered to be the number three: Effi's wedding day is October 3; Kessin has 3,000 inhabitants; the entry hall ceiling in Innstetten's house has 3 exposed beams; the house has 3 rooms upstairs, with 3 chairs in one of them; Effi rings 3 times when the Chinaman's ghost scares her one night; Innstetten has been in Kessin for 3 years; he was an officer in the 3rd Rathenow Regiment; the child is born on the 3rd of July, which is the anniversary of the Battle of Königgrätz — and where will Effi live for 3 years after her divorce? In Königgrätzer Strasse — where else? The window through which Hertha called "Effi, komm" must have been one of three, we learn, as it is identified as "the middle one." Crampas swims in the sea at 9 degrees on September 27th; we hear there were 3 fires in 3 weeks in the vicinity of Kessin. The glass Effi drinks from cost 30 Pfennig, and the party at the forester's house is on the third day of Christmas, with Effi arriving at 3 P.M. There are more threes of this sort — many more — but no matter how many, I fail

[17] "Erzähldistanz in Fontanes *Effi Briest*," *Formen realistischer Erzählkunst. Festschrift for Charlotte Jolles*, ed. Jörg Thunecke, (Nottingham, 1979), pp. 544–549.

to see that it follows that this is an exquisite "Finesse," a subtle hint that "Effi lives under the sign of three," which in turn "articulates danger-laden irrational motifs," or represents "a transempiric realm," "an inscrutable order in league with the demonic." [18] Does this catalogue of trivialities which come in threes really suggest a myth-like "code of fate" which is then "artistically" related to what is supposedly the structure of the novel, i.e. its arrangement of chapters in sets of three? It would help to be a superstitious mathematician to see such metaphysical powers at work in Effi's fate, rather than social and psychological forces, but I suppose there are few of those among the admirers of Fontane. This structuralist detective work is quite "ingenious," but I doubt it uncovers Fontane's ingeniousness. Nor will most of us be persuaded that the number 7 is the secret counterpoint to 3 in *Effi Briest* — "signifying rescue" (p. 211). True, there is a reference to 7 sailors being rescued in a storm, but the other supposed occurrences of 7 are really 6½ — six and a half years from the adultery to the discovery; and "das ist ein (zu) weites Feld" is said six times by Briest plus one time when Innstetten quotes his father-in-law — specious ingeniousness again.

Much of the same goes for Peter-Klaus Schuster's book entitled *Effi Briest — Ein Leben nach christlichen Bildern* (Tübingen, 1978), expensively produced in a most distinguished series and written with the benefit of advice from eleven learned authorities. The book claims that the novel is shot through with recondite symbolic references to Christian — not fatefully heathenish — archetypes; taken together, these archetypes supposedly give the work the extra dimension of an indictment of those social role-patterns of convention sanctioned by the Christian church (and portrayed in Christian art) which subject women to male authority: the Virgin Mary to the authority of God. Thus, the garden in which Effi is told that Innstetten has asked for her hand in marriage, in Chapter One, is that garden (symbolic of virginity) in which the Virgin Mary is sometimes represented, in Christian art, receiving the Annunciation. This analogy, if real, would then identify Effi and the Virgin Mary, although it is the "lymphatic" Hulda, not Effi, who is introduced as looking "als erwarte sie jeden Augenblick den Engel Gabriel" — a

---

[18] Donald C. Riechel, "*Effi Briest* and the Calendar of Fate," *Germanic Review*, 48 (1973), 204–208. The next quotation is from p. 206. See above, note 5.

wisecrack a Prussian officer made some time earlier, we are told in this scene (VII, 10). Effi, to continue on this esoteric expedition, is wearing a blue and white dress. It is the striped cotton sailor suit that Fontane saw on an English Methodist girl on the terrace of his hotel in Thale and which, he decided immediately, would be Effi's outfit in the opening scene of his projected novel (DD, 449). However, blue and white, we are now informed, are the colors of the Virgin Mary as she hears the Annunciation, at least most of the time, according to Christian pictorial art — which reinforces Schuster's point, as it happens (the colors of Bavaria have nothing to do with it). Once you get into this frame of mind, it is also significant that the gate in the churchyard wall through which Bertha, Hertha and Hulda enter into the Briests' garden is painted white, the color of chastity — just as, by the same logic, the wild vines around the windows must refer to Jesus Christ, not to "freedom," not to Hedda Gabler and not to Bacchus either, but, specifically, to the Passion of Jesus Christ — and to it Schuster, in his intrepid search, promptly finds other symbolic references: Innstetten has the Iron Cross, "das Kreuz" (p. 13), and the ship's mast which Briest promised his daughter to install in the garden symbolically suggests the Passion of Christ, all the more so as it is to be put up next to the swing — the "Schaukel," "deren . . . Brett zu Häupten und Füssen an je zwei Stricken hing" (says Fontane), "womit" (says Schuster) "das harmlose Spielgerät im Tonfall eines Chorals in einen Galgen transformiert erscheint. Er sei für den Strick geboren, wird Crampas sagen." Clearly an allusion to "Verkündigung und Passion," all this! This sort of interpretation gets much more sophisticated as the book proceeds. Baroness Briest is the Angel Gabriel, in case you had not noticed:

> Der folgende Dialog variiert offensichtlich die berühmte Stelle des Lukasevangeliums. Die dort (Luk. I, 28) im Gruss des Verkündigungsengels Gabriel ausgesprochene Auszeichnung Mariens vor allen Frauen — in Luthers Übersetzung: "Gegrüsset seist du, Hochbegnadete! Der Herr ist mit dir, du gebenedeite unter den Weibern" — hört sich bei Effis Mutter folgendermassen an: ". . . und wenn du nicht 'nein' sagst, was ich mir von meiner klugen Effi kaum denken kann, so stehst du mit zwanzig da, wo andere mit vierzig stehen. Du wirst deine Mama weit überholen." (p. 7)

Geert von Innstetten "is" God Almighty, under whose authority and judgment Effi (who, incidentally, has to do double archetypal duty as Mary *and* Eve) will have to suffer; Effi calls him "den Herrn," to be sure, when talking to the servants:

> Und Gott is Innstetten schliesslich auch in jenem Bekenntnis, das Effi kurz vor ihrer Hochzeit gegenüber ihrer Mutter macht: "Er ist so lieb und gut und so nachsichtig, aber . . . ich fürchte mich vor ihm." Den eigentlich Fontaneschen Beweis, dass Geert Gott ist, liefern jedoch die Pastoren- und Kantorstöchter. Lachend gestehen sie der erstaunten Effi, dass sie von einem Menschen, der Geert heisst, in dieser Gegend noch nie etwas gehört hätten. Pastor Niemeyer dagegen, der dabei seine Stirn "in Respekts- und Bewunderungsfalten" zog, erklärt Effi: "Ja der Baron! Das ist ein Mann von Charakter, ein Mann von Prinzipien." (p. 8)

These are just a few examples chosen from several more in a five-page section (pp. 4–8) of this book with a strikingly strained thesis. I'll spare you the cumulative effect of dozens of such imagined "Finessen" as Schuster calls them (p. 173) — the home in Kessin equals the stable in Bethlehem, by the way, with no ox and ass, but with a shark and a crocodile (both stuffed) as fully satisfactory substitutes, with a black chicken (unstuffed) thrown in for good measure (p. 90) etc. etc. — the cumulative effect of such ingenuity numbs you like novocain, without allowing you to forget that you are in a dentist's chair. It is a clear case of that relentless use of historical knowledge which, Erwin Panofsky remarked in a different context, should be "tempered by common-sense," "if possible."[19] Without common-sense, it turns into second sight, which is as spooky in literary criticism as it is in real life.

These and similar ultrasubtle "Finessen," then, are not real. They are the intricate fata morganas of an oddly productive school of criticism. Its lack of a firm foothold in the text reminds you of Karl Kraus's critical want-ad "Passende Wüste für Fata Morgana gesucht." If these "Finessen" were real, one would be at a loss to explain why Fontane could *also* create, in the same novel even, other "Finessen" which are like Ibsen's (in Fontane's view) so deliberately contrived that they strike us as crude — as "Künstelei" rather than "Kunst," to apply Fontane's own

---

[19] As quoted by Schuster, p. 173, who adds that he himself might in fact have sinned against this critical commandment.

critical terminology. These other "Finessen", which I now turn to, come at least close to bad taste — and they are real and cannot be explained away by a reminder that, unlike Goethe's, supposedly, Fontane's symbolism is "conscious symbolism," requiring interpretation through the figures of the novel.[20] For one thing, this interpretation is not always provided, as in the case of the Chinaman or the swing motif; for another, even when Fontane's hints are "consciously" interpreted, as it were, in the novel itself, there are some cases where this is done unobtrusively (artistically, Fontane would have said), and others where he "rubs it in," which is painful and aesthetically revolting, however well-meant.[21] They are involuntary self-parodies — worthy of Baron Güldenklee in *Effi Briest*: Güldenklee is satirized by making a speech in which the name of the host, Oberförster Ring, provides the structural inspiration, the speech proceeding, as it does, from Ring to curtain rings, on to wedding rings (one of which is to be worn by one of Ring's daughters soon, on a "Ringfinger . . . in einem *doppelten* Sinne"), and on, logically, to *Nathan the Wise* and Teutonic antisemitism (VII, 162–163).

There are times when Fontane himself does little better than Güldenklee. Take, e.g. (following a clue from Güldenklee's speech), Fontane's use of names. Is it always a matter of "Kunst"[22] or doesn't he occasionally slip into cut-rate entertainment in his choice of names — simply because he cannot resist a little witticism that his good taste more often dissuades him from? *Frau Jenny Treibel* is full of such instances: Fräulein Honig whose features are "herb" (VI, 296) and "süsssauer" (p. 408), Professor Rindfleisch and Professor Kuh (p. 322) — who, to make matters worse, are brothers-in-law, leaving you wondering whether their wives were brought up as vegetarians, Frau von Ziegenhals, who is fat, and Frau von Bomst, who is skinny (p. 286), Friedeburg, who is unable to live in peace, etc. Sometimes, of course, Fontane, plays very deliberately with these "Namenswitze", having someone say, e.g., "Wie kann ein so feiner Mann einen so störrischen Namen führen,"

[20] Hubert Ohl, *Bild und Wirklichkeit. Studien zur Romankunst Raabes und Fontanes* (Heidelberg, 1968), p. 211. For a similar view see Jürgen Kolbe, *Goethes "Wahlverwandtschaften" und der Roman des 19. Jahrhunderts* (Stuttgart, 1968), pp. 189–195.

[21] Even Ohl (p. 219) perceives this, when he notes instances of symbolism that seems "absichtlich" and of "penetrante Direktheit"; he finds, however, that this impression is softened by the chatty tone.

[22] Cf. Demetz' chapter on "Die Kunst der Namen" (pp. 193–203).

namely Wedderkopp, first name Marcell (p. 275) — but the incongruity of first and last name in this case, or in the case of Corinna Schmidt, is simply not as telling and meaningful as are superficially similar names in Thomas Mann (with whose technique *all* of these names have been favorably compared):[23] Tonio Kröger, Gabriele Klöterjahn, etc.

Still, this may be pardonable fun, like Herr von Lichterloh, in *Irrungen, Wirrungen*, marrying Fräulein Holtze — no "Strohfeuer" in this marriage (v, 152)! More disturbing are those "hints with a fence-pole" that Fontane finds equally irresistible, as in *Frau Jenny Treibel*, where the engagement of Corinna and Leopold, which they know will be opposed by his family, takes place against the ominous background music of a Lenau song that happens to drift over to them in the moonlit night from nearby Grunewald castle:

> Wenn nach *dir* ich oft vergebens
> In die Nacht gesehen,
> Scheint der dunkle Strom des Lebens
> Trauernd stillzustehn . . . (vi, 396)

"Trauernd" — needless to say, the engagement will be cancelled soon enough. Too "absichtsvoll," "Künstelei," Fontane might have said in a moment of sober reflection — which would not, by any means, condemn the technique of anticipation *as such*. Even more disturbing is a similar case in *Schach von Wuthenow:* Schach luxuriates in a description of the wedding trip to the Mediterranean he is to take soon with Victoire von Carayon; the description includes, most prominently, a reference to the "Luftbilder und Spiegelungen" of far-away Africa which can be seen in the vicinity of Malta, "und diese Spiegelung aus der geheimnisvollen Ferne, *das* sei das Ziel!" Victoire is elated, yet "im selben Augenblick überkam es sie lang und düster, und in ihrer Seele rief eine Stimme: *Fata Morgana*" (iii, 498f.). The wedding trip will not materialize; Schach will commit suicide on the day of the wedding. Actually, the reader familiar with Fontane's tricks of the trade could have guessed earlier — when Victoire's mother is seen examining some paintings while waiting for an audience with the King, who she hopes will persuade the wayward Schach to marry her daughter, pregnant with his child: among the

---

[23] Jost Schillemeit, *Theodor Fontane. Geist und Kunst seines Alterswerks* (Zürich, 1961), p. 55

paintings, "eine büssende Magdalena" rivets her attention more than all the others (p. 489).

Fontane likes to use pictures in this disconcertingly obvious way. Thus, in his novel *Stine*, the young Count Haldern, who committed suicide when the working-class girl, Stine, rejected his proposal of marriage, is buried in the burial vault of his family, which has rejected him even more unequivocally than did Stine. During the funeral service, the thin smoke of the candles "wirbelte neben dem grossen, halbverblakten Altarbilde auf. Es stellte den Verlornen Sohn dar. Aber nicht bei seiner Heimkehr, sondern in seinem Elend und seiner Verlassenheit" (v, 265). (Stine, incidentally, who has been wasting away throughout the novel and will not survive her lover, lives in Invalidenstrasse.)

The most notorious instance of such use of pictorial art is, of course, in *L'Adultera*, which takes its very title from Tintoretto's painting of the adulteress Mary Magdalen before Jesus Christ. A copy of this painting is introduced and discussed at length in the second chapter of this novel of middle-class adultery, the question being: "Wer von euch ohne Sünde ist" (der werfe den ersten Stein). In the final chapter, after the adultery, a copy of the copy is sent to Melanie by her husband as a token of his forgiveness, and Melanie (or the narrator) remembers *verbatim* what she said about "L'Adultera" in the second chapter: "Ist es nicht, als begriffe sie kaum ihre Schuld?" (III, 251). She had also said, before her own adultery, that there was something "encouraging" in the picture . . . Too clumsy? Fontane called this "Finesse" "eine kleine Geistreichigkeit" which was to bring about "eine rundere Rundung" of the novel (*DD*, 266). "Ich bedurfte dieses Apparats, um die Geschichte nicht bloss aufhören, sondern auch kunstgemäss (Pardon) abschliessen zu lassen" (*DD*, 264). "(Pardon)", indeed! Contrary to some admirers of this technique,[24] one might argue that it is no more subtle than the repeated use of the rhetorical question "Wohin treiben wir" — referring to Melanie and her lover drifting, in a rowboat first and in real life a little later — a cute point which Fontane does not spare us: "in Melanies Herzen erklang es immer lauter: wohin treiben wir" (III, 175); it echoes in the next chapter (p. 176) and once more two chapters later (p. 191).

The "rundere Rundung" which the *L'Adultera* painting achieved Fontane finds difficult to resist elsewhere as well. In *Quitt* the murdered

[24] Ohl, p. 221; Schuster, pp. 69–70.

forester is found in almost exactly the same position (identical down to the surrounding scenery and the game-bag tucked under his head) as his murderer's body will be found in, years later, and similar also are the last words written by both as each lay dying (v, 516–517, 521; 365–369) — too neat a parallel really, as even Fontane felt later when he wrote about *Quitt*: "Das Aufgehen . . . wie ein Rechenexempel, ganz ohne Bruch, ist gewiss ein Fehler" (*DD*, 410). In these and other instances of overly contrived "Finessen," (of "arranged" reality), Fontane did in fact what he thought George Eliot was doing, using too much decorative detail: "an einen Ohrring noch einen andern anzuhängen und so fort und fort, bis das halbe Dutzend voll ist."[25] But perhaps he avoids "Künstelei" more consistently in his most successful novels? What about *Effi Briest* and *Irrungen, Wirrungen?* (On *Der Stechlin*, see above, p. 77f.)

In *Effi Briest*, the duel between Innstetten and Crampas takes place in the dunes among "Immortellen" und "blutrote Nelken," one of which Innstetten puts in his buttonhole ("Die Immortellen nachher," vii, 253). The play that Effi plays the main role in, under her lover's direction, is Wichert's *Ein Schritt vom Wege*, allowing Fontane suggestive ambiguities like "Der 'Schritt vom Wege' kam wirklich zustande" (p. 151). Schuster feels the choice of this particular play is a gem of a "Finesse," designed for the "attentive reader," and is therefore "no coincidence" (p. 140). Of course it isn't! Unfortunately not! And we are no more reconciled to this labored subtlety about the wrong step, I think, when we hear from Schuster that, after all, Effi did sprain her ankle on the ice sometime in the past, that Innstetten speaks of a *faux pas*, referring to his wife's sleigh ride with her lover Crampas, and finally, that the name Crampas itself subtly alludes to the wrong step, too: "Crampas" is to suggest "Krampus," meaning "Wadenkrampf," which in turn is to suggest the Devil and his horse's hoof, even though — Schuster says "denn auch"! — Crampas has no leg trouble but a smashed arm instead (pp. 94–95, 145). I don't see that this "Finesse," if it should be real, accomplishes anything artistically, and even if it did, that effect would be annihilated by the "meaningful" use of Crampas' name that does occur in the novel. Vacationing on the Baltic Sea, after her romance with Crampas is long over, Effi hears about a nearby village by the name of Crampas. She panics; the past is not past, it keeps haunting her — and

[25] To Emilie Fontane, 10. Juni 1862, in *Briefe an seine Familie* (Berlin, 1905), I, 121.

it will eventually catch up with her. "Effi glaubte nicht recht gehört zu haben" (p. 220). Neither do we, being accustomed to greater subtlety in Fontane (although this "Finesse" does have its admirers among critics).[26] And then there are the all-too-deliberate symbolic anticipations of Effi's fate in the first chapter. When Otto Pniower pointed them out, however vaguely, Fontane was delighted.[27] Should he have been? Early on, Effi tells the story of her mother and Innstetten, a "Liebesgeschichte mit Entsagung" (p. 10). "Hochmut kommt vor dem Fall," says one of the girls to Effi, who promptly gives a sample of her arrogance on the very next page (p. 11–12). The "Fall" does occur later, but it too is hinted at even here: the girls eat gooseberries and spit out the skins. Be careful, says Effi, one can slip on them, "und ein Bein brechen" (p. 11). So the skins are wrapped and dumped into the lake:

> "Hertha, nun ist deine Schuld versenkt", sagte Effi, "wobei mir übrigens einfällt, so vom Boot aus sollen früher auch arme unglückliche Frauen versenkt worden sein, natürlich wegen Untreue."
> "Aber doch nicht hier."
> "Nein, nicht hier," lachte Effi, "hier kommt so was nicht vor." (p. 15)

Of course it will happen here, Fontane is suggesting. Is this a "Finesse," all the more subtle because "Stachelbeeren" suggest roses, whose thorns are symbols of sin?[28] Or isn't Fontane doing here what he accuses Spielhagen of: making his characters say, all too obviously, what he, *the author*, "has on his mind." "Virtuosity bordering on inconsiderateness," he calls it (XXI:1, 254). One might give this left-handed compliment back to Fontane, although there is at least one "Finesse" in this opening scene that is charming and intriguing: Effi foreshadowing her future when she says that the rhubarb leaves are larger than fig leaves (p. 17). And so one could go on; one could mention, for example, the much-discussed Schloon episode: the mud- or rather, sand-slide, the abyss ("Abgrund") that Effi and Crampas get into so ominously: literally, with their coach almost sinking in on the way home from the party at the forester's house, and metaphorically, erotically, too, of course, as Fontane makes clear with a profusion of painfully forced hints like

[26] Schillemeit, p. 101; Riechel, p. 196; cf. Tau, pp. 50–51: "gewollt", "allzu bewusst".

[27] See note 15 above.   [28] Schuster, p. 148.

Innstetten's dreaming the following night that Effi and Crampas "sank" into the Schloon together (p. 170) and Gieshübler's suggesting that the sleigh-ride through the woods, after passing through the Schloon, would also be fraught with danger . . . (p. 172).[29] Questionable "Finessen" one and all.

Finally, what about *Irrungen, Wirrungen*, the story of the love relationship of a Prussian baron and a lower-class girl, Lene, doomed to a tragic ending by social convention? This novel should be Fontane's supreme accomplishment from the point of view of art of "Finessen." For it is about *Irrungen, Wirrungen* that he wrote the frequently quoted remark: "Gott, wer liest Novellen bei die Hitze, wer hat jetzt Lust und Fähigkeit, auf die hundert und, ich kann dreist sagen, auf die tausend Finessen zu achten, die ich dieser von mir besonders geliebten Arbeit mit auf den Lebensweg gegeben habe" (*DD*, 363). Walther Killy, and Jost Schillemeit before him, have pointed out the unobtrusively "natural" beauty of many of the thousand, without breaking the butterflies on the wheel—but also without mentioning the many gypsy moths that flutter around with them. These critics' conclusion that the "Finessen" of *Irrungen, Wirrungen* are evidence of Fontane's supreme narrative "art"[30] seems, as a result, to be that of lepidopterists carried away by their favorite species.

True, there are supreme examples of the "Kunst des Anknüpfens, des Inbeziehungbringens, des Brückenschlagens" which Fontane admired in *Wilhelm Meister* (XXI:2, 109). Fontane employs this art most subtly and ironically to weave the two distinct parts of the novel together, joining at the same time the two milieus, the aristocratic and the petit-bourgeois. Thus he refers to the gardener Dörr's dilapidated residence as the castle and speaks, in mock-dynastic style, of "vordörrsche Zeit" (v, 8, 11), or notes, over 150 pages apart, that Mrs. Dörr's aristocratic lover, as well as Lene's eventual petit-bourgeois husband, have their "fuffzig auf'm Puckel" (pp. 10, 170)—"zuletzt ist einer wie der andere," maybe (p. 58)? A similar unobtrusive "Finesse' is the repetition of the motif of the lover taking a strawberry from his girl's lips: Botho from Lene's and another officer from a lady's of doubtful respectability—

---

[29] The Schloon episode is admired by (among others) Riechel, p. 197; Gilbert, pp. 72–73; Thum, p. 123; Gertrude Tax-Shultz, "Andeutung und Leitmotiv in Fontanes *Effi Briest*," *Fontane-Blätter*, III:7 (1976), 520.

[30] Schillemeit, p. 42; Killy, p. 206; Henry Garland, *The Berlin Novels of Theodor Fontane*, (Oxford, 1980), chap. 5.

thus casting an ominously ambiguous light on Botho's and Lene's love for each other, which they think is so different from the usual affairs across class-barriers — it is, and yet in the end, it is not (pp. 32, 87). Or take the repeated use of the words "gebunden" and "binden" in their literal and their metaphorical meanings, in no fewer than four memorable instances, fraught with suggestiveness each time (pp. 46, 70, 149, 151). In this case, however, one might, *in parte infidelium*, have the suspicion that "Kunst" comes perilously close to "Kunsthandwerk" or even "Künstelei," to that artifice or mannerism which Spielhagen praised Fontane for avoiding in *Effi Briest!*[31]

Elsewhere, suspicion becomes certainty. Early in the novel there is a party at which crackers are exploded: the slips of paper that fall out of them contain verses of the fortune-cookie variety that are eminently applicable to the situation of the lovers, like "In Liebe selbstvergessen sein / Freut Gott und die lieben Engelein" (p. 25). "Forget who they are" is precisely what Lene and Botho cannot do, except for fleeting moments: the social barriers that define them are ever-present and will eventually separate them, when Botho marries a local baroness. When Lene says as much in the subsequent chapter, she points — as though changing the subject — to a fire-cracker, exploding quite unexpectedly in the night sky over the Berlin Zoo — exploding in splendor and dying away (p. 35).

Another day, as the doomed lovers go for a walk, they come upon a pile of debris in which they find — what else? — a broken cupid's head, discarded by a sculptor, apparently (p. 54). A similar moment of dire foreboding occurs on the same walk as they decide on a song to sing — Botho picks "Denkst du daran," which pointedly puts happiness ("frohe Stunden") into the past; and much later, when Botho and Lene have parted, though their love remains undiminished, it is this song that Botho "happens" to hear as he passes a band of musicians on his way to Lene's mother's grave; "es war dasselbe Lied," the narrator reminds us, as Botho reminisces about the unforgotten, unforgettable happiness that he has lost (pp. 58, 146). "Vergissmeinnicht," we recall, was one of the flowers that Lene picked on an outing in those earlier days, "falsches" as well as "echtes Vergissmeinnicht" (p. 69). It is only after the separation of the lovers (whose love, it is hinted, was anything but Platonic) that we hear what Lene's full given name is — not Helene, but Magda-

---

[31] "*Die Wahlverwandtschaften* und *Effi Briest*," in Spielhagen's *Neue Beiträge zur Theorie und Technik der Epik und Dramatik* (Leipzig, 1898), p. 122.

lene — the biblical fallen woman who was forgiven, familiar from
L'Adultera and *Schach von Wuthenow* (p. 103). Botho, too, is dogged
by obtrusive symbolism after the separation. As he rides in a cab to the
grave of Lene's mother, what does the narrator place in front of his cab
in the line of traffic? A load of broken glass — which, the narrator feels
he has to tell us, is disconcerting to Botho, who thinks, literally, of
"Glück und Glas . . ." (p. 145). Tactfully, Fontane spares us the completion of the saying. A little later, as he burns Lene's letters, Botho
notices for the first time that there is a picture of Minerva on his fireplace
screen, Minerva putting her spear down ("Speer bei Fuss"). "Vielleicht
bedeutet es Ruhe," says Botho (p. 151). And so on and so on until the
end. The ending itself is a "Finesse." Or is it? Over breakfast, Botho's
wife, Käthe — socially acceptable, rich and more than a little silly —
reads in the paper that Lene Nimptsch — she has no idea who she is, of
course — has married a certain Gideon Franke; she giggles about the
funny name, "zu komisch, was es für Namen gibt!" To which Botho
replies: "Was hast du nur gegen Gideon, Käthe? Gideon ist besser als
Botho." Some critics have felt that this cleverly ambiguous casual judgment ("besser als Botho") with which the novel concludes, hinting ironically at tragedy, is a stroke of genius in its subtlety.[32] But isn't it rather
too contrived or even "cute" in its deliberateness? Isn't the tragedy of
this marriage hinted at much more effectively and subtly a couple of
pages earlier, as Käthe, just back from an extended stay at a resort,
prattles away about trivialities as always, suddenly interrupting herself:
"Aber Botho, du sprichst ja nicht, du hörst ja gar nicht . . . ," while
Botho replies: "Doch, doch, Käthe . . ." (p. 169). This exchange might
actually have made a far better conclusion: less contrived, more subtle,
or using Fontane's own terms: with less "Künstelei," and more
"Kunst" — a tiny scene from this marriage which says it all, without
saying it.

4

What we find instead are the two conclusions, one with, one without "Finesse." Why is this so? And why do we find, in virtually all of

[32] Killy, p. 201; Charlotte Jolles, "'Gideon ist besser als Botho'. Zur Struk-
tur des Erzählschlusses bei Fontane," *Festschrift für Werner Neuse*, ed. Herbert
Lederer and Joachim Seyppel (Berlin, 1967), p. 82. Cf. also Carin Liesenhoff,
Fontane und das literarische Leben seiner Zeit (Bonn, 1976), pp. 90–92, and
Garland, p. 124.

Fontane's novels, this side-by-side of art and artifice, of the natural and the contrived—as Fontane understood the terms. It is hardly plausible that he wrote on two levels at the same time—for the readers of the *Gartenlaube* and similar popular magazines (where his novels usually made their debut) on the one hand, and, on the other, for the elite of discriminating readers (of whom he hoped he might have *one*, or three, on another occasion: "drei Leser, wenn man ein Buch geschrieben hat, und drei Thränen, wenn man stirbt").[33] It is conceivable, of course, that the problem lies with us, Fontane's late twentieth-century readers who are used to greater subtlety and therefore expect it even of an earlier writer. Fontane himself was aware of some such relativity, resulting from the progress of "Bildung" and taste. Commenting on Spielhagen's comparison of *Wahlverwandtschaften* and *Effi Briest*, he noted that the art of Goethe's novel was considered "Natur" at the beginning of the century whereas by Fontane's time it would be considered "gekünstelt" (*DD*, 456). Thus, Fontane himself, unlike Goethe, had avoided "Manier" und "Künstelei," as Spielhagen contended in his essay of 1896, but maybe we could add from *our* vantage point, that Spielhagen's judgment of *Effi Briest* was just as time-bound as was that of Goethe's contemporaries who failed to see the supposed "Künstelei" of *Wahlverwandtschaften*. . . .

Nonetheless, the *root* of the problem is surely to be found not so much in us as in Fontane's credo.[34] For he identified himself, if I may recapitulate, as something more than a naive Realist—as a deliberate, highly conscious shaper of the narrative material and a calculator of symbolic and compositional effects: "Gott, wer liest Novellen bei die Hitze . . . ." After all, he is implying, novels require the reader's acute attention and aesthetic awareness, if all the "tausend Finessen" are to be appreciated: if the *art* of the novel is to be appreciated. The crux is, of course, that Fontane defines art as the impression of artlessness, naturalness, realness: its triumph being its vanishing act: "Ja, das ist Leben." "Die Kunst soll da sein, aber man soll sie nicht als solche fühlen" (XXII:1, 839). If one does, art has turned into various degrees of artifice, "Künstelei," which is always "forced" and shows the "intention," which is the telltale mark of "versagende Finessen." Unlike Goethe

---

[33] *DD*, 373, 672.

[34] See above pp. 71–76 and, for the general context, Heinz Eugen Greter, *Fontanes Poetik* (Bern and Frankfurt, 1973).

on the one hand and the Symbolists such as C. F. Meyer on the other, Fontane clearly does not wish to *show* "die Mache", his conscious art, because for him it has a different function than for Goethe or the Symbolists. This difference comes out most clearly in his use of symbolic motifs, symbolic art-works in particular. Goethe, the later Goethe especially, uses symbolic motifs to point to archetypes, "Urformen menschlichen Zusammenlebens," "überpersönliche, allgemeine Weltgesetze," [35] such as the living picture of the "Holy Family" at the opening of the *Wanderjahre* or the engraving after Van Dyck in *Wahlverwandtschaften* (II,5 and 18). C. F. Meyer, Fontane's contemporary, yet ahead of him as a forerunner of Symbolism, often uses art-works symbolically, to anticipate what will happen in the poem or the novella, implying "philosophically" that art prefigures life, interprets and shapes it, with life sooner or later conforming to art, and to the truth that art anticipates, as in *Die Versuchung des Pescara* or "Auf Goldgrund." [36]

Fontane's "Finessen" have none of these functions. Instead, they are the elements or the tricks of the craftsman's trade that bring about the artistic organization of the material into a well-articulated aesthetic totality, as Tintoretto's painting "L'Adultera" gives the novel of the same name "rundere Rundung" by appearing at the beginning and the end. Literature, for Fontane, is to be well-made — so well that it seems to be an organic product. The paradox of his "Finessen," unlike Meyer's and Goethe's, is therefore that they have to be *there* to be appreciated and should at the same time be so unobtrusive as to flatter the reader with his own ability to discover art in what appears to be natural, meaning in what appears to be haphazardly accidental. And that impossible demand, a literary art of the impossible, is, of course what accounts for both "Finessen" and "versagende Finessen." For as a conscious artist trying to give the impression of naturalness, Fontane constantly treads the line of art — the fine line between crude reality and artifice — sometimes losing his balance in the process: what could be more natural? His critics have by and large not been willing to admit this occasional loss of balance, this lapse from art into artifice. They have claimed instead, ever since Spielhagen, that his supreme artistic

---

[35] André Gilg, *"Wilhelm Meisters Wanderjahre" und ihre Symbolik* (Zürich, 1954), p. 28.

[36] Cf. Karl S. Guthke, *Wege zur Literatur* (Bern & München, 1967), pp. 187–204.

achievement is precisely the naturalness of his shaping ("Modelung") of reality, without any "Absicht" showing: that in his fiction he charges "things" (objects of the real world) with the power to be symbolically suggestive in a subtle way, i.e. "without depriving them of the seeming unintentionality of their natural appearance" ("in ihnen zeichenhafte Kräfte zu wecken, ohne ihnen die scheinbare Zufälligkeit der natürlichen Erscheinung zu nehmen").[37]

If this were always the case, Fontane's rank next to Flaubert and Jane Austen and Tolstoy, say, would be assured. The fact is, however, that unlike them Fontane does lapse into artifice in virtually all of his mature works. And of that he himself was very much aware — aware that the fine line of "Finessen" was a slippery line. I mentioned earlier some examples of his criticism of others (Lessing, Ibsen, Keller) as well as of himself. He offered these examples in the spirit of realistic tolerance, as do I. The longer he lived, Fontane wrote to Schlenther in 1888, the clearer it became to him that it is not possible nor indeed necessary "dass einem ein Ding in allen Teilen glückt"; even "the great and the greatest" are subject to this "law" of failure (*DD*, 384). "Aus feinem aesthetischen Gefühl heraus," he says about *Graf Petöfy*, "wird sich manches, *vieles*, zwar nicht ohne Weitres verwerfen (dazu ist es viel zu sehr überlegt [!] . . .) aber doch *anzweifeln* lassen." But he continues: "Und doch darf ich erhobenen Hauptes die Frage stellen: wer ist denn da, der dergleichen schreiben kann?" "Und so denk' ich denn," he concludes with healthy, craftsmanlike self-assurance, "man nehme es wie es ist, tadle was nichts taugt und freue sich an dem was gelungen ist" (*DD*, 323). Negative criticism is in fact welcome. For "aus solchen Bedenken," he writes to a critic of *L'Adultera*, "spricht oft mehr als aus Anerkennung die echte und rechte Teilnahme, und diese Teilnahme ist das Beste, was der Arbeit und einem selber werden kann" (*DD*, 273).

Sympathetic interest in Fontane is, of course, as alive today as it was during the last years of his lifetime. In fact, it has grown over the decades as Fontane has emerged as a master of fiction, a master of the

---

[37] Killy, p. 204; cf. Schillemeit, pp. 101, 104; Schuster, p. 158; Gilbert, p. 75; Hans Heinrich Reuter, *Fontane* (München, 1968), pp. 602–603. H. H. H. Remak argues against Reuter, stating "Fontane war weit mehr absichtlicher, obwohl diskreter [!] Allegoriker als Symbolgestalter" (*Monatshefte*, 65 [1973], 34). On Fontane's tendency toward allegory and its lucidity see esp. Diethelm Brüggemann, "Fontanes Allegorien, I", *Neue Rundschau* 82 (1971), 290–310; "Fontanes Allegorien, II", *Neue Rundschau* 82 (1971), 486–505.

art of "Finessen"—a master, however, who failed and erred occasionally, as I have pointed out in order to restore common-sense to the criticism of St. Theodore of Berlin. But as we realize that his artistic triumphs are the other side of his artistic failures, that art and artifice are intimately related in the very concept and nature of Fontane's craft, our understanding becomes enhanced and our admiration less blind: more critical, discriminating, more commonsensical but no less strong—the sort of admiration Fontane himself had for others, including "the greatest."

It may, to be sure, be in the nature of things, in the nature of Fontane's precarious art, that we do not all agree with this critical assessment of Fontane as "a very fine artist of not quite the first rank"[38] (and being second, trying harder, hence the problems). But perhaps we are all agreed that Fontane's finest "Finesse" was written by life itself, or rather by death, Fontane's death. While his finest novel was in press, Fontane died reading the evening edition of the *Vossische Zeitung* of September 20, 1898, only seconds after he had written a critical remark in the margin of the lead article, commenting on part, not all of it. The remark was: "ausgezeichnet."[39]

---

[38] Henry Hatfield, *Crisis and Continuity in Modern German Fiction* (Ithaca, New York and London, 1969), p. 18. See Fontane's "liberal" view on the relativity of aesthetic judgment: XXII:1, 839.

[39] Remak, p. 29. A slightly expanded German version of this article is to appear in *Jahrbuch der Deutschen Schillergesellschaft* (1982) as well as in my essay collection *Erkundungen* (Bern: Lang, 1983).

Richard Beer-Hofmann's Translation
of Shakespeare's *Richard II*

EUGENE WEBER

RICHARD BEER-HOFMANN (1866–1945) is remembered mainly as a poet and playwright, but in the twenties and thirties he was also known as a highly successful director of German theater. His first production, in 1924, of Sutton Vane's *Outward Bound* at Max Reinhardt's newly opened Theater in der Josefstadt, in Beer-Hofmann's native Vienna, was followed in 1928 at the same theater by a production of Goethe's *Iphigenie auf Tauris*, which was later taken over by the Salzburg Festival and by Reinhardt's Kammerspiele in Berlin. Beer-Hofmann's most ambitious undertaking and the crowning achievement of his career as a director was a festival production in 1932 at Vienna's Burgtheater, commemorating the hundredth anniversary of Goethe's death, of both parts of Goethe's *Faust*.

Although Beer-Hofmann did not make his appearance as a director until the twenties, he had been taking an active interest in theater since the beginning of his career. While writing his own plays he was as much concerned with the details of producing and directing, with staging, costuming and lighting, movement and gesture, as he was with putting down on paper the words his actors were to speak. The detailed descriptions for costumes and sets as well as the extensive stage directions one finds, for example, in *Der junge David*, represent but a fraction of the time and thought he devoted to the problems of producing his own plays.

Much of this work was performed in close collaboration with Max Reinhardt, the most imaginative and influential force in early twentieth-century German theater, whose concepts still live on in the annual performances of *Jedermann* in front of the Salzburg Cathedral and in productions of *Der Rosenkavalier* in opera houses around the world. Reinhardt, who showed as much interest in contemporary playwrights as he did in the German classics and in Shakespeare, directed the premiere production of Beer-Hofmann's *Der Graf von Charolais* in 1904.

He also began to work on what was to be the premiere of Beer-Hofmann's *Jaákobs Traum* but abandoned this undertaking toward the end of World War I.

The plays of Shakespeare, many of them in productions directed by Reinhardt, were among the most popular works in the repertoire of Reinhardt's theaters, and it is most likely that Beer-Hofmann's plans to direct plays of Shakespeare grew out of his professional association with Reinhardt, who was also one of Beer-Hofmann's closest personal friends. It should be noted, too, that Beer-Hofmann was well acquainted with the world of Elizabethan drama, his own *Graf von Charolais* being based on *The Fatal Dowry* by Philip Massinger and Nathaniel Field. And one would assume that Beer-Hofmann planned his productions for one of Reinhardt's theaters. During the twenties Beer-Hofmann worked on plans for producing and directing three Shakespearean plays: *Macbeth*, *The Winter's Tale* and *Richard II* (see plate, p. 97). None of the plans were realized.[1]

For each of the productions Beer-Hofmann directed, he made extensive revisions in the author's text. He reworked in detail the entire German translation Otto Klement had prepared of Sutton Vane's *Outward Bound*, and he took the liberty of making numerous cuts in Goethe's *Iphigenie auf Tauris*. For the production of Goethe's *Faust*, which runs to some 12,000 lines, Beer-Hofmann so ingeniously cut and arranged the text that the work could be performed in the course of a single evening.

For his Shakespeare productions Beer-Hofmann planned less to simply shorten the existing translations than to create his own. In his plans for *Macbeth* he did not progress beyond making notes, but for *The Winter's Tale* he expanded the encounter between Autolycus and the young shepherd (IV.iii) into a delightful piece of folk comedy, complete with detailed directions for staging and acting.[2] For *Richard II*, the play which, with its theme of loyalty and fidelity, shows the closest affinity to Beer-Hofmann's own *œuvre*, he completed translating three crucial scenes: I.i, in which Richard II calls before him his rival Boling-

---

[1] Materials relating to the plans of these productions are found in the papers of Beer-Hofmann at the Houghton Library (bMS Ger 131 (118)) and in the collection of Miriam Beer-Hofmann Lens, with whose kind permission the text presented here is printed.

[2] Beer-Hofmann's adaptation is printed in *Neue Zürcher Zeitung*, Nr. 283 (December 5 and 6, 1981), pp. 65–66.

Sketches for a Production of *Richard II*. 280×219mm. *Houghton Library.*

broke and Norfolk to hear the charges of high treason they have hurled against each other; I.iii, the tournament between Bolingbroke and Norfolk, which ends with Richard II banishing them both; and III.ii, in which Richard II learns of his defeat and resigns himself to his fate.

Although German theater is well served by faithful and excellent translations of Shakespeare, most notably by those which were created by August Wilhelm von Schlegel and Ludwig Tieck around 1800 and which have since become classics, Beer-Hofmann undertook the creation of new German texts, which he felt would be more appropriate for his conception of theater. In preparing this translation his primary concern was the impact the text would make on a contemporary audience, rather than the fidelity with which the German reproduces the original.

Comparing Beer-Hofmann's text with the original and with Schlegel's translation shows that Beer-Hofmann's efforts centered on creating a text that would be immediately comprehensible to a broad theatergoing public. He consistently simplified and modernized Shakespeare's and Schlegel's highly literary and often archaic language and either recast images and conceits into a more readily understandable frame of reference or omitted them entirely. Shakespeare's "Free speech and fearless I to thee allow' (I.i. 123), which Schlegel rendered into "Furchtlose Red' erkenn' ich frei dir zu," Beer-Hofmann reduced to "Sprich ohne Scheu!" Schlegel's translation of "A dearer merit, not so deep a maim / As to be cast forth in the common air, / Have I deserved . . . (I.iii. 156–58), "Erwünschten Lohn, nicht solche tiefe Schmach, / Dass man mich ausstösst in die weite Welt, / Hab' ich verdient . . . ," Beer-Hofmann compresses into *"Lohn* hab' ich verdient — nicht *Leid!"* Both these examples also illustrate Beer-Hofmann's tendency, apparent throughout, of using heavy alliteration, occasionally to the point of mannerism and excess.

While shortening Shakespeare's text by modifying or eliminating a good portion of the highly literary and at times lyrical language in which the play abounds, Beer-Hofmann produces a more compact text which concentrates on dramatic action and conflict, conflict which is heightened by language which is more forceful and direct in its use of rhetorical devices than is the language of either Shakespeare or Schlegel. Verbal nuance and subtlety are sacrificed for the sake of dramatic tension and an intensified emotional pitch.

In part the play's impact is created through its rhetorical language and by the sharpening of the dramatic conflict. These devices are in keeping with Beer-Hofmann's constant attempt to produce, here as in his own works, highly emotional theater; as he explains it, they are an attempt, "das Wort zu höchster Prägnanz und Durchschlagkraft zu steigern."[3] But language on stage makes its impact only in conjunction with the other arts: sets, costumes, movements and gestures, in short, all the visual elements that are called into the service of theater. And although in preparing this specific text Beer-Hofmann kept stage directions for movement and gesture to a minimum, such additions as he did make (Bolingbroke's farewell in I.iii, and Scroop's entrance and announcements in III.ii, for example) show that pantomime and movement were to play a large part in this planned production. How central a role Beer-Hofmann assigned to pantomime in the drama, and how greatly he mistrusted the subtlety of the word if drama is to appeal to a broad public, is clear from the following note, made in the late twenties: "je mehr der schweigende Ablauf von Situationen auch vom Drama über-

---

[3] Richard Beer-Hofmann, *Gesammelte Werke* (Frankfurt am Main, 1963), p. 879.

nommen wird — also, pantomimisches Element verstärkt ins Drama einströmt, . . . desto mehr wird die Allgemein-Verständlichkeit des Dramas wachsen, der Kreis sich erweitern, zu dem das Drama zu reden vermag . . . . Das Eindringen des mimischen Elementes als Ersatz für Vieles bisher Gesprochene — neben unendlich viel andern Vorteilen — [wird] auch eine Exclusivität der Kunst verhindern, sie verhindern übersubtil zu werden, wozu das Wort oft verführt." [4]

It is regrettable that Beer-Hofmann's work never progressed beyond the three scenes which he completed and which are presented here, for in reading them it is easy to imagine that this text could have formed the basis of a theatrical experience as successful as his much-acclaimed production of Goethe's *Faust*. And he could well have written for the German stage a translation much more suitable for making Shakespeare accessible to a contemporary public than the superb but not always immediately comprehensible translations produced by Schlegel almost two centuries ago.

[4] Ibid., p. 625.

Richard II

London. Ein Zimmer im Palaste.

KÖNIG RICHARD *mit Gefolge;* JOHANN VON GAUNT *und
andere Edle mit ihm treten auf.*
KÖNIG RICHARD.
Alt-ehrwürdiger Johann Gaunt und Lancaster!
Hast du — wie dir's dein Eid gebot — hiehergebracht
Heinrich von Hereford, deinen hochgemuten Sohn,
Wilde Beschuldigungen zu erhärten,
Die jüngst —
    (zu BAGOT, GREEN, BUSHY, *mit einem Lächeln des
    Einverständnisses, leichthin)*
        — uns fehlte damals Zeit ihn anzuhören —   5
Er wider Herzog Norfolk, Thomas Mowbray
Hier vorgebracht?
GAUNT.   Ja, gnädiger Herr!
KÖNIG RICHARD.   Und weiter:
Hast du's ergründet: spricht nur alter Groll
Aus ihm? Wie? Oder will er als getreuer
Diener des Königs seinen Herrn bewahren   10
Vor drohendem Verrat?
GAUNT.   So weit *ich* ihn
Geprüft: um offenkundig drohende
Gefahr von Eurer Hoheit abzuwenden.
KÖNIG RICHARD. Ruft vor uns, beide!
    (Einige aus dem Gefolge ab)
                        Aug' in Aug' und
Stirn, dräuend gegen Stirn — so sollen sie   15
Hier offen reden — Kläger wie Beklagter!
    (zu BAGOT *und* GREEN *geneigt)*
Gebt Acht — wie jetzt, gehusst von Hass und Hochmut,
— Daran fehlt's *beiden* nicht — ein Feuer aufloht!
    (Die vom Gefolge kommen zurück mit
    BOLINGBROKE *und* NORFOLK*)*

BOLINGBROKE. Noch manches Jahr voll froher Tage lebe
Mein gnädiger König, vielgeliebter Lehensherr! 20
NORFOLK.
Herr! Jedes "Gesterns" Glück soll klein Euch dünken
Vor *dem* Glück, das Euch jedes "Heute" bringt!
KÖNIG RICHARD.
Nehmt beide vielen Dank! Doch *einer* von euch —
Zumindest einer — hat jetzt arg geheuchelt!
Ihr kommt doch her, ein jeder, um den andern 25
Des Hochverrats zu zeihen?! — Vetter Hereford,
Was werft Ihr, Thomas Mowbray, Herzog Norfolk, vor?
BOLINGBROKE.
Vorerst — Gott sei mein Zeuge: nicht der Hass,
Nur eines Untertans ergebene Liebe,
Lässt mich als Kläger heute stehn vor Eurer 30
Fürstlichen Gegenwart. — Und nun zu dir,
Thomas Mowbray! merk gut auf meinen Gruss:
Ein Schurke bist du, Hochverräter, schändest
Deines Geschlechtes alten edlen Namen!
Nochmals: *"Verräter!"* Hast du es gehört? — 35
Dass wahr mein Wort — dafür steh' einst im Himmel
Die Seele ein — auf Erden, jetzt, mein Schwert!
NORFOLK. Stehn hier zwei zänkische Weiber, die sich vor
Dem Richter heiser krähen? Hielt mich nicht
Die Scheu vor Eurer Majestät, ich spie' ihm 40
"Feigling", "Verleumder", ins Gesicht — ich zwänge
Ihn vor die Klinge mir, und müsst' ich ihn
Von nie erklommenen, in tödlich Eis
Erstarrten Bergeszacken erst herab
Mir holen — *nur* sein fürstliches Geblüt 45
Schützt ihn ——
BOLINGBROKE.   Da liegt mein Pfand — heb's auf!
Ich will nicht solchen Schutz. Und jedes Recht, das
Herkunft von Königen verleiht — es schlummre —
Bis Gott im Kampf uns beiden Urteil sprach!
NORFOLK. Ich nehm' es auf, und *bin* ich ein Verräter, 50
So möge Gott ——
KÖNIG RICHARD.   Ich höre arge Worte:
"Verräter", "Schurke", "Feigling" und ein Handschuh

Saust durch die Luft — lasst endlich, werter Vetter,
Mich wissen, Thomas Mowbrays Schuld.
BOLINGBROKE.   So hört und —
Für jedes Wort setz' ich mein Leben ein.   55
Zuerst: Wo kamen hin denn die achttausend
Gold-Rosenobels, womit in Calais
Die Söldner er bezahlen sollte? Man hat
Nichts mehr davon gehört! Als Zweites: *Was* an
Verrat und Ränken es seit achtzehn Jahren   60
In England gab — von *ihm* war's ausgeheckt!
Zum dritten: König! Blut von unserm Blut —
Blut der Plantagenet — schuldlos vergossen,
Schreit ungerächt — noch immer auf zum Himmel!
Mowbray ist Schuld an Herzog Glosters Tod!   65
Von ihm ging's aus, und — sehr gern gläubige Seelen
Hat er vermocht an Glosters Schuld zu glauben.
Ich kann beweisen, dass ——
KÖNIG RICHARD.   *(jäh einfallend)* Nun, Herzog Norfolk,
Wollt Ihr nicht Antwort geben ——
NORFOLK.   Wendet Euch,
Mein König, ab — es fliesst durch ihn wie Euch   70
Desselben königlichen Ahnherrn Blut.
Und dass ich dies in ihm — trotz allem — nicht
Doch ehre — wird, so fürcht' ich, Euch ——
KÖNIG RICHARD.   Nein, nein —
Das fürchte nicht! Du weisst doch, Thomas Mowbray,
Des Königs Aug' und Ohr ist unparteiisch!   75
Wär' er mein Bruder — ja, des Thrones Erbe —
Was er durchaus nicht ist, da er nur Sohn ist
Von einem der vier Brüder meines Vaters —
Auch denn — ich schwör's bei meinem Szepter — sollte
Es ihn nicht schützen, dass sein Blut ein wenig   80
Benachbart unserm heiligen Blut entsprang.
Heinrich Hereford ist *so* uns Untertan,
Wie Thomas Mowbray — du. Sprich ohne Scheu!
NORFOLK. Dann, Bolingbroke, stoss ich all deine Lügen
Dir durch den Hals hinab — ins falsche Herz!   85
Dreiviertel des Empfangenen zahlt' ich an die
Besatzung von Calais. Den Rest behielt ich,

Mit Eurer Majestät Erlaubnis, zum
Begleich für Summen, die ich vorgestreckt,
Als ich aus Frankreich die erlauchte Königin   90
Nach England brachte. — Dies, die Antwort auf
Die erste Lüge! — Nun zu Glosters Tod:
Nicht *ich* schlug ihn —— Doch dass ich's *nicht* tat, war
Vielleicht Verletzung einer heiligen Pflicht!
— Was Euch betrifft, mein edler Herr von Lancaster,   95
Sehr ehrenwerter Vater eines — meines Feindes —
Wahr ist's: Ich *habe* Eurem Leben heimlich
— Doch ist dies lang her — nachgestellt. *Die* Sünde
Gesteh' ich ein! Sie brannte mich, und eh' ich
Zuletzt das Sakrament empfing, hab' ich   100
Gebeichtet sie, und hab' von Euer Gnaden
In aller Form, Verzeihung mir erbeten —
Und auch erhalten — hoff' ich! Dies — *nur dies*
Hab' ich verfehlt! Doch — für den Rest der Klage,
Nenn' ich dich, Heinrich Hereford, einen Lügner,   105
Verräter, feigen, abgefeimten Schurken!
Da *hast* du deine Titel — da,
    (*Er wirft ihm den Handschuh hin*)
                    den Handschuh —
Hebt's mit einander auf! — Und dich, mein gnäd'ger König
Dich fleh' ich an — setz' bald ihn an, den Tag —
Ich fürcht' ihn nicht — wo zwischen mir und dem dort —   110
Der Herr da droben richten mag!

KÖNIG RICHARD.

Ihr wutentbrannten Herren — kuriert Euch mit
*Un*blutiger Kur die Galle! Dies Rezept
Verschreiben wir Euch — sind wir gleich kein Bader:
Vergebt, vergesst, vertragt Euch, gleicht Euch aus —   115
Der Doktor sagt:
In diesem Monat *lässt* man nicht zur Ader!
    (*zu* GAUNT *gewendet*)
Mein guter Ohm — hier hub es an, helft mir,
Gleich hier es wieder zu beendigen:
Setzt Ihr nur Eurem Sohn den Kopf zurecht —   120
Thomas Mowbray — will *ich* schon bändigen!

GAUNT. Ich bin ein Greis. Ein Greis soll Frieden stiften.

Mein Sohn — wirf hin des Herzog Norfolks Pfand!
KÖNIG RICHARD. Und Ihr, Norfolk, das seine!
GAUNT.   Nun? — *Nun?*
— Gehorchend meinem König, *bitt'* ich dich!   125
(*Er legt die Hand auf* BOLINGBROKES *Schulter.*
Gedämpft, eindringlich, mit seinem Blick den seines
Sohnes suchend)
Mein Heinz! — Lass mich nicht zweimal bitten!
KÖNIG RICHARD.   (*mit gerunzelten Brauen, gedämpft,*
      eindringlich)
Wir — bitten! — Gibt's da Zögern noch? — Norfolk,
Wirf's hin!
NORFOLK.   (*auf den Knien*)
        Mich werf' ich, Herr, vor deine Füsse hin!
Schick in den *Tod* mich — nur in *Schande* nicht!
Der Name meiner Väter, die dir dienten,   130
Soll fleckenlos auf meinem Grabstein stehn!
Willst du Entehrte denn noch zu Vasallen?!
Und ich — *ward* hier entehrt, geschmäht, besudelt —
Und *Blut* nur, wäscht ——
KÖNIG RICHARD.   (*ungeduldig, auffahrend*)
        Genug jetzt — Mowbray!
(*zu* BOLINGBROKE, *gedämpft, rasch*)
Macht *Ihr* den Anfang, Vetter — werft sein Pfand hin!   135
BOLINGBROKE.   (*auffahrend, aber nicht Haltung*
      verlierend; rasch, stark, nicht schreiend)
Gott wende von mir solch abgründige Sünde!
Wich' ich vor dem dort — könnt' ich meinem Vater
Noch in die Augen sehn?! Die Schmach hinab
Zu würgen, tun, als wäre nichts geschehn —
Das *dürft* Ihr mir, mein König, nicht befehlen!   140
KÖNIG RICHARD. *Geboren* ward ich, zu *befehlen* — nicht
Zu *bitten!* — Doch ein alter Spruch besagt:
"Erzwungene Lieb' tut Gott im Himmel leid!" —
So tragt die Sache aus. Zu Coventry,
Auf Sankt Lambertus' Tag! — Lord Mareschall!   145
Die Wappenherolde bestellt — und auch —
Was solche feierliche Tagung sonst erheischt —
Sorgt, dass es sei, nach Recht und Fug und Brauch!

I. AKT, 3. SZENE
Gosford Aue bei Coventry

[KÖNIG RICHARD, LORD MARSCHALL,
NORFOLK, BOLINGBROKE, GAUNT, HEROLDE]

KÖNIG RICHARD. Lord Mareschall, befragt den Ritter dort,
Warum er herkommt. Warum so in Waffen.
Wie er sich nennt. Und nehmt den Eid ihm ab,
Dass er in Wahrheit glaubt, er sei im Recht!
LORD MARSCHALL. Im Namen Gottes und des Königs! Sag: 5
Wie nennst du dich? Warum kommst du hieher?
Warum so ritterlich in Wehr und Waffen?
Und gegen wen kommst du? Und was verfichst du?
Bei deiner Ritterschaft und deinem Eid
Die Wahrheit sprich — willst du, dass Gott dich schütze!   10
NORFOLK. Ich heisse Thomas Mowbray, Herzog Norfolk!
Ich komme her — getreu geschworenem Eid.
Und dass ich Gott, dem König, und dem Haus
Des Königs Treue hielt und halte — will ich
Verfechten wider Herzog Hereford, der   15
Mich anklagt! Gottes Gnade und mein Arm
Erweisen Herzog Hereford als Verräter
An Gott — dem König — und an mir! Gott schütze
Mich also, wie dies lautre Wahrheit ist!
KÖNIG RICHARD. Lord Mareschall! Befragt den andern Ritter,   20
Warum er herkommt. Warum so in Waffen.
Wie er sich nennt. Und nehmt den Eid ihm ab,
Dass er auch wahrhaft glaubt, er sei im Recht.
LORD MARSCHALL. Im Namen Gottes und des Königs! Sag:
Wie nennst du dich? Warum kommst du hieher?   25
Warum so ritterlich in Wehr und Waffen?
Und gegen wen kommst du? Und was verfichst du?
Bei deiner Ritterschaft und deinem Eid
Die Wahrheit sprich — willst du, dass Gott dich schütze!
BOLINGBROKE. Heinrich von Hereford, Lancaster und Derby   30
Bin ich!
Mit Gottes Gnade und mit meiner Kraft
Will ich verfechten hier, dass Thomas Mowbray,

Herzog von Norfolk, ein Verräter ist
An Gott — dem König — wie an mir! Mag Gott   35
Mich schützen — wie dies lautre Wahrheit ist!
(Trompetenstoss)

LORD MARSCHALL.
Bei Todesstrafe: Niemand unterfange sich,
Die Schranken zu berühren. Ausgenommen: Ich,
Lord Mareschall, die Herolde und Ordner!

BOLINGBROKE. Lord Mareschall! Lasst meines Fürsten Hand   40
Mich vorher küssen noch, und niederknien
Vor Seiner Majestät! Mowbray und ich
Sind wie vor Antritt ungewisser, langer
Und schwerer Pilgerfahrt — nicht jeder kehrt zurück!

LORD MARSCHALL.
Der Kläger grüsst in Ehrfurcht und erbittet,   45
Zum Abschied, Eurer Hoheit Hand zu küssen.

KÖNIG RICHARD. In unsre Arme ihn zu schliessen steigen
Wir selbst herab! Mein Vetter, ist das *Recht*
Mit dir — sei *mit* dir, auch das Glück! Lebt wohl
Mein Blut! Wenn's heut' aus deinen Adern bricht,   50
Kann ich's *beklagen* — *rächen* kann ich's nicht!

BOLINGBROKE. So sicher wie der Edelfalk herab,
Auf niederes Wild stösst — stoss ich heut' auf Mowbray!
   (zu LORD MARSCHALL*)*
Von Euch, mein gütiger Herr, nehm' ich nun Abschied,
   (zu AUMERLE*)*
Von Euch, Aumerle, edler Vetter — und —   55
Zuletzt — vom Teuersten: von dir — mein Vater!
Dein jugendkühner Sinn, in mir erneut,
Braust auf, wirft mich empor, den Sieg aus Lüften
Herabzureissen auf mein Haupt! Durch *dein*
Gebet mach meine Rüstung fest — *dein* Segen,   60
Mein Vater, härte mir das Schwert!

GAUNT.   Mag Gott
Dir Glück zu deiner guten Sache geben!
Spring *an* den Feind, lass deine Hiebe hageln,
Sei Donner ihm und Blitz und Sturm in einem —
Los — *los*, du kühnes Blut, wirf ihn, und lebe!   65

BOLINGBROKE. Mein Recht und Sankt Georg — steh mir bei!

NORFOLK.

Wie auch mein Los — durch Gott, durch Gott — jetzt fällt,
Hier lebt, hier stirbt — treu König Richards Thron —
Ein Edelmann, rechtschaffen, ohne Falsch!
Die hier mir Freund sind — grüss' ich, lebt im Glück!   70
Dir, König, Dank, dass du den Kampf gewährt hast!
Erlöst, tanzt meine Seele so ihm zu,
Als ging's zu Fest und Feier! Treue wohnt
In dieser Brust — drum wohnt in ihr auch Ruh'!

KÖNIG RICHARD.

Leb wohl! Aus Eurem Aug' — ich seh' es gut —   75
Mowbray, strahlt Mannheit, Treue, Mut!
  (KÖNIG RICHARD *steigt die Stufen hinab*)
Lord Mareschall! Anordnen und beginnen!

LORD MARSCHALL.

Heinrich von Hereford, Lancaster und Derby,
Die Waffe nimm! — Gott gebe Sieg dem Recht!

BOLINGBROKE.   *(erhebt sich)*

Das tue Er! Aus tiefstem Herzen: Amen!   80

LORD MARSCHALL.

Herold! Die Waffe bring an Thomas Mowbray,
Herzog von Norfolk!

1. HEROLD. Heinrich von Hereford, Lancaster und Derby,
Steht hier, um zu verfechten, dass Thomas
Mowbray, Herzog von Norfolk, ein Verräter   85
An Gott, an seinem König sei, und ihm.
Er fordert ihn heraus, mit ihm zu kämpfen!

2. HEROLD.

Thomas Mowbray, Herzog von Norfolk, steht hier,
Sich zu verteidigen, und zu verfechten,
Dass Heinrich Hereford, Lancaster und Derby   90
Treulos an Gott, am König sei, und ihm!
Er nimmt die Forderung an, und harrt des Zeichens!

LORD MARSCHALL.

Trompeten ruft! Beim dritten Ruf — schlagt los!
Halt, halt! Der König warf den Stab herab!

KÖNIG RICHARD. Lasst Helm und Waffen sie beiseite legen,   95
Zu ihren Sitzen sich zurück begeben!
Ihr Herren: zur Beratung — und Trompeten

EUGENE WEBER

So lang, bis unseren Beschluss wir kund tun!
[*Pause; Trompetenstoss*]
Tretet herzu! Vernehmt, was wir beschlossen:
Weil wir nicht wollen, dass des Reiches Boden   100
Befleckt vom Blut der eignen Söhne werde —
Weil unser königliches Auge, Anblick
Von brudermörderischen Wunden, widert —
Weil wir erkannt, dass Hoffart, Neid und Träume,
Die höher fliegen, als Euch *beiden* ziemt,   105
Euch reizten — was in unsres Landes Wiege
In süssem Kinderschlaf tief atmend ruht:
Den *Frieden,* unsern holden Frieden, aus
Dem Schlaf zu scheuchen —— *weil* wir dies erkannt:
Verbannen wir aus unserm Land — Euch *beide!*   110
Vetter Hereford! Eh' nicht zehnmal der Sommer
Die Früchte unsres schönen Reiches reift,
Ist Rückkehr Euch versagt — bei *Todesstrafe!*
Zehn Jahre müsst Ihr ferne, in der Fremde
Einsame Wege der Verbannung wandeln!   115
BOLINGBROKE. Ich füge mich dem Willen meines Königs!
GAUNT. Die Sonne scheint der Fremde, wie der Heimat!
KÖNIG RICHARD. Norfolk!   (NORFOLK *tritt nahe*)
Dich trifft ein härtres Los! Wie schwer's uns fällt —
Den hoffnungslosen Spruch: "Nie wiederkehren   120
Bei Todesstrafe" — sprech' ich über dich!
NORFOLK. Mein König — *Lohn* hab' ich verdient — nicht *Leid!*
"Nie wiederkehren"! Herr — *ermesst* das Wort!
Mit vierzig Jahren, Herr, bin ich zu alt
Zu lernen, fremde Worte nachzulallen!   125
Ihr bannt mich nicht bloss aus der Heimat — Herr —
Ihr stosst aus aller freundlichen Gemeinschaft
Mich aus! Ein liebes Wort, das man dem armen
Verbannten in der Fremde schenkt — versteht er's denn?!
Und klagt er — ach — wer *horcht* dem fremden Stammler!   130
Stumm, taub, als Bettler, jagt Ihr mich hinaus —
"Nie wiederkehren"! Nehmt das Wort zurück!
Mein König — bannt mich lange — lange —— aber sprecht:
"Bist du am Sterben — komm — stirb in der Heimat!"
KÖNIG RICHARD. Wir fühlen tiefes Mitleid — doch versuch,   135

108

Uns umzustimmen, nicht. Nur ungern sprachen
Dies Urteil wir — doch *gilt* des Königs Spruch!
NORFOLK.　　　*(senkt den Kopf; dann hebt er ihn, alles mit*
　　　einem Blicke umfassend, leise)
　　　Heimat — leb wohl!
KÖNIG RICHARD.　　　Halt — Norfolk, bleibt noch!
　　　(zum MARSCHALL*)*　　　　　Mein Schwert!
　　　(Man bringt es)
　　　Norfolk und Vetter Hereford — eh' Ihr geht,
　　　Legt Eure Hände hier auf meines Schwertes　　　　140
　　　Kreuzgriff — und schwört, bei allem, was Euch heilig,
　　　Den Eid zu halten, den wir von Euch fordern:
　　　Niemals — so Gott Euch helfe — sollt Ihr in der
　　　Verbannung zur Versöhnung Euch umarmen!
　　　Niemals einander grüssen — mehr noch, *niemals*　　　145
　　　Einander auch nur in die Augen sehen —
　　　Niemals Euch Botschaft — schriftlich, mündlich — senden!
　　　Nie über Eures Hasses Grab die Hände
　　　Einander reichen, bösen Anschlag aus-
　　　Zusinnen wider mich — mein Volk — mein Land!　　　150
　　　Schwört Ihr mir das?!
BOLINGBROKE.　　　Ich schwöre es!
NORFOLK.　　　　　　　　Und ich auch!
　　　(Er wendet sich zum Gehen)
BOLINGBROKE.
　　　Norfolk — bist du mein Feind auch — denke, dass du
　　　Für *immer* gehst — dein Weg ist weit — nimm *nicht*
　　　Die schwere Last der Lüge mit — *bekenne*
　　　Deinen Verrat!　　　　　　　　　　　　155
NORFOLK. Nein, Bolingbroke, war je ich ein Verräter,
　　　Mag — wie mein Leib aus diesem Land — die Seele
　　　Verbannt einst aus dem Himmel sein, für immer!
　　　Nein — ich bin kein Verräter — doch was *du* bist —
　　　Heinrich von Hereford, Lancaster und Derby —　　　160
　　　Weisst *du* sehr wohl, weiss *ich*, weiss *Gott* — zu *bald* nur
　　　Mein König — fürcht' ich — wirst auch *du* es wissen!
KÖNIG RICHARD. Oheim, aus deinen Augen blickt mich ein
　　　So tief bekümmert Herz an —— nun so seien
　　　Vier Jahre von den zehn hinweggenommen!　　　165

Sechs eisige Winter nur währt Euer Bann —
Dann, Vetter, seid mir wieder hier willkommen!

BOLINGBROKE.
Welch *Wunder* wirkt ein König doch! Es braucht
Sein Atem nur ein Wort zu wehen — *schon* sind
Vier Sommer, Herbste, Winter, Lenze — weggehaucht!   170

GAUNT. Gedankt sei dir, mein Fürst, dass uns zulieb,
Vier Jahre dieses Banns du tilgst — gedankt
Für meinen *Sohn* — mir, *Altem* hilft es nicht!
Denn eh' sechs Jahre sich vollenden, lischt
In eisige Nacht dies kärglich flackernd Licht!   175

KÖNIG RICHARD.
Ei, Oheim — wie du dastehst: aufrecht, rüstig —
Geb' ich dir noch so manches Jahr zu leben!

GAUNT. *Nehmen* — mein König — kannst du Jahre mir —
Doch keine einzige *Sekunde* geben!
Ja — *kürzen kannst* du meine Tage mir mit Sorgen,   180
Und Nächte rauben — *ja!* Doch keinen Morgen
Mir leihen. Helfen kannst du, Furchen ziehen
Der Zeit — *das kannst* du, ja——

KÖNIG RICHARD.   Was *willst* du, Oheim?
Berieten wir nicht reiflich? Stimmtest nicht
Du selbst dem Urteil bei?   185

GAUNT. Verfluchtes Prahlen war es, Euch zu zeigen, wie ich
Dem eignen Sohn ein ungerührter Richter sei!
"Ja," sagt' ich Eurem Spruch und sah dabei Euch an,
Ob keiner von Euch riefe: "Tu's nicht, alter Mann,
Dein Restchen Leben bannst du fort mit deinem Sohn!"   190
Ihr schweigt —
        (sich die Brust schlagend)
                Nun zahlst du, altes, eitles Herz, den Lohn!

KÖNIG RICHARD.
Vetter, lebt wohl — nehmt Abscheid, Ohm, auch Ihr!
Geht — und sechs Jahre bleibt gebannt von hier!
        (KÖNIG RICHARD *und Gefolge ab. Der Türsteher gibt*
        ein Zeichen. Draussen der Königsruf der Trompeten
        und Trommelwirbel, die während des Folgenden bis
        zum Schlusse, immer ferner verklingend, weitergegeben
        werden.)

BOLINGBROKE.
 (dem König nachblickend; vor sich hin leise)
 Verbannt!
GAUNT.   "Verbannt!" Ein *Wort!* Ein jedes Ding
 Wird schliesslich das, wofür man's hält!   195
 Sag *so:* der *König* ward gebannt in Englands Grenzen —
 Und du darfst wandern, frei in alle Welt!
 Sag: Dunst aus Mooren, Nieseln, Nebelgrauen
 Verleiden Englands Luft dir, und zu blauen
 Besonnten Himmeln, Meeren, zieht dich's hin!   200
 Wie du's benennst — gibt deinem Schicksal Sinn!
 Komm, Sohn — ich selber will den Weg dir weisen!
 So jung wie du — wie *froh* wär' ich zu reisen!
BOLINGBROKE.   *(den Kopf leicht schüttelnd, gedämpft)*
 Was dunkel, wird nicht hell — nennst du's auch "Licht"!
 Benennst den Frost du: "Hitze" — friert dich's nicht?   205
 Doch mag auch, frostig, freundlos, Fremde drohn —
 Was *in* mir glüht, *bleibt* Glut — in aller Fremde
 Bleib' ich, mein Vater, *dein* — bleib' *Englands* Sohn!

III. AKT, 2. SZENE
Die Küste von Wales. Ein Schloss im Prospekt.

Trompetenstoss und Kriegsmusik. KÖNIG RICHARD, *der Bischof von*
CARLISLE, *und* AUMERLE *treten auf mit Truppen.*

KÖNIG RICHARD.
 Barkloughly Schloss nennt Ihr das, was dort herblickt?
AUMERLE. Ja, gnädiger Herr! Wie mutet Euch, nach all dem
 Durchrütteltwerden in der Brandung, nun
 Die Luft des Landes an?
KÖNIG RICHARD.   *(tief Atem holend)*
 Gut! — Muss ich nicht beglückt sie in mich trinken,   5
 Luft meines Landes, drauf ich *endlich* stehe!
 Wie eine Mutter, lang vom Kind getrennt,
 Wenn sie es sieht, es fasst, und unter Tränen
 Und Lächeln mit ihm spielt —— so, lächelnd, weinend,
 Teuere Erde, fass' ich, grüss' ich dich —   10

Dein König streichelt dich mit seinen Händen.
Rebellen wider Seine Majestät sie schlagen
Mit ihrer Rosse Hufen, wund dich — Erde!
Gib ihnen Nahrung nicht! In dich zurück
Reiss du den Quell, der labt, Gift schleudre du   15
Aus deinen Klüften: Kröten, Spinnen, Nattern,
Gezücht, das toll, mit Biss und Stich und Speien
Tötlich nach ihren Fernen fährt!
Lacht *nicht* — meint nicht, dass Taubes ich beschwöre!
Die Erde *hört,* sie *fühlt, kennt* ihren Herren!   20
Und Stein und Fels hier, schafft sie eher um,
Zu erznen Kriegern, eh' sie's duldet, dass
Empörung ruchlos ihr den eingeborenen,
Den gottgewollten König niedertritt!
CARLISLE. Getrost! Die Macht, die Euch zum König setzte,   25
Ist Macht genug, als König Euch zu halten.
Doch — dass der *Himmel* will, enthebt uns nicht,
Selbst, auch zu wollen, und ——
AUMERLE.   Er meint, mein Fürst,
Wir sind zu lässig, unser Zögern stärkt
Mit jedem Tage Bolingbroke!   30
KÖNIG RICHARD.   (die Hand auf AUMERLES
        Schulter; lächelnd, überlegen, leise anhebend)
Vetter, voll Kleinmut! Sieh, die Sonne dort —
Wenn sie — wie jetzt — zum untern Erden-Halb
Hinabsteigt, Antipoden dort zu leuchten ——
Dann schweifen hier, gedeckt vom Dunkel, Diebe
Und Räuber, blutig frevelnd, frech umher!   35
Doch steigt sie erst, die Wipfel glühend, dort
Im Ost empor — dann reisst ihr Strahl den Mantel
Der Nacht herab von schuldigen Schultern, und
Verrat, Mord, Sünde stehen nackt und schauernd!
So — nur, weil ferne *andern wir* geleuchtet,   40
Hat feig im Dunkel hier ein *Bolingbroke*
Gewagt zu brüsten sich! Steig' *ich* erst auf
Im Ost — erträgt er meines Auges Strahl nicht!
Erröten wird er schamerfüllt, erschaudern
Vor dem, was er gewagt! Ein *Gegenkönig?!*   45

Nicht Sturm und Sturzflut wilder Meere spült
Den Balsam von gesalbter Königsstirn!
Irdischer Odem setzt nicht ab, wen *Gott* zum
Statthalter, hier auf Erden, sich geweiht!
Für *jeden* Mann, den Bolingbroke sich presst,   50
Hat Gott für seinen Richard einen Engel
Im Himmelssold! Irdisches Schwert zerspellt
Am Flammenschild, das vor mich hin, ein Cherub
Leuchtend in Gottes Glorie, schirmend hält!
    (SALISBURY *tritt auf*)
    (KÖNIG RICHARD *ihn froh zuversichtlich grüssend*)
Willkommen Salisbury, wie weit von hier   55
Steht Euer Heer?
SALISBURY.   *(ernst, kurz, gedämpft anhebend, rasch)*
           Nicht weiter und nicht näher —
Als ich *hier* steh'. Mein gnädiger Herr, was kamt
Ihr *gestern* nicht! Dies "*Gestern*" ruft zurück —
Und *zwanzigtausend* stehen hier! Zu spät —
Um *einen* armen Tag nur — und der eine   60
Wölkt alle Eure künftigen Erdentage,
Schwarz, unheilträchtig, ein! Herr — Tag um Tag
Verhiess ich Euer Kommen den Wallisern!
Bis gestern ging's — da hiess es, Ihr wäret tot —
Aus war's! Kein Halten mehr! Zu Bolingbroke!   65
AUMERLE.
    (nahe an den König herantretend; nur zu ihm, gedämpft)
Mut, Mut, mein Fürst! Ihr seid ja totenbleich!
KÖNIG RICHARD.   *(mit geschlossenen Augen,*
    gedämpft, leise, die Lippen kaum bewegend)
Noch eben prangte in den Wangen hier
Von Zwanzigtausenden das Blut — nun ist es
Mit ihnen — fort! Ich darf wohl blass sein!
    (zu den andern, ohne umzusehen, noch immer gedämpft)
                Geht!
Bringt Euch in Sicherheit — lasst mich allein ——   70
    (für sich)
Was jetzt mir hier geschah — brennt mir — dem Stolzen —
Ich fühl' es — tief das Todeszeichen ein!

AUMERLE.
(noch näher am König, sich zu ihm neigend, gedämpft)
Mut, Mut, mein Fürst! Vergesst nicht, wer Ihr seid!

KÖNIG RICHARD.
(mit einem Versuch, sich aufzurichten)
Ja — ich vergass!
(mit einer Geste, als wische er den Schlaf sich aus den Augen; noch immer gedämpft)
    Auf — träge Majestät!
Wach auf — du schliefst! Bin ich nicht König? Wiegt nicht   75
Des Königs Namen vierzigtausend andre
Gleichgiltige auf?!
(sich Mut zusprechend, rascher)
    Was ist denn viel geschehen?
Ein ein-zi-ger armseliger Untertan
Hebt wider meine Herrlichkeit die Hand!
(zu den andern, mit wiedergewonnener Zuversicht, rasch)
Blickt auf! Hat Eures Königs Gunst so *hoch* Euch   80
Gestellt — so habt auch *hohen* königlichen Mut!
Das Heer allein, das unter Oheim York steht,
Reicht aus, um ——
(Von rechts stürmt keuchend SIR STEPHEN SCROOP.
Er beugt vor dem König das Knie. Der KÖNIG *winkt ihm aufzustehen. Das Folgende in atemloser Hast)*
    Stephen Scroop was *ist* denn?!

SCROOP.   *(nach Atem ringend)*   Herr —
Mehr Heil und Glück Euch, als ——

KÖNIG RICHARD.   *(drängend)*   So rede!

SCROOP.   — *ich* heut'
Euch ——

KÖNIG RICHARD.   *(ihn anherrschend)*
    Ohne Umschweif!

SCROOP.   Herr, ich wag' nicht ——

KÖNIG RICHARD.   *(aufstampfend)*   Rede!   85
(rasch, stark, knapp, entschlossen)
Mein Ohr ist offen und mein Herz gefasst!
Nur *weltlichen* Verlust kannst du mir melden!
Sag — ist mein Reich hin? Nun — *nur Sorge* war mir's.

Verlust nicht nenn' ich — sorgen*frei* zu sein!
Ringt Bolingbroke, so gross zu sein als wir? —   90
Sei er's! Doch *grösser* nicht! Nur Gottes Diener
Sind wir! Dient er Gott *auch* — so sind wir gleich!
Empört mein Volk sich?
          (achselzuckend)   Das — kann ich nicht ändern!
Sie brechen *Gott* die Treue — so wie mir!
Sprich, sprich! wie unheilvoll es lauten mag ——   95
Unwiderruflich ist *nur* Tod — und *mir* —
Ich weiss — brach noch nicht an mein letzter Tag!

SCROOP.   *(ein wenig ruhiger)*
Wie gut, dass Ihr gefasst seid! Gnädiger Herr:
Ein *Wahnsinns*wind fegt über Euer Land,
Und wirbelt alles hin zu Bolingbroke!   100
Greise verjüngt es, ihre kahlen Schädel
Zu helmen wider dich — und *wider dich,*
Mein König, gürten noch unreife Knaben
Mit schweren Panzern ihre Mädchenlenden!
Des Palasts Bettler, Volk, von je entlohnt,   105
Für dich zu *beten* — *gegen* dich gespannt
Sind ihre eibenen Bogen! Weiber reisst es
Von Herd und Spinnrad weg! Gelösten Haares!
Medusenhäuptig, heisser jauchzend, schütteln
Sie rostige Piken gegen dich! *Alles* —   110
Mein König — *gegen* dich! Es steht viel schlechter
Als ich es sagen kann ——

KÖNIG RICHARD.   Zu *gut* kannst du's!
Zu *gut* sagst du so Böses! *(drängend)* Aber Scroop,
Wo ist der Graf von *Wiltshire?* Wo ist *Bagot?*
Was ward aus *Bushy?* Wo blieb *Green?* Wie *konnten*   115
Sie meinen Todfeind denn, so ungestört, sich
Ausbreiten lassen in des Reichs Gemarken?
Gewinnen wir — *bezahlt* es uns ihr Kopf!
Sie haben Frieden wohl mit ihm gemacht?!

SCROOP.   *(nickend, gedämpft, gesenkten Blickes)*
Sie *haben* Frieden wohl ——   120

KÖNIG RICHARD.   *(wild aufschreiend)*
Hundspack! das feig vor jedem wedelt! Nattern,
Gewärmt an meines Herzens Blut? *Stecht* Ihr

Mir nun ins Herz!? *Drei* Judasse, und jeder
Dreifach ein Judas!
    (bitter auflachend)   *Frieden* haben sie
Mit ihm gemacht!
    (die geballte Faust schüttelnd)
              Verfluchte Brut——
SCROOP.   *(einfallend)*   Mein König   125
Flucht ihnen nicht! Sie haben Frieden — dort,
Wo einzig Friede *ist* — in kühler Erde!
    (AUMERLE, CARLISLE, SALISBURY *auffahrend,*
    einen Augenblick es nicht fassend, dann schreiend)
AUMERLE.   *(fasst* SCROOP *an den Schultern und*
    schüttelt ihn in furchtbarer Erregung)
Wie? Bushy——?
SCROOP.   Tot!
CARLISLE.   Der Graf von Wiltshire——?
SCROOP.   Tot!
SALISBURY. Green ——?
SCROOP.   Tot! — Zu Bristol hat man sie enthauptet!
                                  [— *Alle!*
    (Es ist still, alle haben das Haupt entblösst)
AUMERLE.   *(gesenkten Hauptes vor sich hin, leise,*
    gedämpft)
Nun ist mein Vater York die letzte Hoffnung!   130
Wo *bleibt* er?
KÖNIG RICHARD.   *(vor sich hinstarrend, leise,*
    gedämpft, müde abwehrend)
        Gleichviel wo! — Jetzt *nichts* von "Hoffnung"!
Von Gräbern sprecht, von Würmern, von Verwesung!
Land, Leben, alles hat jetzt Bolingbroke!
Uns bleibt nur Tod und nur das Häufchen Erde,
Das unser Leib — der drin verwest — bedeckt.   135
    (Er setzt sich)
Um Himmels Willen, lasst uns niedersitzen,
Im Dunkel gruseln uns an Schauermären,
Wie Könige sterben: — *die* vom Feind erschlagen
Und *die,* entthront, — und *die* in Tod und Wahnsinn
Gehetzt von Geistern der Entthronten — *die*   140
Vergiftet von der eigenen Frau — und *die*

Erwürgt im Schlaf —— ermordet, alle — *alle!*
Denn im gewölbten Kronenrund, das golden
Sterbliche Schläfen eines Königs zirkt,
Hält seinen Hof — der Tod! Da sitzt er, bleckt   145
Die weissen Zähne wie ein Schalksnarr, höhnt,
Begrinst all unsern Pomp, lässt auf der Bühne
Uns einen Atem lang den König mimen,
Herr über Tod und Leben prahlend sein,
Bläst uns mit Hoffart eitlem Dünkel auf —   150
Als wär' dies Fleisch, drin unser Leben haust,
Un-ein-nehm-bare Burg — gebaut für ewig ——
Und *hat* er uns so weit — kommt er zuletzt
Und bohrt mit einer kleinen spitzen Nadel
Den Burgwall an — und —— König, gute Nacht!   155
Bedeckt die Häupter! Höhnt hinfällig Fleisch nicht!
Lasst feierlichen Gruss, gebeugte Nacken —
Kniet *nicht* im Staub — tut Ehrfurcht von Euch ab!
Verkannt habt Ihr mich ja durch all die Zeit!
Wie Ihr, leb' ich von Brot — fühl' Schmerz wie Ihr,   160
Bedarf der Freunde — einsam — so wie Ihr!
In Angst und irrend, keiner Sünde frei,
Jedweder irdischen Notdurft untertan —— wie *könnt*
Ihr sagen noch, dass ich ein "König" sei!
CARLISLE. Wer weise ist, mein König, jammert nicht   165
Um Unheil, das ihn traf — *künftigem* beugt
Er vor. Furcht ist das Schlimmste, denn sie schlägt uns
Zu Boden, eh' der Feind uns niederschlug!
AÜMERLE. Euch blieb doch meines Vaters Heer, als Kern!
Um ihn herum baut Eure Macht von Neuem!   170
Ihr frugt ja Scroop noch gar nicht, wo mein ——
KÖNIG RICHARD.   Ja!
Recht habt Ihr — Recht! Ein Fieberschauer war's nur,
Der mich durchschüttelte — er ist vorbei!
Sprich, Scroop, wo blieb mit seinem Heer mein Oheim?
Nun? Nun? Blickt nicht so mutlos drein ——
SCROOP.   Mein König!   175
Das Ärgste hielt ich noch zurück — nun muss
Auch dies heraus: — Sein ganzes Heer hat York
Vereint mit Bolingbroke. All Eure Burgen

Im Norden sind in seiner Hand — im Süden
Steht Euer ganzer Adel gegen Euch!
KÖNIG RICHARD.   (aufschreiend) Genug!   180
Nun, Bischof! Vetter, nun! Was sagt Ihr jetzt?
Hab' ich zu früh verzweifelt? Wie? Wollt Ihr
Mit Hiobspost und Trostwort im Wechsel,
Von Hoffnung zu Verzweiflung, immer wieder
Hinauf — herab, mich wippen?! — Nichts von Trost mehr!   185
Nach Flint Burg will ich, dort schliess ich mich ein
Mit meinem Leid. — Dankt meine Truppen ab!
Und Ihr ——
AUMERLE.   Mein König, nur ein Wort noch ——
KÖNIG RICHARD.   (stark)   Nein!
Nicht Worte jetzt! Schweigend verlasst mich! Jeder —
Ich geb' Euch alle frei — tu was er mag!   190
Die Sonne sank — um uns ward Nacht! Euch lockt es
Ja doch zu Bolingbroke —— Um *ihn* ist leuchtend Tag!

Fifteen Letters
by Richard Beer-Hofmann

WALTER GROSSMANN

THE EXHIBITION "Vienna 1888–1938" in December of 1967 gave splendid testimony to the early recognition the Viennese *fin-de-siècle* achievement had received at the Houghton Library. Above all, the *Dreigestirn*, Hugo von Hofmannsthal, Arthur Schnitzler and Richard Beer-Hofmann were represented by rare editions of their works and manuscripts. During the years of World War II the Houghton Library played a unique role as custodian of the Hofmannsthal manuscripts, some of which it retained permanently. These manuscripts were joined later by manuscripts of Richard Beer-Hofmann,[1] thus laying a most solid foundation for an ever-growing collection of works on Austrian literature and history. It is appropriate, therefore, to publish a group of letters by Richard Beer-Hofmann on this occasion when we honor James E. Walsh, bibliographer of Hofmannsthal and imaginative collector of Austrian literature.

Herbert Steiner once beautifully epitomized Beer-Hofmann's character: "He was an Austrian, a Jew of Moravian descent, a poet of the German tongue, full of passion and dignity." As a letter writer, Beer-Hofmann chose words as carefully as he did when writing poetry. The text is based on originals when possible, and on his copies in letterbooks *(Brief-Konzepte)* when despite generous cooperation from recipients and archivists, the originals could not be located. The letterbooks served a dual purpose for Beer-Hofmann. As the name indicates, they contain a draft of each letter, sometimes showing major revisions (see plates, p. 128–9). They were also his permanent record of letters, because he did not try to make carbon copies of the handwritten letters that were dispatched. A word of caution is therefore warranted. In cases where

---

[1] The bulk of these are his Literary papers (bMS Ger 131), acquired in 1958, his Correspondence — largely letters received — bMS Ger 183, acquired in 1968, and finally his Letterbooks — i.e. drafts of letters sent — accessions no. *78M–64.

the letter cannot be located, there is no full assurance that the text in the letterbook corresponds to the final version. However, in cases where the letter has been found, a comparison with the text in the letterbook verifies exact copying by Beer-Hofmann. The fifteen letters here printed are loosely separated into four groups: letters expressing thoughts on the works of their writers (1–4), letters reflecting on his own work (5–8), letters in connection with arrangements for speaking engagements at Yale University and Harvard University (9–11), and letters which evoke memories of his Austrian homeland. A letter to Mrs. Herter Norton that needs no categorization concludes this offering.[2]

[2] The editor is grateful to Mrs. Miriam Beer-Hofmann Lens and the Houghton Library, with whose permission these letters are published.

In the following transcription, capitalization, punctuation, and spelling have been silently normalized, except where spelling may reflect a difference of pronunciation (e.g. *giebt/gibt*). R. B.-H. regularly wrote *Somer* and often *wol*; and his punctuation is rather rhetorical than logical; but such idiosyncrasies are not preserved here. Obvious typographical errors (e.g. *gelsen* for *gelesen*) are silently corrected, and there is no attempt to indicate the numerous erasures and *pentimenti* in the letterbooks. Directions, containing the names of addressees and their addresses, are omitted, and the displaying of salutations and conclusions is normalized. The dateline is transcribed as it appears in the base-text, with the place of writing in square brackets if it is supplied, e.g. from the printed letterhead.

---

1   To Franz Werfel

Wien, 14. Juni 1934

Sehr verehrter Franz Werfel!

Seit wir über "Die 40 Tage des Musa Dagh"[1] miteinander sprachen, sind Monate vergangen. Damals hatte mich das Werk in gebieterischem Anstürmen mit sich fortgerissen. Nun schlage ich es wieder auf und fühle, wie dort wo beim ersten Begegnen Spannung und Reiz des Geschehens fast schmerzlich stark an mich rührten, nun das stete mächtige Glühen und Leuchten dieses grossen Werkes mich ergreift. Denn es scheint, als würde mit unerhörter Kühnheit hier versucht, die von jeher

[1] Franz Werfel, *Die vierzig Tage des Musa Dagh* (Berlin-Wien-Leipzig, 1933).

springenden Quellen alles Epischen zu entfesseln und in weitem Becken aufzufangen.

Kampf eines Häufleins Todesmutiger gegen eine mordende Übermacht, und — wie in würgender Not, als letztes Aufgebot, aus tiefverborgenen Schächten, die innersten Gewalten des Menschen, helle und dunkle, verzweifelt und hüllenlos hervorbrechen — sind auch wir, bangend und hoffend mit hinein geworfen in allen Wirbel in alles Auf und Ab des Kampfes.

Und alle Knaben-Ergriffenheit unserer Jugend entzündet sich von Neuem, am Abenteuer wenn — wie Schiffbrüchige auf einer verlorenen Insel, die Sterben und Martern umbranden — eine kleine Schaar Notdurft und Fristen des Lebens, sich erfindungsreich erobern, erlisten, ertrotzen muss.

Und als Drittes, Kampf und Abenteuer durchtönend: Schwermütiger Zwiegesang und endliches Verstummen zweier armer Herzen, die in Bitternis erkennen, dass, was sie "Liebe" nannten, nur reichte, sie in Lust Eins werden zu lassen, aber nicht reichte, sie in Leid und Tod, über allen Tod — "stärker als der Tod" — zu einen.

Kaum übersehbar, der Heereszug der Gestalten: Hinter den Voranschreitenden, die Masse eines Volkes — auch in ihr das Antlitz Einzelner immer wieder, wie im jähen Licht eines Blitzes erkennbar. Und Mitläufer, Tross, Nachzügler — Menschen von allüberall geholt, eingereiht und in den Dienst gestellt: "—— das unfassbare Schicksal des armenischen Volkes dem Totenreich alles Geschehenen zu entreissen."

Diese Worte, Ihrem Werk vorangesetzt, bekennen in Stolz und wehmütigem Verzicht die gottgewollten Grenzen die dem Dichter gesetzt sind. Wohl vermag er — gleich einem Gott der Sage — Gestalten noch einmal aus dem Schattenreich heraufzuführen in ein Leben, das, zeitlos erhöht, über kommenden Geschlechtern schwebt —— alles Schicksal der Menschen bleibt auch ihm "unfassbar." Doch, wenn der Dichter das ewige Dunkel alles Geschehens auch nicht zu hellen vermag — zu verklären dies Dunkel ist ihm gegeben. Und so überschimmert auch "Die vierzig Tage des Musa Dagh" ein frommes Lämpchen dessen Licht verkündet: Wenn "der Sieg" auch irdisches Erbe und Teil der Starken und Mächtigen ist — für jene, denen "— "stark" und "schwach" wie Schatten sind des Rauchs, "Macht", "Ruhm" leer schellt—" für jene ruht noch immer auf den Knien der Gottheit "das Wunder" bereit.

Ihr edles Werk, lieber Franz Werfel, hat seinen Weg nun angetre-

ten — es trägt an der Stirn leuchtend das Zeichen, vor dem das Tor
aufspringt, durch das Kostbarstes der Völker, ihre Märchen, Legenden,
und Heldenlieder, geschritten sind. Über die Schwelle dieses Tores wird
auch — ich fühle es — Ihr Werk schreiten.

Ich grüsse Sie herzlich

R. B.-H.

Houghton Library, *78M–64: Letterbook (special folder) labeled "Brief
an Franz Werfel" (autograph).

---

2 To Thornton Wilder

The first meeting of Beer-Hofmann with Thornton Wilder probably
dates back to an evening at the home of the Viennese publisher, E. P.
Tal. Reference to this gathering is made in a letter of Dec. 15, 1928 by
E. P. Tal to Dr. Bermann-Fischer, son-in-law of the publisher Samuel
Fischer, in which he reported that Thornton Wilder wrote: "But Dr.
Beer-Hofmann was so human and kindly that I look back on that hour
with the greatest pleasure, and would like to have asked him questions
all through the night. The same is true of Dr. Bermann." [1]

In a letter of November 1937 Thornton Wilder thanked Beer-Hofmann for a copy of the play *Der Unbedeutende* (1849) by Johann
Nestroy, preserved in a case made of old Viennese decorated paper. The
gift came to him at an auspicious moment, when he had just finished
The Matchmaker, an adaptation of Nestroy's *Einen Jux will er sich
machen* (1844). Wilder expressed his delight at having met the messenger
who brought the book to him in Zurich, where he had come to give a
lecture on November 17th. The messenger was Herbert Steiner, who
had already published a story by Wilder, *Die Frau von der Insel Andros,*
in *Corona* and was glad to meet the author. Steiner wrote to Beer-
Hofmann of the meeting: "Gestern früh also läutete W. an, er war in
London, kam Sonntag Nacht zurück, fand mit Entzücken "the lovely
book," um so mehr mit Entzücken als er an einer Nestroytransposition

[1] Houghton Library, bMS Ger 183 (757).

ist . . . . W. liebt *Jakob* sehr . . . war auch beglückt über den Karton." [2] The letter by Beer-Hofmann of August 27, 1940, printed here, is in response to a letter by Wilder from Cohasset, Massachusetts, dated August 6, 1940. That letter tells of his work during six weeks at McDowell Colony on a play that would become *The Skin of Our Teeth*. It mentions his interest in audience collaboration, in combining contrasting elements from violence and low comedy to lyric poetry, and his difficulty in encompassing this Aristophanic mixture. [3]

Woodstock, N.Y. 27. VIII. 40

Lieber Thorton Wilder!

Wie schade, dass wir uns nicht getroffen haben — die Schuld liegt an mir — ich habe wohl die Adresse nicht genau angegeben.

Zu wissen, dass Sie tief in Ihre Arbeit versenkt sind, ist mir eine wirkliche Freude. Auch ich bin überzeugt, dass der Rahmen der überkommenen dramatischen Form gesprengt werden muss, dass vor allem die traditionelle wohltemperierte Relation zwischen Epischem, Lyrischem, Dialogischem nicht mehr aufrecht zu halten ist. Stoff, Affekt, Aufnahmswille des Zuschauers, vor allem aber anders gewordenes Zeit und Raumgefühl des Dichters wie der Menge diktieren umstürzlerisch neue Relationen, Mischungen, Dimensionierungen.

Auch bisher war jede wirkliche Dichtung — nicht nur die dramatische — unumschränkt Herr über Zeitliches wie über Räumliches. Aber das "Theater" als zumindest intentionierte potentielle Erfüllung einer dramatischen Dichtung hatte zwei grobe handgreifliche Symbole für die räumliche und zeitliche Irrealität: Die fehlende vierte Wand für räumliche, die Vieldeutigkeit der Dauer eines Zwischenaktes für die zeitliche Irrealität.

Wenn Sie die Zuschauer — wie Sie beabsichtigen — in Ihr Spiel einbeziehen, so greifen Sie nur zurück auf alte Rechte: auf Elemente die in allem Chorischen verborgen ruhen. Sie laden den Zuschauer für eine Weile an Ihren Tisch, sie machen ihn scheinbar zum Partner Ihres Gespräches. Es wölbt sich unvermutet eine Brücke vom Dichter zum Zuschauer, der nun aufgeschlossener, vertrauender vom Dichter an die

[2] Steiner refers to the play *Jaákobs Traum: Ein Vorspiel* (1918) by Beer-Hofmann; his letter is dated Winckelwiese (Zürich) 16.XI.37. Houghton Library, bMS Ger 183 (555).

[3] See further sixteen letters by Thornton Wilder to R. B.-H.; Houghton Library bMS Ger 183 (632).

Hand genommen, mit ihm willig den Weg des Spiels zu Ende zu gehen bereit ist.

Dass Sie auf ihre Palette alle Farben von "violence" und "anguish" bis zu "buffoonery" und "lazzi" gesetzt haben — und entschlossen sind nach Ihrer Laune (oder doch wohl nach Ihrem innersten Gesetz) mit spitzem oder breitem Pinsel zu arbeiten, die Farben pastos oder dünn aufzutragen, oder gar den Malgrund durchschimmern zu lassen —— all das wird Ihnen — Sie empfinden es ja jetzt schon — jene grosse Freude an der Arbeit geben, ohne die wirkliche Schöpfung nicht entstehen kann.

Das lyrische Element, das Sie als so essentiell empfinden, soll Ihnen keine Sorge machen. Wie es sich in die anderen Elemente einfügen, oder sie rings umspülen soll, wird vielleicht davon entschieden werden, wie stark in Ihnen der Drang werden wird, Musik heranzuziehen. Ich denke nicht an Komposition einzelner Teile, auch nicht an Melodramatik, aber zeitweilig eine leise melodische bescheidene Untermalung, oder ein kurzer Satz eingepasst zwischen einzelnen Szenen, sie verbindet —— oft nur ein einziger Akkord — ein kurzer Trommelwirbel, ein Paukenschlag — kann von ungeahnter Wirkung sein.

Nehmen Sie all das als nichts Anderes als Gedanken, die mir durch den Kopf gehen, angeregt durch Ihren Brief. In mir ist vielleicht die Montiertheit Eines, der nicht mehr reiten wird — auch nicht mehr reiten *will* — dem aber das Herz ein wenig höher schlägt, wenn er sieht wie ein Jüngerer — mit dem alle seine guten Wünsche sind — sich froh in den Sattel schwingt und losreitet.

Und nun von diesem Sommer: Ich wohne eine Stunde vom Ort, am Waldrand, still, fast zu schattig. Mein Vetter, der Kulturhistoriker Erich von Kahler, wohnt nahe von uns. Eine Pleuritis, die mich über zwei Wochen zu Bett hielt, ist nun — hoffe ich — vorbei. Mitte Sept. will ich in N.Y. sein. Ich weiss noch nicht, wo ich wohnen werde. Post erreicht mich aber dann c/o Wachtell 1 Cedar street.

Zu Mozarts Briefen: Es giebt Briefe des ganz jungen Mozart an seine Kousine von entzückender Ausgelassenheit.

Und Kleist: Der Erzähler, wie der Dramatiker, wie der Mensch — etwas Einmaliges, Erschütterndes — trotz vielem Unerträglichem.

Und nun — mein lieber Thornton Wilder — gute Arbeit. Ich hoffe, Sie suchen mich auf, wenn Sie eine Ruhepause einschalten.

Von Herzen Ihr

R. B.-H.

Houghton Library, *78M–64: Letterbook v (19.IV–31.VIII.1940) (autograph).

3   To Hermann Broch [1]

New-York 27 Dez. 1943

Vielen Dank, sehr Verehrter, für Ihre freundlichen Zeilen die leider ein wenig zu fromm resignierend, Sich und mich mit Ihrem Nicht-zu-mir-kommen, abfinden.

Im "Heart of Europe" lese ich eine "Introduction" von Robert Pick — [2] irgendjemand nannte den Namen einmal im Zusammenhang mit Ihnen. Wer ist er? Wie alt? Es scheint mir ausserordentlich wie, in 2½ Seiten, so viel verhaltene Liebe, und darum wohl so viel verstehendes Wissen um das wahre Wesen dieses Oesterreichs ist, das — ein trockenes Mittelmeer — von vielen Völkern durch Jahrhunderte umküstet, ihrer Buntheit, dem reichen wechselnden Tonfall ihrer Sprachen und — mehr noch — dem Hellen und Verschleierten oder selbst Dumpfen ihrer Seelen willig sich erschloss, bereit zu vergewaltigen und wiederum sich hinzugeben — und so Alles in ein Etwas zu verschmelzen, grösser als das, was jedes Einzelne der Rand-Völker zu schaffen vermocht hätte. Also, nochmals: Wer ist Robert Pick? Aber schreiben Sie es mir nicht — *sagen* Sie es mir. Versuchen Sie, wenn Sie hier sind, eine halbe Stunde mir zu geben — auch wenn Andere dadurch verkürzt werden sollten.

Herzlichst Ihr
Richard Beer-Hofmann

Houghton Library, bMS Ger 201 (48) (autograph).

[1] Hermann Broch (1886–1951). R. B.-H.'s draft has no direction, but is clearly a reply to a letter of Dec. 22, 1943, in which Broch disingenuously expressed his disappointment at not seeing Beer-Hofmann more often. Houghton Library, bMS Ger 183 (86).

[2] Robert Pick, "Austria: Introduction," in *Heart of Europe: Anthology of Creative Writing in Europe 1920–1940*, ed. Klaus Mann and Hermann Kesten (New York, 1940), pp. 556–558. Pick (1898–1978) would later write several novels, among them *The Terhoven File* (Philadelphia and New York [1944]), a biography, *Empress Maria Theresa: The Earlier Years, 1717–1757* (New York [1966]), and a historical account, *The Last Days of Imperial Vienna* (London [1975]).

4   To Robert Pick

[New York City] 24. XII. 1944

Lieber, verehrter Robert Pick,

dies ist kein Brief, nur die Geschichte dieses Briefes: an einem No-
vember-Sonntag wurden "Die beiden Ringe" mir anvertraut.[1] Ich wollte
das Buch erst am nächsten Tag lesen, aber, als ich einen Blick hineinwarf,
wurde ich sofort vom Brio des Vortrages erfasst, las die Nacht durch,
und als ich am Ende dieser — im wahrsten Wortsinn — "bezaubernden"
Erzählung war, wusste ich, dass ich mit sehr Überragendem zusammen
gewesen war.

Am nächsten Tag las ich das Buch nochmals, und die Schlagworte,
die ich notierte — als Gedächtnis-Stütze, wenn ich mit Ihnen darüber
sprechen sollte — nahmen 8 Seiten eines grossen Blockes ein. Ich wollte
Ihnen schreiben — aber Ende November fand ich mich in einem Netz
physischer und psychischer, gegenseitig sich steigernder Verstimmungen
so arg verfangen und gelähmt, dass ich es hinaus schob. —— Aber ich
will das Schuldgefühl, nicht gedankt zu haben, nicht weiterschleppen, so
lassen Sie mich — an einem Jahres-Ende — als einen Wunsch sagen: Ich
möchte, dass Sie der Dichter von hohem Rang, der Sie heute sind,
bleiben, und die "ganze Zuversicht in die Entwicklung des Menschen-
geschlechtes, die Überzeugung vom Primat des anständigen Empfindens
vor allem Vorurteil" weitertragen in die Zukunft.

Herzlich, Ihr
Richard Beer-Hofmann

Bitte, übermitteln Sie meinen sehr respektvollen herzlichen Dank
der Besitzerin, die mir gestattete "Die zwei Ringe" kennen zu lernen.[2]

Houghton Library, bMS Ger 201 (47) (autograph).

[1] Robert Pick, "Die beiden Ringe." This story remains unpublished; a
typescript is among the papers of the author in the Houghton Library, bMS Ger
201.

[2] The title-page of the manuscript bears the inscription: Aus dem Besitze
von weiland Lily Sporer.

5 To Gottfried Bermann-Fischer [1]

N.Y. 17.II. 41

Verehrter Herr Doktor:

Ich entdecke soeben bei der Durchsicht der "Verse" einen scheusslichen Tippfehler.

Im "Lied a.d. Hund Ardon" muss es in der viertletzten Strofe heissen "Weltentakt" nicht "Weltenakt." [2]

Belächeln Sie nicht den Eifer meiner Richtigstellung; der Dichter kann nur leben in tiefen Glauben an die Sacrosanktheit des Wortes, das für ihn — des täglichen stumpfenden Dienstes enthoben — magisches Zeichen für das Erbeben seiner Seele sein muss.

Herzlichst Ihr

R.

Houghton Library, *78M–64: Letterbook VI (2. Sept. 1940–Sept. 1941) (autograph) (see plates, p. 128–9).

[1] Dr. Gottfried Bermann-Fischer (1897–   ), proprietor of Bermann-Fischer Verlag, Vienna (1936–38) and Stockholm (1938–48); cf. S. Fischer Verlag, *Almanach: Das neunzigste Jahr, 1886–1976* (1976).
[2] "Lied an den Hund Ardon — da er noch lebte," *Verse* (Stockholm–New York, 1941), pp. 45–49.

6 To Franz Schneider [1]

N.Y. 28. XII. 41

Sehr verehrter Herr Professor!

Verspäteten Dank für die beiden sommerlichen Briefe und für Ihr freundliches Empfinden.

Die Worte Hegels wären mit Worten Goethes zu konfrontieren: "Die Kunst ist eine Vermittlerin des Unaussprechlichen; darum scheint

[1] Franz Schneider (1883–1976), Professor of German, University of California, Berkeley.

Richard Beer-Hofmann to Gottfried Bermann-Fischer, Feb. 17, 1941.
213×171mm. *Houghton Library.*

Dr. Bermann Fischer 214

N.Y. 17. II. 41

Verehrter Herr Dr. Zu spät – ich entdeckte sodann bei der Durchsicht der Verse einen ~~se~~ schwerwiegenden ~~Druck~~ Tippfehler. Im „Lied a. d. Hauer“ am Anfang muss es in der vorletzten Strophe heissen: „~~[illegible]~~ Wellentakt ~~[illegible]~~“ nicht „Wellenakt“. ~~Nehmen Sie es Belächeln~~
~~Belächeln Sie es nicht~~
~~Bele~~ ~~Belächeln~~
~~Wenn Ihnen die H.~~
~~Nehmen Sie diese Z~~
~~Lächeln Sie nicht über~~

es eine Thorheit sie wieder durch Worte vermitteln zu wollen. Doch indem wir uns darin bemühen, findet sich für den Verstand so mancher Gewinn, der dem ausübenden Vermögen auch wieder zu gute kommt." Ich sende Ihnen die "Gedenkrede auf Wolfgang Amadé Mozart." [2] Sie wurde anlässlich eines Mozart-Gedenktages 1906 verfasst. Fachleute hatten es übernommen, über die Musik, die Texte, die Zeit, die Briefe, das Biographische zu schreiben. Mein Auftrag ging dahin, vor all diesen fachlichen Würdigungen noch eine Art Triumpfbogen, eine "Ehrenpforte" aufzurichten. Was mich lockte, war von dieser einmaligen Jünglingsgestalt in einem Ton zu sprechen, als wäre sie der Prinz eines Zaubermärchens, und alles Wohldokumentierte ihres irdischen Erlebens und Schaffens, ein rasch vorüberrauschender leuchtender Traum.

Alle guten Wünsche für dieses neue Jahr. Hoffentlich bringt es Sie nach New York — es wird mir dann eine Freude sein, Sie wiederzusehen.

Ihr sehr ergebener
R. B.-H.

Houghton Library, *78M–64: Letterbook VII (Sep. 41–Oct. 42) (autograph).

[2] Richard Beer-Hofmann, *Gedenkrede auf Wolfgang Amade Mozart* (Berlin, 1906).

---

7   To Richard von Mises [1]

N.Y. 2.April 1944

Sehr Verehrter —

Dank für den Vornamen — ich versprach das "Schlaflied." [2]

Ich sende Ihnen die "Novellen," die Sie noch nicht besitzen, unauf-

[1] Richard von Mises (1883–1953), mathematician and philosopher of science, was Gordon McKay Professor of Aerodynamics and Applied Mathematics at Harvard University. He collected German and Austrian literature, and particularly devoted his efforts to the work of Rainer Maria Rilke (cf. his *Katalog der Rilke-Sammlung* [Frankfurt am Main, 1966]), now in Houghton Library.

[2] The first edition — an offprint from *Pan* — was published in 1898.

geschnitten — ich wollte sie blieben es.[3] Wenn Sie aber doch einen Blick in das Buch werfen —— nun, es ist eben vor mehr als einem halben Jahrhundert geschrieben — ein erster Versuch.

Jemand der viel Musik gehört hat, Musik liebt, Partituren gelesen hat, tastet unsicher willkürlich herausgegriffenen Themen, die Form einer Sonate, oder einer Fuge zu geben. Aber, ohne inneres Verhältnis zum Thema, ja, noch ohne wirklich starken Drang etwas zu gestalten, mehr von unbestimmter Unrast getrieben, und dem Drängen von ein paar Menschen nachgebend, die er gern hat, die alle von ihm — er weiss nicht recht warum — Besonderes erwarten. Freilich, verbirgt er ihnen, wie wenig er an seine Arbeit glaubt, und versucht, zumindest anständiges Handwerk zu geben — aber, ehe das Buch noch erschienen ist, hat er sich, wie von ihm Fremden abgewandt, und das einzige was ihn noch ein wenig mit dieser Arbeit verbindet, ist das dem Buch vorausgesetzte Motto aus "Faust": "Sind wir ein Spiel von jedem Druck der Luft?"

Das von mir zusammengestellte Programmheft der Faustaufführung am Burgtheater, (im Jahre 1932)[4] wird Ihnen — ich hoffe, schon vom Bibliophilen Standpunkt aus — mehr Spass machen. Die Umpanzerung der Bearbeitung mit Belegstellen hat ihren Zweck wirklich erfüllt. Philologische, literarhistorische, dramaturgische Kritik wurde abgeschreckt — da mir, sichtlich, die Bestände des Arsenals ihrer Angriffswaffen allzugut bekannt waren.

Und nun: Keinen Dank — da Sie ihn immer abwehren — nur die sachliche Feststellung, dass die Tage in Harvard[5] mir gute freundliche Erinnerung bleiben.

Herzlich ergeben Ihr
R. B.-H.

Ich überlese den Brief, und finde, dass die Art, wie ich die "Novellen" erkläre, entschuldige, mich gegen sie verwahre, noch auf einen Rest von geheimen Attachement an sie schliessen lassen könnte. Aber wenn meine Worte so wirken sollten, als hielte ich — trotz Allem — meine Hand schützend über meine Arbeit —— so täuscht das. Meine Hand ist

---

[3] The first edition was published in Berlin, 1893.

[4] *Fest Aufführung des Faust von Goethe I. und II. Teil* [Burgtheater, 27. Februar 1932]. Mit Benutzung des Ur-Faust und Faust-Nachlasses . . . eingerichtet von Richard Beer-Hofmann [Vienna, 1932].

[5] Refers to his reading at Harvard, March 22, 1944.

vielleicht nur— mir unbewusst— schützend gebreitet über die Zeit meiner Jugend, die ich nicht verleugnen mag, und der ich Treue halte.

Houghton Library, bMS Ger 183 (382) (typescript).

---

8   To Hermann J. Weigand [1]

New York 16.IV.44

Sehr verehrter Herr Professor,

ich bin mit Ihrer Einteilung [2] völlig einverstanden.

Sie haben in Ihrem vorletzten Brief an dem weiteren Schicksal des "David" sehr freundlichen Anteil genommen. "König David" und der daran anschliessende "Davids Tod"— zu denen Mappen mit Realien, Dispositionen, Entwürfen des Ganzen, wie einzelner Szenen reichlich vorhanden sind—[3] werden wohl nicht mehr geschrieben werden. Der Stoff und ich sind seit 1938 einander fremd geworden, und das einfache Aufzeichnen der Erinnerungen an meine Frau,[4] der dürftige Versuch ihrer Gestalt noch ein wenig Dauer zu verleihen, füllt mein Leben so sehr, das alles Andere mir kaum wesentlich erscheint.

Ich schicke Ihnen das "Vorspiel auf dem Theater zu König David": [5] Ursprünglich nur als überleitende Brücke zu "König David" gedacht, geriet das "Vorspiel" in die launenhaft-mäandrische Trift des Einfalls, wandelte sich in eine Auseinandersetzung des Dichters mit Bühne und Publikum, um erst mit der Invokation an David zu seinem Ursprung zurückzufinden.

[1] Hermann John Weigand (1892–   ), Professor of German at Yale University. Beer-Hofmann expressed his appreciation of Weigand in "Zwei Briefe von Richard Beer-Hofmann an Hermann Weigand," Curt von Faber du Faur (ed.), *Wächter und Hüter: Festschrift für Hermann J. Weigand* (New Haven, Conn., 1957), pp. 165–167.

[2] "Einteilung" probably refers to the arrangements for the April 25, 1944 reading by Beer-Hofmann at Yale.

[3] These materials are now in Houghton, bMS Ger 131 (15)–(55).

[4] These "Erinnerungen" would be published posthumously, as *Paula: ein Fragment* (New York, 1949).

[5] *Vorspiel auf dem Theater zu König David* (Vienna [1936]).

Das "Lied an den Hund Ardon" will ich gerne Ihnen und Ihrer verehrten Frau vorlesen.

Dank für Ihr freundliches Bemühen und herzliche Grüsse.

Ihr

R. B.-H.

Houghton Library, *78M–64: Letterbook VIII (1943–44) (autograph).

---

9 To Taylor Starck.[1]

412 Cathedral Parkway
New York 25, N.Y.
November 22, 1943

Sehr verehrter Herr Professor:

Überzeugt, dass Sie den richtigsten Zeitpunkt für die Vorlesung wählen werden, bin ich mit der Ansetzung für März durchaus einverstanden.

Da es vielleicht eine Vereinfachung bedeutet, wenn ich jetzt schon mitteile, was ich zu sprechen gedenke, so bitte ich um die Freundlichkeit, eine der zwei beiliegenden Informationen Herrn Professor Viëtor zu übermitteln.

Mit diesem Brief zugleich sende ich einige Exemplare eines kleinen Heftchens "Besprechungen."[2] Es wurde von einem Journalisten rasch zusammengestellt für eine Vorlese-Tournée in der Schweiz, zu der es nicht mehr kam. Vielleicht ist es für "publicity"-Zweck geeignet.

Nochmals, sehr verehrter Herr Professor, herzlichen Dank, und wiederum die Versicherung, dass ich gerne komme. Mit freundlichen Grüssen,

Ihr sehr ergebener

R. B.-H.

Bei der Wahl dessen, was ich sprechen möchte, ist, vor allem der Wunsch entscheidend, innerhalb begrenzter Zeit, formal Geschlossenes,

[1] Taylor Starck (1889–1974), Professor of German, Harvard University.

[2] *Richard Beer-Hofmann: Besprechungen seiner Werke* ([Zürich] 1939).

oder in seinem Gefühls-Inhalt sich schliessendes zu geben, das — unschwer zu verstehen — bereits bei früheren Anlässen sich jedesmal stark genug erwiesen hat, den Hörer zu fassen, und festzuhalten. Ich möchte sprechen die "Gedenkrede auf Wolfgang Amadé Mozart" (17 Minuten), die erste Szene des ersten Bildes aus "Der junge David" (26 Minuten), einige Gedichte (12 Minuten). Der "Gedenkrede" würde ich einige einleitende Worte vorausschicken ebenso der Szene aus "Der junge David." Ausserdem würde ich in dieser Szene, die vermutlich befremdenden Namen durch die geläufigeren der Luther-Bibel ersetzen.

Die "Gedenkrede" erschien im S. Fischer Verlag, Berlin, zweite und dritte Auflage 1921. "Der junge David" im S. Fischer Verlag, Berlin, erste bis dritte Auflage 1933. Die Gedichte sind enthalten in "Verse" im Bermann-Fischer Verlag, Stockholm–New York 1941. Sollte ein oder das andere Werk in der Universitäts-Bibliothek nicht vorhanden sein, so würde ich es gerne zur Verfügung stellen.

Houghton Library, *78M–64: Letterbook VIII (autograph).

---

10   To Karl Viëtor

This letter was first published among "Briefe Richard Beer-Hofmanns aus dem Exil. Mitgeteilt von Eugene Weber," in *Neue Zürcher Zeitung* (Sept. 17, 1972), pp. 49–50.

In a letter of Nov. 30, 1943, Karl Viëtor (1892–1951), Kuno Francke Professor of German Art and Culture, suggested that Beer-Hofmann change the program that he had proposed to Taylor Starck:

> Die Wahl, die Sie getroffen haben, wäre für ein rein europäisches Publikum, deren Muttersprache Deutsch ist, gewiss ausgezeichnet. Die Gedichte und die Szene aus Der junge David werden auch für unser Harvard Publikum ausgezeichnet sein. Aber ich bin nicht sicher, dass die Rede auf Mozart von unsern amerikanischen Hörern verstanden werden kann; ich bin sogar fast sicher, dass sie nicht verstanden werden wird. Ich meine nicht um ihrer grossartig dichterischen Substanz willen. Sondern rein sprachlich. Die angelsächsischen Völker, und erst recht die Nordamerikaner, haben (bis auf ganz wenige Ausnahmen wie Walter Pater und seine Freunde oder Thornton Wilder hier) im Zuge der gegennaturalis-

tischen Strömungen keine artistische Prosa entwickelt. Sie haben keinen Sinn dafür und keinen Gefallen daran. Eine so hoch stilisierte, dichterisch gesteigerte Prosa wie die der Gedenkrede, befremdet den gegen ein gehobenes Sprachniveau äusserst empfindlichen amerikanischen Hörer derart, dass er dann gar nicht erst zur Würdigung des Gehalts gelangt.

Darf ich gleich etwas Anderes anschliessen. Wir hatten, als wir uns erlaubten Sie um die Lesung zu bitten, daran gedacht, mit dieser Veranstaltung zugleich auf den Wiener Kreis und seine grosse dichterische Bedeutung hinzuweisen. So wenige hier wissen etwas davon, der Naturalismus allein war in diesem Lande populär, und neuerdings erst Rilke. Aber Hofmannsthal ist fast ganz unbekannt. Es läge uns drum sehr am Herzen, wenn wir bei dieser Gelegenheit auch an H. erinnern könnten. Und wir hatten uns gedacht, dass niemand diese schöne Aufgabe lieber übernehmen und niemand sie besser erfüllen könnte, als grade Sie. Wir hatten uns ferner gedacht, dass man praktisch das Programm zwischen der Lesung Ihrer Dichtungen und der Hofmannsthals teilen könnte. Auch daran, dass es sehr interessant für alle Hörer sein müsste, wenn Sie sich entschliessen könnten, ein paar Erinnerungen an die Zeit des gemeinsamen Lebens zu erzählen. Sie haben uns wissen lassen, dass Sie das nicht tun möchten. Aber wie wäre es, wenn Sie einige Gedichte H.s, ein paar Prosastücke aus einem der Loris-Essays und vielleicht noch eine kurze Stelle aus dem Tod des Tizian oder einem der andern lyrischen Dramen lesen wollten? Und vielleicht zugleich ein paar Worte erklärend und schildernd beifügen würden über den Kreis, dem der junge Hofmannsthal damals in Wien zugehörte, dem auch Sie damals zugehört haben? [bMS Ger 183 (602)]

New-York, 11. Dez. 43

Sehr verehrter Herr Professor:

Ihr Schreiben vom 30. November konnte nicht gleich beantwortet werden — ich brauchte Zeit, zu überlegen. Sie erwähnten, dass dieser Abend "ein erster Versuch" sein sollte, derartige Veranstaltungen, nach längerer Pause, wieder aufzunehmen. Dass dieser nicht ungewagte Versuch mir anvertraut wird, empfinde ich als ehrend, aber zugleich ein wenig bedrückend. Lassen Sie mich, um für Sie und für mich Alles klarzustellen, Ihre Wünsche und Vorschläge Punkt für Punkt durchgehen.

Die wichtigsten Stellen Ihres Schreibens lauten: "Wir hatten uns ferner gedacht, dass man praktisch das Programm zwischen der Lesung Ihrer Dichtungen und der Hofmannsthals teilen könnte" und "Ich glaube diese Teilung des Programms wäre schön für alle Hörer, und klug, was den Erfolg des Abends als eine Veranstaltung des German Departments von Harvard anbetrifft. Und möchte auch meinen, dass es Ihnen lieb sein sollte, eine Gelegenheit zu haben, Hofmannsthals grosse Bedeutung in helleres Licht zu stellen."

Vor mir liegen die beiden bisher veröffentlichten Auswahl-Bände der Hofmannsthal-Briefe — 26 von ihnen an mich gerichtet. In einem aus dem Jahre 1897 spricht er von den "hunderten von Gesprächen, die wir in diesen fünf Jahren miteinander gehabt haben" —— in einem, aus dem Jahre 1900, steht: — "von wieviel hundert Stunden kommt manchmal eine flüchtige Erinnerung zurück: so viele Stunden in der Früh in Ihrer oberen Wohnung, und wieder Abends auf der Strasse beim Nachhausegehen, in Ischl vor 3 und 4 Jahren, in Salzburg, in Italien" —— und in mir ruht, manchmal noch emportauchend, das Erinnern an Stunden, unzählbar viele, in denen ich — von Hugos ersten Versen an, bis zum Turm, so oft um seinetwillen zur Rede gestellt — zu Andern *von* ihm, und — wie hätte es anders sein können — *für* ihn sprach. Wenn nun — mehr als ein halbes Jahrhundert nach dem Tag, an dem *er*, der sechzehnjährige, und *ich*, der vierundzwanzigjährige, einander trafen — wenn nun die Stimme eines Menschen von Rang, der Hofmannsthals Werk verehrt, von mir die Hälfte der mir eingeräumten Stunde, für Hofmannsthal verlangt, so kann ich ja wohl nicht anders, als noch die eine armselige halbe Stunde, zu all den andern, vielen für ihn herzugeben.

So mag denn die Vorlesung geteilt werden.

Eine normale Vorlesung soll nicht länger als eine Stunde dauern —— aber diesmal würde ich — ich habe alle Lesezeiten genau kontrolliert — eine Stunde und zwölf Minuten brauchen: 34 Minuten, für Hofmannsthal, 34, für mich, und 4 Minuten Pause zwischen den beiden Teilen.

Meine Hälfte enthielte: die erste Szene aus "Der junge David" — aber nun sehr gekürzt, und nur kürzere Gedichte, da ich 34 Minuten nicht überschreiten will.

Von Hofmannsthal würde ich lesen: Gedichte, den Prolog zu "Der Tor und der Tod" (Nachlese), dann nicht "ein paar Prosastücke aus einem der Loris-Essays," da der strahlende Intellekt dieser Stücke, bestenfalls, den Intellekt des Zuhörers entzündet, anspannt, aber auch ermüdet, da der Hörer nicht, wie der Leser, Tempo und Rythmus die ihm zugemutet werden, sich anpassen kann. Christiane Zimmer[1] (die ich seit der Nacht, da sie zur Welt kam, kenne, und der die Intentionen ihres Vaters vertraut sind) rät mir statt dessen ein paar kürzere Briefe zu lesen, die — in ihrer, aus einem Anlass entspringenden Unmittelbarkeit, ihrer seltenen Gefühlsbetontheit, ihrem wundervoll leichtem Dahinströmen, Prosa-Stücke ersten Ranges — Hofmannsthal von einer wenig gekannten Seite zeigen.[2]

Das dramatische Fragment "Der Tod des Tizian" habe ich durch einleitende zusammenfassende Worte und Kürzungen auf eine Dimension gebracht, die es nun ermöglicht das Fragment als ein, immerhin doch Geschlossenes, wirksam an das Ende der Hofmannsthal-Rezitation zu stellen.

Auch Ihrem Wunsch nach, "Persönlichem" kann ich nun doch zum Teil nachkommen, da alles so gewält ist, dass sich nebenher, zwanglos, parenthetisch, bisher nicht Gekanntes aufhellend einstreuen lässt. Vor allem viel, in dem Prolog zu "Der Tor und der Tod," auch in den Gedichten und Briefen.

Beim Vortrag müsste ich unbedingt Hofmannsthal den Vortritt lassen, schon, weil es junge Menschen sind, die seine Verse sprechen, und ich also nicht bloss meine Stimme höher stellen, lebhafter rythmisieren, auf ihrer Palette hellere Farben mischen muss, sondern auch, weil die Stimme frisch, ausgeruht klingen soll, und nicht mögliche Spuren einer vorhergegangenen halbstündigen angespannten Rezitation tragen darf.

Als Termin wird wohl März in Betracht gezogen sein.

Mit besten Grüssen und vielem Dank für Ihr freundliches Bemühen,

Ihr sehr ergebener

R. B.-H.

Houghton Library, *78M–64: Letterbook VIII (autograph).

[1] Hofmannsthal's daughter; the wife of Heinrich Zimmer, the authority on Indian myth.

[2] The reading took place in the evening of March 22, 1944 at the Houghton Library. Beer-Hofmann was a splendid interpretive reader. Among the letters of Hofmannsthal he chose to read from was the letter of May 10, 1896: "Und, bitte, arbeiten Sie: das ist vielleicht das einzige Wirkliche, was es auf der Welt gibt." When Beer-Hofmann came to this passage he paused and smiled, savoring his own indulgence and his friend's admonition.

11   To Hermann J. Weigand

New-York C. 28. XI. 1943

Sehr verehrter Herr Professor,

Die Erinnerung an Ihren freundlichen Besuch ist durchaus nicht verblasst, und ich weiss, wie sehr mich die verstehende Liebe berührte, mit der Sie dem Phänomen "Kleist" sich hingaben, und das Problem des "Vertrauens" als den Kern seines Wesens erkannten.[1]

Lassen Sie mich vor Allem bitten, der Universität für die ehrende Einladung zu danken. Ich werde mich freuen, in der zweiten April-Hälfte oder Anfang Mai im Rahmen des Germanic Club aus meinem Werk zu lesen.[2] Dass vielleicht — wie Sie mich vorbereiten — nur eine "Handvoll Zuhörer" da sein wird, ist nichts, worum ich sorge. Ob es nun, nur eine "Handvoll" ist, oder eine Menge die den Saal überfüllt — wenn es sich fügt, dass darunter auch nur ein einziger ist, dem mein Wort etwas wirklich zu geben vermag: fruchtbare Ruhe — oder weiterzeugende, nachdenkliche Unruhe — so wird mein Lesen Sinn gehabt haben.

Ich denke 55 Minuten werden wohl die richtige Dauer sein, und der Nachmittag die Zeit, die ich vorziehe. Ich möchte lesen: die "Gedenkrede auf Wolfgang Amadé Mozart," die erste Szene aus "Der junge David," und einige Gedichte — Dinge, die sich bereits als geeignet erwiesen. Ich weiss nicht, ob ich Ihnen seinerzeit das Heftchen "Besprechungen" gegeben habe, das für eine Tournée in der Schweiz zusammengestellt wurde — so sende ich jetzt für alle Fälle ein Exemplar.

Dank für den "Florian Geyer"[3] — er wird in allernächster Zeit in Ruhe gelesen werden —— nun auch für Ihr so freundliches Bemühen — sehr Verehrter — herzlichen Dank, und Grüsse

Ihr sehr ergebener
Richard Beer-Hofmann

Houghton Library, Autograph file.

[1] "Das Vertrauen in Kleists Erzählungen," *Monatshefte für deutschen Unterricht,* 34 (1942), [49]–63, [126]–144.

[2] The reading at Yale University by Beer-Hofmann was on April 25, 1944 at five o'clock in the afternoon.

[3] "Auf den Spuren von Hauptmanns *Florian Geyer,*" PMLA, 57 (1942), 1160–1195 and 58 (1943), 797–848.

12   To Marie Heller [1]

Wien 22. III. 1939

Sehr verehrte gnädige Frau:

Dreimal um die Nachmittagsmitte und einmal am Vormittag versuchte ich Sie zu treffen. Immer kam die Auskunft der Telephonistin "nicht zu Hause" oder "Das Telefon abgestellt, dürfte schlafen." Als ich das Fünftemal am frühen Vormittag anrief, hiese es "abgereist." So bleibt mir nichts übrig als Ihnen mit diesen Zeilen zu sagen, wie gerne ich Sie noch gesehen hätte. Ihre freundliche Erscheinung ist in die Erinnerung unseres letzen Ausseer Sommer mit verflochten. Im gleichen Raum nahmen wir unsere Mahlzeiten, auf unserm Tischen standen in kleinen bäurischen Krügen dieselben Blumen-Uhren die Jahreszeit zeigend. Wenn wir im Frühsommer kamen: Trollblumen und Narzissen — Nachzügler des Frühlings im Tal, an den höheren Hängen gepflückt, Alpenrosen und Fingerhut, Annika Akonit — Heilkräuter der Berge — im Sommer und im Herbst eh wir gingen herbstliche Enziane: violetter und Schwalbenschwanz-Enzian, dessen Bläue einem matt schien, wenn man an die tiefblauen grossen Kelche des kurzstieligen Enzians der durchwässerten Frühlingswiesen dachte. Sie selbst kamen und gingen still, lautlos einen kleinen Raum gewollten Alleinseins um sich legend und wenn wir am Nachmittag vom Balkon des Hauses über die Wiesen hinsahen, wussten wir: dort drüben im Durchblick zwischen verstreuten kleinen Häusern, gerahmt von den grossen Kronen, zweier alter grauummoderten Apfelbäume ist das Stück Wiese das zu Ihrem Hause gehört, dort drüben steht ihr Streckstuhl, und was jetzt über die Wiesen zum Stuhl hingeht müssen Sie sein — kenntlich an der weissen Sonnen durchleuchtenden Krone Ihres Haares.

So gehört Ihr Bild für uns mit zu dem wunderbaren Tal, es fügt sich ein in jene [   ] Landschaft deren Berge, Wiesen, und weissgrüne Wasser seit unserer Jugend uns Heimat geworden waren, uns lieber und vertrauter mehr Teil an uns habend als die Stadt, in der wir lebten. Von diesen Sommern, in denen wir nicht nur das Gelände, sondern unsere eigene Jugend liebten, von diesen Sommern, deren letzte — jetzt erst im

---

[1] Marie Heller has not been identified; the letter to her is addressed in care of Askonas, Trianon Palace Hotel, Paris–Versailles — the name of a family Beer-Hofmann was friendly with.

Erinnern wird es uns bewusst, — schon rätselhaft überschattet waren von einem heimlichen Abschiednehmen von der süss schmerzlichen Trauer einer letzten Liebe —— von diesen Sommern hätten wir wohl miteinander gesprochen, wenn wir uns noch gesehen hätten. —— Statt dessen stehen jetzt nur diese dürftigen Zeilen hier, als Gruss von uns Beiden, als herzlicher, alles Gute erhoffende Wunsch für Sie, sehr verehrte — und für Alles, was Ihnen teuer ist.

In Verehrung Ihr
[unsigned]

Houghton Library, *78M–64: Letterbook II (1939 bis August) (autograph).

---

13   To Adolph Oko [1]

Woodstock, N.Y. 3. VII. 1940

Mein Lieber!

Seit Dienstag (25.VI.) sind wir hier. Das kleine Haus liegt nahe der Strasse, aber ganz eingeschlossen von stundenweit sich streckendem Wald, der hinter dem Haus weglos, unbegangen aufsteigt: riesige Felsblöcke — wohl Reste eines alten Bergsturzes — dazwischen ein Verhau aus aufrechten lebenden und gestürzten verwesenden Stämmen, dazwischen — die hohe Schicht von verrottetem Laub durchstossend — junges Gehölz, Schlingkraut, Farne, die um ein wenig Sonne ringen müssen. Es erinnert Alles an viele glückliche Sommer in den Bergen — auch das helle Rinnen des kleinen Rohrbrunnens vor dem Haus, und manchmal, wenn ich morgens erwache, braucht es einen Augenblick, bis mir wieder bewusst wird, dass ich weit weg von dem, was mir Heimat war, weit weg von meiner Jugend bin — und allein bin.

Erich Kahler, seine Frau und seine Mutter wohnen wenig Minuten von uns und sind sehr lieb.[2] Auch er würde sich sehr freuen, wenn Ihr

---

[1] Professor Adolph S. Oko (1883–1944), Librarian of Hebrew Union College, Cincinnati, 1909–33. His Spinoza bibliography was published posthumously in Boston, 1964.

[2] Erich von Kahler (1885–1970) was a cousin of Beer-Hofmann; cf. above, Letter 2.

für eine Weile hieher kommen würdet. Von Woodstock, das in Grünem gebettet liegt, und gute Hotels hat, sind wir 7 Autominuten entfernt. Wir wollen nicht vor Mitte September von hier weggehen — das sind 2½ Monate — und ich habe schon gelernt 2½ Monate als Zeitspanne nicht mehr jugendlich leichtfertig zu unterschätzen. So wäre es eine sehr grosse Freude, wenn Ihr kämet und mit Euch Freundliches und Zuversichtgebendes.

Wenn die Archiv-Aufzeichnungen noch nicht zurückgekommen sind, fordere sie — bitte — gelegentlich zurück. Es giebt mir ein besseres Gefühl sie in Deinen treuen Händen zu wissen.

Alles Liebe, Euch Dreien. Antworte mit keinem Brief, nur ganz kurz, am liebsten mit einem Telefonanruf, der Euer Kommen meldet.

Von Herzen
Richard

Tel. 335.

Houghton Library, *78M–64: Letterbook v (autograph).

---

14   To Raoul Auernheimer [1]

New York 27. IV. 1941

Mein lieber Raoul Auernheimer!

Hier — zu Ihrem Geburtstag — ein sehr alter Prospekt Wiens, "Vienna Austriæ metropolis urbs toto orbe notissima celebratissimaque," steht in der Überschrift des Prospektes.[2]

Dem Angriff überheblicher Horden, vorbereitet durch Dummheit, Tücke, Verrat, seit Jahrzehnten gezüchtete widerliche Seuchen, die Seele und Antlitz der Menschen dieser Stadt und auch noch das Antlitz der Stadt selbst zerstörten, ist diese Stadt, ist das Land dessen reiche

[1] Raoul Auernheimer (1876–1948), Austrian writer of plays, biographies, essays.

[2] "Vienna Austriæ Metropolis. . .", Plate 42 in vol. 1 of Georg Braun, *Beschreibung und Contrafactur der vornembster Stät der Welt*, 6 vols. (Cologne, 1574–1618).

Erfüllung sie erschien, schliesslich erlegen. Aber ihre Art, die Art ihrer Besten — wie diese Stadt durch die Dauer der Zeiten "invictum propugnaculum" (so benennt sie der Stich) "unbesiegtes Bollwerk" war, dahinter erdgeborene, naturhafte freie Anmut und einmalige, nie wiederkehrende, unirdische begnadete Schönheit sich entfalten durften — wird in der Erinnerung der Menschen bleiben.

Alle guten Wünsche, mein lieber Raoul Auernheimer, Ihnen und Ihrer lieben Frau!

Herzlichst Ihr
R. B.-H.

Houghton Library, *78M–64: Letterbook VI (autograph).

---

15 To M. D. Herter Norton [1]

N.Y. 21. IV. 41

Ich danke Ihnen, sehr verehrte gnädige Frau, für die schöne Sternen-Karte, und die freundlich-tröstenden Worte die sie begleiteten.[2] Dass rings um uns Sterne entrückt aller vergänglichen irdischen Gewalt — solange Menschen denken — ungerührt die gleichen Bahnen ziehen, giebt uns manchmal scheues Ahnen eines Etwas, das menschliches Tun und Lassen nicht mit Erden- sondern mit Sternen-Maassen misst.

Für alle, die ihr Leben nicht stumpf dahindämmern, kommt ja irgendeinmal die Zeit, wo sie von äusserem, von innerem Schicksal vertrieben — oder sehnsüchtig, aus freien Stücken — das hinter sich lassen, was ihnen so lange wert, wichtig unentbehrlich schien und — ungebeugt — "refugees" in ein ihnen seit je offenes Kosmisches ziehen, in

---

[1] Mary Dows Herter Norton (1892–   ), translator of poems, prose, and letters by Rainer Maria Rilke.

[2] In a note dated Apr. 16, 1941, Mrs. Norton had written, "In spite of everything, behold, the stars are continuing in their courses, and having found that this is so, I am sending you this chart, in the hope that it will make you feel more at home each day and night in our part of the world!" Houghton Library, bMS Ger 183 (227).

dessen ungeheuerem blendenden Licht, sie vergessen, wie stark oder wie schwächlich ihr Erden-Schicksal flackerte.

Ich werde mich sehr freuen, Sie bald zu sehen — inzwischen herzliche Grüsse

Ihr

R. B.-H.

Houghton Library, *78M–64: Letterbook VI (autograph).

Così leuando me ſu uer la cima
Dun ronchion auiſaua unaltra ſcheggia
Dicendo ; Soura quella poi taggrappa :
Ma tenta pria, ſè tal, chella ti reggia .

paratione, ci ricorderemo, che il principio de lanno, alcuni pigliandolo da la nattiui ta di Chriſto, ſanno che ſia il primo di del meſe di Genaro . Altri pigliandolo da la incarnatione , ſanno che ſia il primo di

Marzo. Gliaſtrologi pigliano il ſuo principio, quandol ſole entra nel primo grado de l' Ariete, il che ſuol eſſer comunemente tra lundecimo e duodecimo del detto meſe di Marzo. Ma il poeta , laſciando queſto tal ordine de gliaſtrologi, e prendendo lanno da la nattiuita di Chriſto , ſecondo luſo Roma no, intende la parte de lanno giouanetto per la fin di Genaro , uicino a mezo delqual meſe il ſol en tra ſotto l' Aquario, & allhora tempra I Crini , cio è, I raggi ſotto tal ſegno , perche cominciano pur un poco a riſcaldare , E Gia le notti ſe ne uanno al mezo di , Intende al mezo del di naturale, ilqual è da lun a laltro naſcimento del ſole , perche allhora cominciano a diminuir le notti , & a

creſcer

La comedia (1544), N4ᵛ. Woodcut, 126×107mm. *Houghton Library.*

The Presence of Vergil
in the Marcolini Dante of 1544

RUTH MORTIMER

IN VENICE in 1544, the printer Francesco Marcolini designed a new edition of Dante's *Commedia* for the purpose of printing the extensive commentary of Alessandro Vellutello. The title-page reads, "La Comedia di Dante Aligieri con la nova espositione di Alessandro Vellvtello" in four lines of solid capitals with Vellutello's name equal in size to Dante's.[1] The commentator took more responsibility for the production than merely submitting the manuscript; the colophon records completion of the printing in June 1544 by Marcolini, "in instantia di Alessandro Vellutello." Vellutello's commentary on Petrarch, first published in 1525, was reprinted in 1543/44 at Venice by Gabriele Giolito de' Ferrari[2] in a newly illustrated edition. For twentieth-century readers who may chance upon these editions, Vellutello's contribution to Italian letters, to the understanding of Dante or Petrarch, is overshadowed by that of his printers, who used the occasion of a fresh commentary to revitalize the illustration of the text.

The Dante volume is a thick quarto in eights. It has the collation: AA-BB⁸, CC¹⁰, A-Z⁸, AB-AZ⁸, BC-BI⁸ (BI8 blank); 442 leaves. The body of the work is set in two sizes of Marcolini's fine italic letter, with Dante's text beginning at the left margin, the longest lines running to about the center of the page. The commentary begins to the right of center, continues parallel to the text and finishes underneath it, full measure. This results in small segments of the original text engulfed in commentary on a page, and in the setting of the commentary in a line which when full is much too long for the type size. The density of the commentary is matched by the woodcuts, but they are marvelously

---

[1] There is a copy of this edition in the Harvard College Library Department of Printing and Graphic Arts, described as no. 146 in vol. 1 of the Department's Catalogue of Books and Manuscripts, Part II, *Italian Sixteenth-Century Books*, by Ruth Mortimer (Cambridge, Mass., 1974). Six illustrations are reproduced as part of that description. There is also a copy in the author's collection.

[2] *Italian Sixteenth-Century Books*, vol. 2, no. 375.

complex, where the commentary is perhaps merely exhaustive. The blocks are unsigned. There are three full-page cuts, approximately 175 by 105 mm., at the beginning of the *Inferno*, the *Purgatorio*, and the *Paradiso*. The other blocks measure 126 by 107 or 109 mm. Ten of these were designed for Vellutello's introductory "Descrittione de lo Inferno." The illustration within the *Commedia* is a total of seventy-four scenes.

There are two levels at which the *Commedia* could be illustrated, through Dante's eyes or from a vantage point where the poet himself is observed in his progress. Twentieth-century artists such as Barry Moser[3] have concentrated on what Dante sees, rather than on Dante seeing. Fifteenth- and sixteenth-century printed illustrations provide reference figures of Dante together with Vergil through the *Inferno* and the *Purgatorio* to the moment when Vergil relinquishes his charge to Statius and ultimately Beatrice. The guidance of Vergil is essential to Dante's and the reader's comprehension of the journey Dante is making, and the first illustrators in manuscript and printed book followed the text closely by including the two poets in every scene. The commentators could state that Vergil represented Rational Philosophy in the allegory, but the illustrator had to humanize Vergil and work him into a visible storyline.

A fully illustrated *Commedia* was a considerable achievement; Volkmann describes Dante manuscripts in which such illustration was attempted and abandoned partway through the manuscript.[4] In their edition completed March 3, 1491, Bernardino Benalio and Matteo Capodecasa introduced a set of blocks 66 mm. square, one for each canto. The March 1491 blocks were copied almost immediately, for the use of Petrus de Plasiis in another Venetian edition dated the 18th of November in the same year. The original Benalio-Capodecasa blocks passed from printer to printer until they reached an edition printed by Jacopo da Borgofranco for Luc' Antonio Giunta in 1529.[5]

As the fifteenth-century blocks came into the sixteenth century, so also did printing conventions about the production of classical texts.

---

[3] The Moser drawings are reproduced in the *California Dante* (University of California Press), accompanying Allen Mandelbaum's translation: the *Inferno* was published in 1980.

[4] Ludwig Volkmann, *Iconografia Dantesca: The Pictorial Representations of Dante's Divine Comedy* (London, 1899), pp. 23–73 *passim*.

[5] *Italian Sixteenth-Century Books*, vol. 1, no. 145. All of the fifteenth-century illustrated editions are at Harvard. A summary of the literature on these editions is given as part of the 1529 catalogue description. Transfer of the Marcolini blocks, found as late as 1696, is noted under no. 146.

The layout of a page of Dante with surrounding commentary mirrored a printed·page of Vergil or Horace, and thus Dante was seen as a classic of vernacular literature worthy of the attention accorded the Latin poets. The 1529 Giunta Dante has on its title-page a border that illustrates the juxtaposition of ancient and modern texts that was the livelihood of Italian printers at this period. The border is architectural, with Apollo leaning out of a shell niche in the upper piece and the Muses in concert on either side of Giunta's Florentine lily device below. The two side pieces are broken into niches containing author portraits, five classical authors on the left, five modern authors on the right. The uppermost figures are Vergil and Dante, facing one another across the title-page. This border is recorded earlier on a Giunta Vergil of 1522, where the right-hand strip was another five classical authors. When the strip of modern authors was cut to adapt the border to the Dante, Giunta advertised a descent of authority through Dante to such living literary figures as Pietro Aretino. A mid-century printer like Francesco Marcolini would be committed to contemporary writers while the classical texts continued through the press and the classical ideal determined the shape of the book. Printer and author learned from the past.

In fifteenth- and sixteenth-century woodcuts illustrating classical texts, the ancient author frequently is portrayed as the master with pupils or is shown writing with figures of commentators at adjoining desks. One illustration used in a Venetian edition of Vergil had detachable commentator-figures, so that the number of commentators pictured could be varied according to the number of commentaries printed with the text.[6] In both representations, the classical figure materialized in front of his audience. The prevalence of such portraits indicates an impulse to envision the literature of the past in terms of the human figure. It is not surprising, then, that Dante's use of Vergil appealed to artists and to printers commissioning illustrators. Vergil in Book VI of the *Aeneid* provides Dante with a groundplan for his *Inferno* and a precedent for his descent into the Underworld, but beyond this role as inspiration, Vergil is also active in the *Commedia* text. Allegorically, he is Reason incarnate; literally, he has in the poem not only dignity and authority but human qualities of sympathy, doubt, and anger.

Probably the most significant feature of the early printed Dante illustrations is the repetition of the Dante and Vergil figures within a

[6] *Italian Sixteenth-Century Books*, vol. 2, no. 524.

single block. Before these woodcut artists began work, Botticelli saw the *Commedia* in this light, and his Dante drawings contain multiple pairs of Dante and Vergil figures. He creates a sense of movement by these repeated figures and by repeating at the edge of one drawing the configuration that was the center of another. The Botticelli drawings were to have provided the first Dante illustration for a printed book, in 1481, but the attempt to transfer them to copperplates failed, and copies of the edition have only a few illustrations in place and blank spaces for others.[7] On a much smaller scale, the figure repetition is operative in the 1491 woodblocks. The little figures are labelled "D" and "V" and they move the eye within the block. Marcolini's artist also recognized the usefulness of this device of repetition and placed and labelled his figures accordingly.

In the first of the circular overviews of Hell in Vellutello's "Descrittione," the first illustration in the Marcolini volume, the Dante and Vergil figures are very small. They appear twice, just inside the gate of Hell and then on the edge of the river Acheron. They are too small to be more than sketched, but the labels lead the reader to look for them, again minute, in the second block; by the third block, where the viewer is closer to the scene, they are beginning to provide a point of identification within the block. By the Third Circle (fourth block), where Vergil crouches to throw earth at Cerberus, the two figures clearly are entering into the spirit of the work, gesturing and conversing with one another and with figures on the scene. Some of the designs for this preliminary sequence reappear in place in the *Commedia* text, recut without the lettered text. Others were abandoned completely in favor of a different perspective. The changes in size of the D and V figures, and the fact that they are nearly lost sight of in a welter of detail on some blocks, give the reader a further sense of participation in the journey. The "Descrittione" blocks prefigure this experience of the reader within the illustrations as well as map out the progress of Dante and Vergil.

The full-page illustration for the *Inferno* shows Dante turning in terror from the three beasts while Vergil waits in his path: "Dinanzi a gliocchi mi si fu offerto;/ Chi per lungo silentio parea fioco." — "before my eyes there suddenly appeared/ one who seemed faint because of the

---

[7] There are several studies and reproductions of this series, the most recent being by Kenneth Clark, *The Drawings by Sandro Botticelli for Dante's Divine Comedy, after the Originals in the Berlin Museums and the Vatican* (New York, 1976).

long silence." The figure responds to Dante's questioning, "Not man; I
once was man./ . . . I was a poet . . ." And Dante says,

> "And are you then that Virgil, you the fountain
> that freely pours so rich a stream of speech?"
> . . . .
> "O light and honor of all other poets,
> may my long study and the intense love
> that made me search your volume serve me now.
> You are my master and my author, you—
> the only one from whom my writing drew
> the noble style for which I have been honored."[8]

The large woodcut introduces both figures into the narrative. There was
in circulation in the sixteenth century a fine Florentine cut of Dante
alone with the beasts in a 1506 Filippo Giunta edition of the *Commedia*
and in several other Dante and Dante-related texts.[9]

The Marcolini block also establishes the physical appearance of the
two poets in a manner carried through the small blocks. Here Marcolini
obscures a distinction that the 1491 artist was careful to make. In 1491,
Vergil as the older poet is bearded, and the identifying feature of his
dress is an outer cloak fastened at the neck. Dante is smooth-shaven and
wears a soft cap with a flap to one side. In 1544, Dante and Vergil are
dressed alike, and both have long hair, beards, and caps edged with
laurel. Volkmann notes that the bearded Dante is rare outside of manuscripts but that there is authority for it in Boccaccio,[10] one of Vellutello's
sources for his own prefatory "Vita." Volkmann also refers to the
medieval view of Vergil as White Magician, which is reflected in some

---

[8] *Inferno*, canto i, lines 62–87. The Italian text for this and subsequent
quotations is taken from the Marcolini edition. The English is the translation by
Allen Mandelbaum (Berkeley, 1980); reprinted by permission of Allen Mandelbaum.

[9] *Italian Sixteenth-Century Books*, vol. 1, no. 259.

[10] Volkmann, *Iconografia Dantesca*, pp. 6–7. Although they are sometimes
too small to tell, it appears that neither figure is bearded in the 1544 prefatory
illustrations and beards are deliberately added in the recutting of the designs as
text blocks. There is also in the Marcolini volume one text illustration, for canto
ii of the *Purgatorio*, where neither figure has a beard and one has an ermine-
collared cloak similar to Dante's cloak in 1491. But the ermine-collared figure
is variously labelled as V or D as the pair moves in the illustration, and the
whole block seems thus to be erroneously drawn, since the familiar figures return
at canto iii.

manuscript representations where Vergil is in fantastic costume, even to a peaked crown.[11] The desire to restore to Vergil the acknowledged dress of the poet of antiquity has here affected the Dante figure also. Instead of a medieval Vergil, we have a classical Dante, a poet of authority.

The decision to ignore the recognizable figure of Dante common to earlier editions is strange for Francesco Marcolini, who was responsible for some of the most important author portraits in Italian mid-century books. The chiaroscuro portrait of Pietro Aretino, attributed to Titian, printed in Marcolini's 1537 edition of Aretino's *Stanze* in praise of Angela Serena, is justly celebrated as an allegorical portrait unique to its text.[12] In 1540, Marcolini had published his own portrait, also possibly by Titian, in his book on fortune-telling, *Le sorti intitolate Giardino di pensieri*.[13] Given Marcolini's ability to produce an authentic portrait, we can look for, and find, textual support for this doubling of the poet figure. To Dante's description of Vergil as his model quoted above from canto i, add the mirror passage, *Inferno*, canto xxiii: "E quei; Sio fosse dimpiombato uetro,/ Limagine di fuor tua non trarrei/ Piu tosto a me; che quella dentro impetro."

> And he to me: "Were I a leaded mirror,
> I could not gather in your outer image
> more quickly than I have received your inner.
> For even now your thoughts have joined my own;
> in both our acts and aspects we are kin —
> with both our minds I've come to one decision.[14]

There are other times at which Vergil reads Dante's mind.

Marcolini's seeming reduction of the figures to two poets distinguished by initials does not lessen the drama, because Vergil's support and encouragement are still evident in the attitudes portrayed by the cutter. The specific acts of protection or intervention by Vergil are faithfully recorded in the woodcuts. In *Inferno*, canto xiii, for instance, Vergil instructs Dante to break a branch in the Wood of the Suicides. In the center pair of figures in the woodcut, Dante's hand is uplifted to the branch and Vergil is close behind him. The illustration is poised at one

---

[11] Volkmann, *Iconografia Dantesca*, pp. 94–95.

[12] *Italian Sixteenth-Century Books*, vol. 1, no. 26.

[13] *Italian Sixteenth-Century Books*, vol. 2, no. 279. The portrait is reproduced together with a second portrait ten years later, p. 413.

[14] *Inferno*, canto xxiii, lines 25–30.

of the passages in the text most closely connected with the *Aeneid,* by Vergil's own statement. The reference is to *Aeneid,* Book III, and as Dante stands terror-stricken while the tree pours forth "words and blood," Vergil responds, "anima lesa,/ Cio che had ueduto, pur con la mia rima . . ."

> My sage said: "Wounded soul, if, earlier,
> he had been able to believe what he
> had only glimpsed within my poetry,
>   then he would not have set his hand against you;
> but its incredibility made me
> urge him to a deed that grieves me deeply.[15]

In the illustration at canto xvi, Vergil has already mounted Geryon, while Dante hesitates on the edge of the pit. In the next woodcut, Vergil holds Dante safely on the monster as they descend into the Eighth Circle. The last of the *Inferno* illustrations has Dante seated, marvelling at Satan's legs, with Vergil standing behind him. He then follows Vergil into a tunnel, emerging at the top of the illustration, where Vergil stands in the starlight and Dante pauses halfway up from the tunnel at the base of Mount Purgatory.

In the fourteen text cuts in the *Purgatorio* in which Vergil appears, the relationship between the two figures has undergone a change. Dante is less dependent on Vergil, and Vergil has assistance. It is St. Lucy who carries Dante up the mountain at canto viii. Statius joins Dante and Vergil at canto v and stays with them from canto xix, and Matilda arrives at canto xxviii. At canto xxix, Vergil is at the outer edge of the two sets of figures in the illustration, and in the next cut he has disappeared. The two outer figures are now Dante and Statius, while Beatrice descends in a cloud of flowers.

It is Vergil who provides the gloss for the major distinction between the Vellutello-Marcolini edition and those preceding it, when in *Inferno,* canto xi, and again in canto xiv, he explains to Dante the geographical features of Hell. In the ten new woodcuts commissioned for Vellutello's prefatory "Descrittione," the emphasis on mapping Dante's progress is seen in the new structure of the illustrations as circular with the inner spiral descent visible within the immediate scene in which the poets find themselves. As the reader turns from the preface to the text, the first of

---

[15] *Inferno,* canto xiii, lines 46-51.

the text-size blocks has Vergil in conversation with Dante at the right and Vergil leading Dante into the cave in the mountainside at the left. The second text block is a recutting of the first of Vellutello's maps with the miniature D and V figures. Beginning with this abrupt change from normal figures to the overview of the *Inferno,* the extraordinary variety of the twenty-eight *Inferno* blocks comes from the varying sizes of the figures on the scene, using Dante and Vergil for scale. In their repetitive motion within the block, Vergil and Dante regularly enter the block on the right and move towards the center. This approach by way of geography rather than story is well within the interests of Vellutello's prospective readers. In the same decade with the Dante, Marcolini was engaged in printing the architectural works of Sebastiano Serlio, and woodcut maps, elevations, plans and diagrams illustrate books of this period.

The first of two woodcuts in *Inferno* canto xxiv (leaf N4ᵛ, reproduced on p. 144), will best serve to illustrate this discussion of the Marcolini presentation. Marcolini places his woodcuts within the canto rather than using them, as earlier printers had, to mark the exact text division. This may be simply expedient within the quarto format, but it has the effect of setting up a different rhythm between text and illustrations. The poets' descent, on the back of the monster Geryon, into the Eighth Circle, was admirably portrayed at canto xvii, and each succeeding woodcut for the Circle is precise in following Dante's description of the stone pouches, ribs, and bridges. In this illustration, showing the ascent from the level of the Hypocrites to the bridge overlooking the Thieves, Dante and Vergil appear three times, but they are almost hidden in the composition, whereas they were clearly on the edge of the pouches in the earlier view of this Circle. This is correct on the part of the illustrator, since Dante and Vergil were prodded into descending to the level of the processional figures by demons in the preceding cut. First, at the right edge of the block, they are climbing over a pile of rocks of a broken bridge. The next two figures to the left are Dante and Vergil as they have ventured onto the bridge, with Dante leaning over to look at the figures below. The third pair of figures is poised on the edge of the next pouch, Vergil behind Dante, as they speak to Vanni Fucci. The next woodcut moves this last pair into focus and adds a second behind them. In each of these illustrations, the number of remaining pouches is accurately indicated in the center. For the first two scenes of the Eighth Circle, the outer border was entirely clear of figures; then the artist began adding activity on the edge, where Dante and Vergil struggled with demons. In the block reproduced and the block following, the entire surface of the block is filled with figures. Here the steady march of the Hypocrites in leaden cloaks is contrasted with the teeming mass of Thieves and serpents.

Canto xxiv has come under considerable scrutiny from Dante scholars for its elaborate opening simile, in which the evanescence of the hoar-frost is used to convey Vergil's mood of frustration and anger at having been deceived by the demons of canto xxiii.[16] The despair and hope concentrated in the peasant (Dante) dependent on his world's countenance (Vergil) are memorable as a sketch of Dante's condition at a crucial point. The symbols for Vergil in this passage are the sun, the frost, the pen. Dante is the peasant, but as Vergil's anger melts, so does Dante's anxiety, and Dante in this poem takes the pen from Vergil. The simile is part of the rich texture of the poem, in Vergil's *Aeneid* and in Dante's *Commedia*. The images are accessible to the illustrator, as sun, hoar-frost, snow, pen, peasant, lambs; these could be pictured successively, but the vital connection the poet is making would be lacking in a pictorial representation. Volkmann records several instances of illustrators attempting unsuccessfully to picture the simile in a manner compatible with the illustration of the narrative.[17]

Marcolini's illustrator, however, is preoccupied not with reading the simile but with tracking the poets. The first sixty-three lines of the canto brought Dante and Vergil to the position they occupy at the edge of the woodcut. The second pair of figures would appear to be in position for line 70, where Dante cranes to see who is speaking from the ditch below. Here in the text, Dante takes the initiative and asks that they move to a better vantage point, and Vergil replies approvingly. The third position reached and illustrated gives Dante and Vergil a full view of the serpent-filled chasm and the metamorphosis of the Thieves. The figure facing them, with monster attached, anticipates the transformations in canto xxv. The 1491 block for this canto has Dante and Vergil climbing, with no memory of the slow march of Hypocrites that encircle their efforts, and then descending to speak with serpent-eaten Thieves,

---

[16] David J. Baker, "The Winter Simile in *Inferno* xxiv," *Dante Studies*, 92 (1974), 77–91, gives a survey of the literature at note 1, pp. 88–89. Richard H. Lansing also discusses the passage in *From Image to Idea: A Study of the Simile in Dante's Commedia* (Ravenna, 1977), pp. 21–22, 74–80.

[17] Volkmann, *Iconografia Dantesca*, pp. 60, 154–156, 179–180.

represented by three figures. The technical refinement of the woodblock fashionable and possible in 1544 renders Dante's experience as incredibly complicated within its framework. The enormity of the vision, with its multiplicity of figures, is made part of the picture. The Marcolini Dante is a scholarly edition, in which the illustrator adds a commentary of his own in his reading of the text and the printer supports an artistic as well as an editorial interpretation. Looking beyond Marcolini's restructuring of the illustrations to his poet figures within them, the twentieth-century reader may see Dante in yet another light.

A Venetian *Tavola di Cebete*

ELEANOR M. GARVEY

VENETIAN ILLUSTRATED BOOKS of the eighteenth century include among their many types slender volumes of a popular philosophical nature. There are, for example, Gioacchino Trioli's *L'educazione delle fanciulle* of 1765, Jean-Jacques Rousseau's *Il buon governo degli affari domestici* of 1784, and *L'arte di rendersi felice* of 1766, a translation of *L'art de se rendre heureux* (Amsterdam, 1764), falsely ascribed to Rousseau. The educational purpose of these little publications is confined to the texts, for the engravings of contemporary genre they contain serve as decoration rather than illustration. They would not be unsuitable for one of the many romances popular at the time and often issued by the same publishers.

A different kind of illustration, instructional in character, accompanies Cornelio Pepoli's Italian editions of the *Tavola di Cebete*. Two illustrated Pepoli editions in eight years attest to the continuing popularity of this ancient text. Each contains a folding engraved frontispiece illustrating the *Tavola,* whose un-Venetian character and source suggest some of the many influences shaping the arts of this most international of cities.

Cornelio Pepoli (1708–1777), of an ancient Bolognese family, settled in Venice in 1739. There he was occupied with public affairs and literary publications as he pursued his interests in philosophy, languages, and natural science. He was praised for his study of geometry, algebra, and physics by his better-known Bolognese compatriot, Francesco Maria Zanotti. A literary career was also cultivated by Pepoli's son Alessandro (1757–1796), founder of the Tipografia Pepoliana and author of the libretto of the opera, *I giuocchi d'Agrigento,* with music by Giovanni Paisiello, which inaugurated the new Teatro Fenice in 1792.[1] *I giuocchi*

[1] Giovanni Fantuzzi, *Notizie degli scrittori bolognesi,* VI (Bologna, 1788), 347. See also *Enciclopedia italiana,* 26 (1935), 712–713 for the Pepoli family and especially for Alessandro. It was another Cornelio Pepoli, of an earlier generation (d. 1707), who formed a notable collection of books and manuscripts (Carlo Frati, *Dizionario bio-bibliografico* [Florence, 1933], p. 447). A younger cousin Carlo (1796–1881) was a patriot of the Risorgimento and the librettist of Bellini's opera *I Puritani.*

d'Agrigento was published by the Stamperia Curti, and it was probably with the assistance of this house that the younger Pepoli developed his imprint. Within the next few years, he published several of his own plays, as well as some others.[2] The official imprimatur was granted to "Alessandro Pepoli stampatore di Venezia," but in at least one book, Luigi Sala's *Saggio di poesie drammatiche* of 1794, the imprint reads: "Dalla Tipografia Pepoliana Presso Antonio Curti Q. Giacomo."

Like most of his literary contemporaries, Cornelio Pepoli was a member of the Accademia degli Arcadi and was *vicecustode* of the Bolognese Colonia Renia, with the academic pseudonym of Cratejo Erasiniano.[3] He used this pseudonym and his academic rank, as well as his own name, on the title-page of the first edition of his *Traduzione della Tavola di Cebete in versi sciolti, ed Alcuni rime profani, morali, e sagre*. It was published by the Negozio Zatta in 1763, and Antonio Zatta had received the imprimatur the previous December. He was one of the three most active and influential Venetian publishers of the mid-century, sharing this prominence and a concern for illustrated books with Giovanni Battista Pasquali and Giovanni Battista Albrizzi. Zatta issued a wide range of literature, both Renaissance and contemporary, as well as a number of fête books designed for the many spectacles that made Venice such a vivid and picturesque scene. In the 1780s the imprint became Antonio Zatta e Figli and as such continued into the 1790s. The firm was only rarely designated the Negozio Zatta; perhaps it indicates that Zatta was commissioned by Pepoli to print and publish this book.

The *Traduzione* is a little octavo of 127 pages, containing the Latin text, "Cebetis Thebani Tabula" set in italic on the verso pages, with Pepoli's Italian verse translation, "Tavola di Cebete Tebano," in roman on the facing rectos. Following the text are additional verses, "Parte profane, parte morali e sacre," which the author tells us he was pleased to add.

Pepoli's second publication of the *Tavola* is a sequel, rather than a mere second edition. Entitled *Lettere instruttive intorno alla Tavola di Cebete*, it was published in 1771 by Francesco Sansoni, whose imprint appears on but few Venetian books. A quarto of 107 pages, it contains supplementary material in the form of letters from a provincial gentle-

---

[2] G. Morazzoni, *Il libro illustrato veneziano del settecento* (Milan, 1943), p. 247–248.

[3] He also used the Arcadian pseudonym Nautilo Sicopeo. Michele Maylender, *Storia delle Accademie d'Italia*, IV (Bologna, 1929), 429.

man to his nephew commenting on the *Tavola*, the text of which is repeated in Latin, along with Pepoli's verse translation, from the 1763 edition. The copies of both these editions in the Department of Printing and Graphic Arts of the Houghton Library are in contemporary white wrappers.[4]

The *Tavola di Cebete* (Κέβητος Πίναξ, *Tabula Cebetis, Cebestafel, Table* or *Tablet of Cebes*) has a long history.[5] Fancifully attributed to the philosopher Cebes the Theban, a disciple of Socrates and a speaker in Plato's *Phaedo*, it is now generally assigned to the first century A.D. The Greek text was first translated into Latin by Lodovico Odassi, edited by Filippo Beroaldo, and published in Bologna in 1497, a year before the first Greek edition. It was a popular Humanist text of the sixteenth century, often issued with Epictetus' *Enchiridion*, and an educational text well into the eighteenth century. Concerned with choices on the path of life, it is an instructional text for the seeker of truth and virtue.

The Tablet is described as a picture in the temple of Kronos (or Saturn),[6] the ancient divinity and the personification of Time. The complex allegory is explained by a wise attendant, who points out that the walled circular enclosure in the picture represents the field of life. It contains two inner concentric circles, each with a gate, and near the outside entrance stands the figure of an old man, Genius, who counsels those who enter. The easy path to the left is to be avoided, and the upward one to the right is to be encouraged. The road is circuitous and dangerous, leading to Felicity at the summit, but threatened with Death and Debauchery; Fortune is but a blind and unstable guide. Only Penitence (assuming each wayfarer must stumble), Patience, and True Learning can assist the Pilgrim over the stony path to the Virtues, the true

---

[4] The 1763 edition, the gift of Philip Hofer, was acquired from the John Saks sale, Christie's, 10 June 1981, lot 35, not itemized. The 1771 edition is in the personal collection of Philip Hofer.

[5] For a brief summary of the history of the Tablet of Cebes and its early editions, see Cora E. Lutz, "The Salmasius-Elichmann Edition of the *Tabula* of Cebes," *Harvard Library Bulletin*, 27 (1979), 165–171 and Lutz, *Essays on Manuscripts and Rare Books* ([Hamden, Connecticut] 1975), p. [79]–86: "Aesticampanius' Edition of the *Tabula* Attributed to Cebes." For a discussion of the origin and content of the text see Robert Joly, *Le tableau de Cébès et la philosophie religieuse*. Collection Latomus, 61 (Brussels, 1963). The only study of the visual interpretation is Reinhart Schleier, *Tabula Cebetis* (Berlin, 1973) with 135 plates and excellent bibliography.

[6] Samuel C. Chew, *The Pilgrimage of Life* (New Haven and London, 1962), p. 207–208.

way to Felicity. The Tablet is one of many traditional metaphors for the choices of life and takes its place with the Y of Pythagoras, the Crossroads of Hercules, with which it was sometimes published,[7] and the familiar "strait gate" of the Gospel of Matthew. To the English-language reader, the path is familiar from John Bunyan's *Pilgrim's Progress,* and the Tablet has been suggested as one of his sources.[8]

Few texts and illustrations are as interdependent as this one. Not only are the images precisely described in words, but the title is *table* or *tablet* and the text elucidates a picture: the tablet at the gate. An illustration of this text is therefore a picture of a picture — a visual interpretation of a literary description of an imaginary image. Indeed, in the eighteenth century, the Tablet was seen as the first successful alliance of philosophy and painting.[9]

The earliest recorded illustration of the Tablet is by an anonymous artist, who designed a title-page woodcut for the 1507 Frankfurt edition.[10] This small, stylized, and crudely cut image is simply conceived as a succession of flat and parallel planes. The path to virtue is vertical and narrow, with no sense of the circuitous, and the attractions of pleasure are caricatured rather than conveyed.

Far more sophisticated is Hans Holbein's *Cebestafel,* perhaps the best-known and most influential interpretation of this theme. He designed four versions,[11] two metal-cuts and two woodcuts, which appeared as book borders in Basel in 1521–1522. They were used not to illustrate editions of Cebes, but to ornament books of grammar and religion, such as Froben's 1521 edition of Erasmus' New Testament. Holbein's borders form vertical backgrounds for the title labels laid over them. Because they accommodate titles of different sizes, the borders are adjusted to fit the title labels so that the narrative is clearly visible. In all cases, the lower margin contains the first circular wall, its masonry

---

[7] Ronald Paulson, *Emblem and Expression, Meaning in English Art of the Eighteenth Century* (Cambridge, Mass., 1975), p. 30, note 44. Lord Shaftesbury wrote a pair of essays, "The Picture of Thebes" and "The Judgment of Hercules" for a projected second volume of his *Characteristics.* See Stephen Orgel, ed., *Cebes in England* (New York and London, 1980) for the essays.

[8] Chew, p. 174.

[9] Jean H. Hagstrum, *The Sister Arts* [Chicago, 1958], p. 34.

[10] Schleier, p. 32 and pl. 1.

[11] Basel, Kunstmuseum, *Die Malerfamilie Holbein in Basel* [1960], p. 300–302, no. 367, 370, 371, 376. Schleier, *Tabula Cebetis,* p. 34–35, pl. 5–8.

clearly articulated, with the entrance gate and the figure of Genius, identified with a label above his head. New-born souls in the guise of Renaissance putti outside the wall press to enter. *Suadela* or Persuasion greets them, and the path of life unfolds, each tempter and guide carefully labeled as the picture leads the pilgrim and the viewer upward to the right, with *Felicitas* in the center of the upper border. Despite the interruption of the title labels, there is a remarkable sense of continuity to the compositions, which weave back and forth across the page with a clarity and regularity of action. The designs soon reached Venice, where one of the woodcuts was copied by Zoan Andrea Vavassore for the title-page of Aldus Manutius' *Dictionarivm Graecvm* of 1525.[12]

A composition in turbulent contrast to the Holbein, the Vavassore, and other Venetian interpretations [13] is the engraving illustrating Pepoli's first edition of 1763, his *Traduzione della tavola di Cebete* (see plate, p. 160). The engraved image measures 177 × 325 mm. while the platemark is 195 × 334 mm. The temptations, the punishments, and the rewards are unlabeled, but vividly depicted. In the right foreground, souls are born of a reclining female figure, watched by an eagle and a phoenix, both suggesting metaphorical rebirth. As the young souls play with children's toys, they are guided by the paternal figure of Genius toward an unruly crowd, clamoring for a drink offered by the lavishly-gowned figure of Persuasion or Deceit. Within the gate surmounted by an A, the Alpha of the beginning, the crowds swirl around the figure of Fortune as they taste a multitude of pleasures or engage in destructive battle and pillage. The next step on such a path is the punishing darkness of the cave at the left, surmounted by gallows and instruments of torture. An uncrowded path leads to the next gate, where the attractive figure of False Learning entices the unwary to vain pursuits. Only the solitary Pilgrim breaks away to ascend the final rocky path to the blazing celestial light of True Felicity, an O formed by a snake biting its tail, symbol of Eternity.

The unsigned plate, more ambitiously composed than executed, may be assigned to one of the many engravers Zatta called on to illustrate his large production. He often copied the plates of previous publications, with no indication of the source, a common practice. The primary model

[12] Victor Masséna, Prince d'Essling, *Études sur l'art de la gravure sur bois à Venise* (Florence-Paris, 1907–14), Pt. 2, p. 514–515, ill. Schleier, *Tabula Cebetis,* p. 79 and pl. 9.

[13] For examples, see Schleier, pl. 38 and 39.

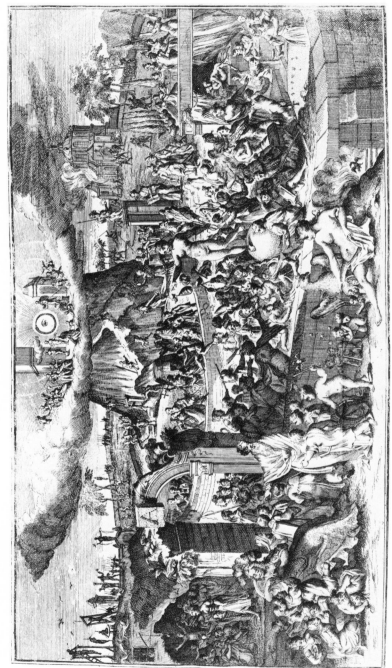

Cornelio Pepoli, *Traduzione della Tavola di Cebete* (Venice, 1763).
Engraving. 177×325mm. *Houghton Library.*

Romeyn de Hooghe, "Cebetis Tabula" (1670), in *Epicteti Enchiridium* (Delft, 1723). Etching, 177×340mm. *Houghton Library.*

for this *Tavola di Cebete* was doubtless the frontispiece of a Venetian edition of 1714, a duodecimo *I caratteri di Epitetto con la spiegazione della Tavola di Cebete* published by Girolamo Albrizzi,[14] founder of the firm carried to international fame by his son Giovanni Battista. The Albrizzi were cosmopolitan in outlook and in touch with northern Europe, where this composition originated.

The ultimate source, however, was Romeyn de Hooghe's engraving of 1670 (see plate, p. 161), which illustrated a Leyden-Amsterdam edition of *Epicteti Enchiridium, una cum Cebetis Thebani Tabula.*[15] This brilliant and prolific Dutch artist (1645–1708) produced a large body of book-illustration of great complexity, ranging from the eroticism of La Fontaine and the *Cent nouvelles* to the majesty of plates commemorating William III, his patron. The posthumous edition of his *Hieroglyphica* in 1735 demonstrates his familiarity with classical and Christian iconography, presented with remarkable originality. His *Tabula* was influenced by other Dutch artists, such as Hendrik Goltzius,[16] especially in the treatment of the rocky, heavenly summit. De Hooghe appears to be the first to depict in this scene the human birth of souls, elsewhere shown emerging from the ground or from the whirlwind of Chaos.[17] His work is characterized by a brilliant manipulation of the etched line, with a wide range of tonal effects never achieved by his copyists.

Also from the hand of a copyist comes the more spacious and skillfully presented illustration of Pepoli's sequel of 1771, the *Lettere instruttive intorno alla Tavola di Cebete* (see plate, p. 164). The image measures 350 × 415 mm. while the platemark area, which includes lettering, is 375 × 425 mm. The legend clarifies the composition, identifying the figures with numbers. Il Genio (2) presides over the crowd of entering souls (1), to whom *L'Impostura* (3) offers her cup. Within the gate await

[14] Schleier, p. 51 and note 181. The Harvard copy lacks the plate. Schleier records it as signed by Alessandro à [or della] Via. Schleier's measurements for the frontispiece of the 1714 edition (17.8 × 33.4 cm.) are close to those of the frontispiece of Pepoli's first edition.

[15] Schleier, p. 51 and pl. 57. John Landwehr, *Romeyn de Hooghe (1645–1708) as Book Illustrator* (Amsterdam and New York, 1970), no. 6, p. 36–37, ill. Schleier records the Pepoli edition, but does not illustrate it.

[16] Schleier, pl. 47 and 48.

[17] John Baptist Knipping, *Iconography of the Counter Reformation in the Netherlands* (Nieuwkoop and Leiden, 1974), I, 73, in discussing Dutch versions of the Table of Cebes states merely: "In 1670 Romein de Hooghe made a much more original composition of the formula."

three seductive young women, the *Stuol di Meretrici* (4). *La Fortuna* (5) is blind to the heedless crowd (*Turba de Inconsiderati*) (6) whom an *Altra Ciurma di Meretrici* (7) lead to the temple of Pleasure adjacent to the *Luoco di Miserie* (8), presided over by a scourging *Penitenza* (9). Chastened and redirected, the Pilgrim is greeted at the next gate by *Sapienza Menzogniera* (10), whose garden is filled with her followers, the crowd of *Folli Amatori del falso sapere* (11). Ready to help the Pilgrim who chooses the steep and stony path are *Continenza* and *Toleranza* (13), leading to *La Verace Sapienza* (14). Within her gates is a *Drapello di Virtù* (15) to guide the Pilgrim to *La Felicità* (16). This radiant figure crowns the Pilgrim kneeling before her throne, set against a turreted and steeply-roofed northern city surrounded with trees. The wide, bird's-eye view is convincingly rendered in isometric perspective, with the background as large and clear as the foreground. The plate bears no engraver's signature, but it can lead us, together with the text, to the source of this image.

The text is in the form of a dialogue in letters exchanged between an uncle (Pepoli) and nephew. The nephew states: "mi venne alle mani un Rame antico" (p.v), and he goes on to describe this print. The uncle identifies the subject and proceeds to explain the imagery, thus taking the place of the traditional interlocutor. Nothing further is said about the *rame antico,* but the careful copyist has recorded his source. On the plinth of the first entrance gate is the monogram DK, and these superimposed initials lead us to David Kandel,[18] active in Strasbourg as a painter and designer from about 1538–1587. He was associated with the illustration of some distinguished woodcut books, such as Hieronymus Bock's *Kreuterbuch* of 1546 and Sebastian Münster's *Cosmografia* of 1550. Among his woodcuts, his *Cebetis Tabula* is perhaps best known (see plate, p. 165).[19] It is signed and dated 1547 and derived from a combination of Holbein's designs (Schleier's C and D, see plates, p. 166–7), but composed with very different dimensions and effect. The composition is horizontal, with the three concentric walls clearly arranged and the imagery easy to follow. Kandel's woodcut, of which

---

[18] G. K. Nagler, *Die Monogrammisten*, II (1860), p. 456, no. 1163.

[19] Schleier, p. 87 and pl. 12. Also noted and illustrated is the Pepoli edition, p. 38, note 134 and pl. 14. J.-E. Gérock, "Un artiste Strasbourgeois du XVI siècle, David Kandel," *Archives Alsaciennes*, 2 (1923), 84–96 and fig. 38. Gérock gives the dimensions as 32 × 40 cm.

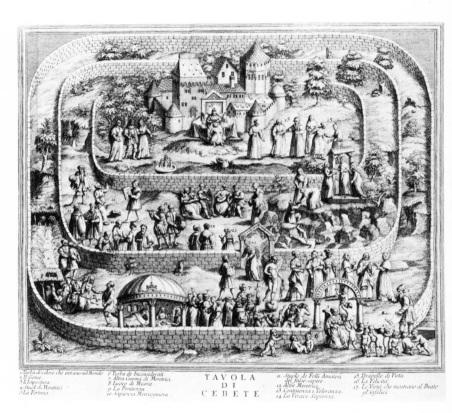

Cornelio Pepoli, *Lettere instruttive intorno alla Tavola di Cebete* (Venice, 1771).
Engraving, 350×415mm. *Houghton Library.*

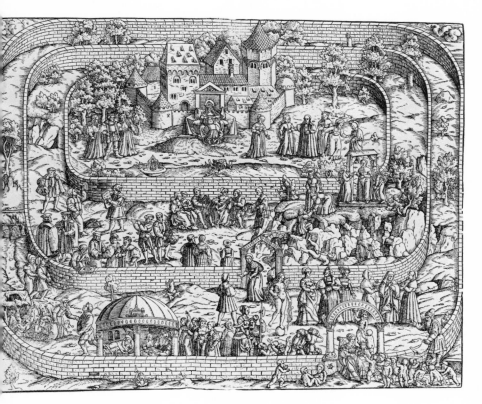

David Kandel (illus.) *Epicteti Enchiridium* (Basel, 1563).
Woodcut, 323×408mm. *Houghton Library.*

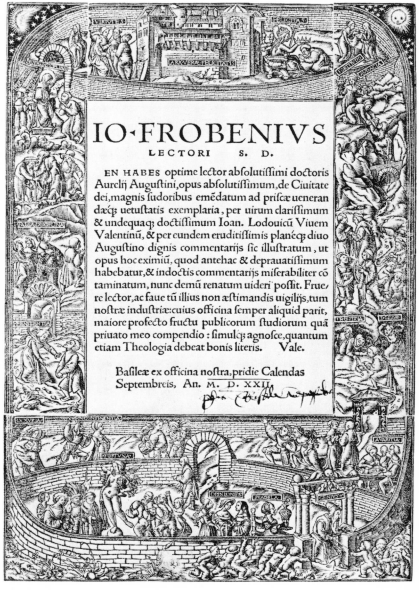

Hans Holbein (illus.) St. Augustine, *De civitate Dei* (Basel, 1522).
Metal-cut title-page border, 250×168mm. *Houghton Library.*

Hans Holbein (illus.) Niccolò Perotti, *Cornucopiæ* (Basel, 1532).
Woodcut title-page border, 275×188mm. *Houghton Library.*

separate impressions are known, also appeared as an illustration in the 1563 Basel edition of *Epicteti Enchiridion ... cum Cebetis Thebani Tabula* edited by Hieronymus Wolf. Of the many graphic versions of the *Tablet*, the Holbein and the Kandel appear to have been the most influential. The Kandel, for example, served as the model for French Renaissance embroidered hangings now at the Metropolitan Museum.[20] Less well known today than the Holbein, its predecessor and model, an impression or a copy of the Kandel came into Pepoli's hands.[21] This was apparently after the publication of his first edition, which he therefore revised to accommodate a picture both larger and clearer than the first example. One can understand his eagerness to elucidate this new and sharply defined image. As a *dilettante* author working with an inexperienced publisher, Pepoli would have been in a more influential position than with the busy Zatta, who had his own formulas.

The *Tavola di Cebete* served as an educational text throughout the eighteenth century,[22] and numerous editions are recorded in Italy. It remained in the Jesuit curriculum,[23] and many a young Venetian was acquainted with it. Because of its traditional, even orthodox, teaching, the illustrator's approach remained conservative, looking back to earlier models and to northern Europe, not a common pictorial influence in

[20] John Goldsmith Phillips, "The Garden of False Learning," *The Metropolitan Museum of Art Bulletin*, 1 (1943), 243–247.

[21] He speaks of a *rame antico*, a copperplate or impression therefrom, and Kandel's original is, of course, a woodcut. The *rame antico* may have been an engraved copy of Kandel, or Pepoli may have used the word *rame* to refer to any print, regardless of medium.

[22] For bibliographies, see Johann Albert Fabricius, *Bibliotheca Graeca*, II (Hamburg, 1791), 702–15; S. F. W. Hoffmann, *Bibliographisches Lexikon der gesammten Literatur der Griechen*, I, (Leipzig, 1838), 438–448. Fabricius lists Pepoli editions of 1743 and 1763, perhaps the source for Brunet's entry (1. 1709). The 1743 edition must be a ghost, since it is not in Paitoni, whom Fabricius cites as his authority. For the use of the Tablet in school curricula of this period in Great Britain, see Hagstrum, *The Sister Arts*, p. 32 and Paulson, *Emblem and Expression*, p. 30, note 44. Paulson relates this iconography, as well as that of similar didactic treatises, to certain eighteenth-century English gardens with elaborately arranged circular walks with sculpture and temples that are the climax of a symbolic path. See also Max Schulz, "The Circuit Walk of the Eighteenth-Century Landscape Garden and the Pilgrim's Circuitous Progress," *Eighteenth-Century Studies*, 1 (1981), 1–25.

[23] "Ratio Studiorum et Institutiones Scholasticae Societatis Jesu" in *Monumenta Germaniae Pedagogica* (Berlin, 1887–1894), XVI, 6–7 and 183, quoting a German rule of 1619: "In Graecis litteris ... auctores praescribantur ... ut sunt Tabula Cebetis ...."

Italy at this time. Germany was, however, a factor in Venetian culture and taste. A number of titles of nobility borne by Venetians of both the city and the *terrafirma* were imperial in origin. Count Alessandro Zanetti, for example, the noted collector, patron and artist, was ennobled by Maria Theresa. Venice has always welcomed a variety of influences and visitors. Her geographic situation had established this pattern in the Middle Ages and the Renaissance, and in the eighteenth century she was a mecca on the Grand Tour. Not only the rich and the pleasure seekers sought her out, but also the most learned and cultivated minds of Europe. When Goethe visited Venice in 1786, he stopped at a bookshop in Padua, the most important town of the *terrafirma* and the seat of the university. He noted that "everyone who is in any way connected with literature . . . drops in," and he had a long conversation with these "friendly men."[24] Goethe's first book purchase in Italy was not a mere pictorial memento of the scene, but a serious and learned treatise, a copy of Consul Joseph Smith's facsimile edition of Palladio's 1570 *Quattro Libri.*[25]

Such interests remind us of the variety of the Venetian presses and of the diversity of their contents and sources. In addition to books of literature, history, science and fine arts, and the popular worldly books of immediate visual appeal, they quietly produced books for serious contemplation. The *Tavola* is one of these, an instructional book for the Italian reader.

---

[24] J. W. Goethe, *Italian Journey* (London, 1962), p. 53.   [25] Ibid.

Geofroy Tory's edition of *Hore in laudem beatissime virginis Marie*
(Paris: by S. Du Bois, 1527). Title-page. *Houghton Library.*

Geofroy Tory's Borders "à la Moderne" and their Later Fortunes in Portugal

ANNE ANNINGER

As I was cataloguing Portuguese sixteenth-century books in the Hofer collection at the Houghton Library, I came across what appeared to be a set of French woodcut borders in a Lisbon, 1539 edition printed by Luiz Rodrigues, bookseller of the King. The same borders were used to frame the title-page of a work printed in the following year by Germão Galharde, a printer from Lisbon associated with Rodrigues. On further investigation, these borders of flowers, birds and insects turned out to derive from a 1527 Book of Hours printed in Paris by Simon Du Bois for the famous bookseller-publisher Geofroy Tory.

Woodcut ornaments of French origin are not common in the work of early Portuguese printers. Their typographic stock, often acquired through Spanish colleagues, is mainly composed of typefonts and ornamental material of German or Italian origin. I began researching the circumstances surrounding the production, the disposal and the Portuguese fortunes of Tory's borders.[1] With the help of King Manuel's bibliography of *Livros antigos portuguezes, 1489–1600*,[2] I soon found out that their afterlife was longer and richer than one might have expected at first. Tory's blocks appeared in Lisbon, Coimbra and Braga, in the works of five printers over a period of thirty-seven years, and were copied by two others.

What had been at first simple evidence of typographical exchange between France and Portugal turned into a documentary on the Portuguese trade of the period: the transfer of blocks established a network

[1] I wish to thank my friends and colleagues Ruth Mortimer, Katharine F. Pantzer, Roger E. Stoddard, Scott D. Ward and Michael Winship for their helpful suggestions. An early draft of this paper was submitted as a course requirement for LS 500, Advanced Independent Study, under the direction of Prof. Estelle Jussim, Simmons College School of Library Science.

[2] Manuel II, King of Portugal, *Livros antigos portuguezes, 1489–1600, da bibliotheca de Sua Majestade Fidelissima*, 3 vols. (London, 1929–35); hereafter cited as *King Manuel*.

of associations among printers, while the use to which the borders were put provided graphic evidence of the evolution of taste in Portugal between 1539 and 1575.

Geofroy Tory's contribution to French book production hardly needs to be restated. Following a period of graceful exuberance at the dawn of the century, the art of printing in France experienced a major decline under the reign of Louis XII. Sense of proportion and balance were lost as printers crowded the page with ill-fitting blocks of different sizes and styles. "La révolution Torienne" was one of aesthetic, if not typographic import: imbued with the artistic ideals of the Italian Renaissance and with the French longing for harmony, Tory brought to the book a new sense of equilibrium and grace. We are all familiar with the noble proportion of his page, the simplicity and delicacy of his borders and vignettes; but what is possibly most characteristic of Tory's style is the sense of harmony, of unity between text and illustration, exemplified in the Books of Hours and the *Champ fleury*.

Our principal sources for Tory's endeavors are two privileges — one dated Avignon, September 23, 1524,[3] the other, Chenonceau, September 5, 1526 — which describe his dealings with two different styles of illustrative material: ". . . certaines Vignettes a Lantique & a la Moderne. Pareillement Frises, Bordeures, Coronemēs et Entrelas, pour faire imprimer Heures en telz usages et grādeurs que bō luy semblera."[4] One is most familiar with Tory's style "à l'antique" — meaning in this context Renaissance style — since it encompasses almost all of his work: conventionalized scroll patterns, stylized arabesques cut in clear lines on white grounds, matching vignettes with Italianate architectural settings, the whole strongly reminiscent of Venetian book illustration of the beginning of the century, in particular of the Aldine edition of Francesco Colonna's *Hypnerotomachia Poliphili*.[5]

---

[3] Printed at head of the *Horae, in laudem beatiss. semper Virginis Mariae secundum consuetudinem curiae romanae* (Paris: S. de Colines for G. Tory, 1524–25).

[4] The 1526 privilege is printed at the front of three works published by Tory: the *Hore . . . secundum consuetudinem ecclesie parisiensis* (Paris: S. du Bois for G. Tory, 1527), the *Horae . . . secundum consuetudinem curiae romanae* (Paris: S. de Colines for G. Tory, 1527), and his *Champ fleury* (Paris: G. Gourmont for G. Tory, 1529).

[5] Francesco Colonna, *Hypnerotomachia Poliphili* (Venice, 1499); see further A. F. Johnson, "Geofroy Tory," *The Fleuron*, 6 (1928), 37–66; the Harvard College Library, Department of Printing and Graphic Arts' Catalogue of Books

In Tory's rather homogeneous production, his quarto *Hore*[6] of 1527, printed in Paris by Simon Du Bois, stands out as a unique phenomenon, both in terms of its style and its rather peculiar history.

By contrast to the vast body of work Tory produced in the style "à l'antique", the Du Bois *Hore* constitutes the sole example of his work "à la moderne" that is, in "Gothic" style. Its illustrative material, in particular, the realism of the borders of flowers,[7] birds, animals and insects, brings the Du Bois *Hore* in line with a long tradition of Book of Hours illustrations dating back to the illuminated manuscript of medieval times.[8] It is also the only book published by Tory to be printed in *lettres bâtardes*. As such, the *Hore* has been treated as a kind of anomaly in Tory's overall production. Auguste Bernard, Tory's nineteenth-century biographer and bibliographer, usually lavish in his praise and overly generous in his attributions, speaks of the Du Bois *Hore* in rather disparaging terms: "Ce livre me semble assez mal exécuté, sous le rapport artistique comme sous le rapport typographique: les cadres s'accordent mal, les proportions en sont fort irrégulières, et la gravure ne m'en semble pas irréprochable . . . ni les cadres ni les sujets ne portent de marques, et je doute qu'ils soient de Tory."[9]

and Manuscripts I, *French 16th Century Books*, comp. Ruth Mortimer (Cambridge, Mass., 1964), no. 304 (hereafter cited as "Mortimer").

[6] Hore in laudem beatissime virginis Marie: secundum consuetudinem ecclesie parisiensis. Paris, S. Du. Bois, for G. Tory, October 22, 1527. 4°: a–r⁸, s⁴.

The Hofer copy (Houghton Library, call no. Typ 517.27.262) is bound in contemporary calf stamped in gilt with the arms of François I within a border of arabesques and interlaced frames. *References*: Mortimer 30; Bohatta 330; Lacombe 364–371. Hereafter cited as Du Bois *Hore*: signature references in the text indicate the first occurrence of a border element in this edition.

[7] Carroll E. Wood, Professor of Biology at Harvard University, to whom I showed the borders, could easily identify a great majority of the flowers — among them, in the upper borders, Delphinium and Veronica; in the inner borders, Legume, Pansy, Violet and Centauria; in the outer borders, Solanum, Hops, Dianthus and Crucifer; and in the lower borders, Anemone and Poppy.

[8] For the illuminated manuscript as a source of inspiration, see Myra Dickman Orth, "Geofroy Tory et l'enluminure: Deux livres d'heures de la collection Doheny," *Revue de l'Art*, 50 (1981), 40–47; and her "Progressive Tendencies in French Manuscript Illumination, 1515–1530: Godefroy le Batave and the 1520's Hours Workshop," Diss. New York University, 1976; for possible prototypes, see Mortimer, no. 304.

[9] Auguste Bernard, *Geofroy Tory, peintre et graveur, premier Imprimeur Royal*, 2d ed. (Paris, 1865), p. 161. He objects to the fact that the borders fit poorly, not being properly cut to size.

The Du Bois *Hore* presents itself as a volume in quarto with well-proportioned pages. The title-page (see plate, p. 170) and each page of text proper is surrounded by woodcut borders. The proportions of the borders are conventional, very much in keeping with those of illuminated manuscripts.[10] The borders are composed of four elements: two lateral pieces (a narrow inner piece and a wide outer piece), an upper piece, relatively narrow, and a much wider lower piece. The illustrated area of each of these elements is framed by rules: a single rule on the inside, which delimits the text area, and a triple rule on the outside. The difference in width and the top-to-bottom orientation of the designs prevent the lateral borders from being interchangeable: those intended for the recto can only be used on the recto, those for the verso, on the verso. The upper and lower borders, on the other hand, are horizontal friezes which fit equally well on recto or verso.

One must concede to Bernard that the borders do not always fit properly. Illustrated areas and inner rules are usually well aligned. The triple rules of the perimeter are most often a source of problems: two of the rules are set very closely together (about 1 mm. apart), while the third is farther away (about 3 mm). Visually, this triple-rule border is all-important, as it delimits and frames the whole of the printed area. Technically the cutting of these three rules is critical: every fraction of a millimeter counts, and it is extremely difficult to achieve perfect alignment. In general, the lower pieces fit relatively well and the triple rules align properly. The upper pieces are the greatest offenders. Poorly proportioned, the two closely set rules are consistently out of line, the exterior rule sometimes one, or even two millimeters higher than those of the lateral borders which they are intended to meet.

The number of designs for each of the four elements of the border varies considerably (see diagram, p. 175). There are twenty-four designs in all for the inner border: sixteen of these have been cut specifically for the rectos, but only half of that number have been cut for the versos. This disparity between the number of recto and verso borders is also present in the case of the outer borders. There again, sixteen designs have been cut for the rectos, but only eight for the versos. Moreover,

---

[10] For further details on page proportions and margin sizes, see Jan Tschichold, "Non-arbitrary Proportions of Page and Type Area," in *Calligraphy and Paleography: Essays presented to Alfred Fairbank*, ed. A. S. Osley (New York, 1966), pp. 179–191.

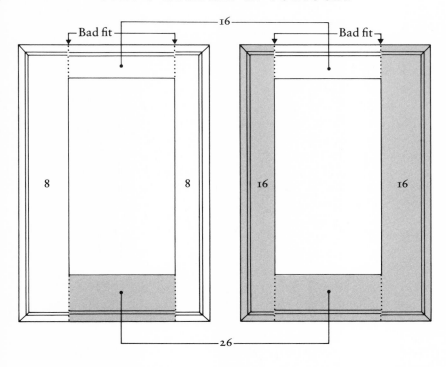

The numbers in this diagram refer to the numbers of designs prepared for each of the four elements of the borders. The elements are coded according to their stylistic similarities: the shaded elements contain designs attributed to the "Master of the rectos." Their elongated arabesques are formed of well-centered, realistic subjects. The unshaded elements contain designs attributed to another artist. Their arabesques are formed of deeper, shorter curves in which the subjects, more stylized, occupy the whole width of the border.

there are sixteen different designs for the upper element and twenty-six for the lower element.

The disparity in the number of designs for each of the four elements is sufficient to disprove Bernard's contention that the borders are composed of "vingt-six encadrements *complets* qui reviennent successivement."[11] Regularity, in any case, was not the printer's intent, as the

[11] Bernard, p. 161 (italics added); apparently he only counted the lower borders.

elements seem to have been set at random. The distribution by inner and outer forme of the various designs of each of the four elements fails to reveal any recognizable setting pattern except in the case of the lower elements. Possibly because of their dedicatory content, the lower borders [12] do regularly recur in a cycle of 26, with some inner variations.

The disparity (32 to 16) in the number of designs for the lateral borders of the rectos and versos is puzzling. Time constraint is a possible explanation. Working at leisure, the artist proceeded to cut thirty-two blocks for the rectos. Pressed by time, he could only prepare half that number for the versos. There is no evidence, however, either to substantiate or disprove such an explanation. All we know is that some of the blocks were already cut or in preparation in 1524,[13] and that they were completed — at least in design, if not all cut — by September 5, 1526, the date of the privilege of the Du Bois *Hore*.[14]

It could also well be that the designer, considering the recto of the leaf as visually more important, prepared a greater variety of designs for that side of the leaf.

A third possibility is that there were two "tailleurs d'images" at work, one doing most if not all of the lateral borders of the recto, the other the remainder and all those of the verso. Careful examination reveals some marked differences in the borders of the rectos and versos: differences in the type of arabesques, the lateral organization of space and the choice of subjects. As a rule, the arabesques of the borders of the rectos are sinuous, elongated, almost rectilinear at times: long-stemmed flowers gently undulating into one long curve, with insects and birds used as incidentals and incorporated in the movement of the curve. In some of the outer borders, we find an occasional single stem (such as

---

[12] Dedicated to the Royal Family, these borders include the Royal arms of France, the Crowned F of François I, his Salamander, the Crowned L, "Ailes" and "Cordelière" of Louise de Savoie, his mother, the interlaced H and M of Henri d'Albret, King of Navarre and Marguerite d'Angoulême, his spouse and the King's sister.

[13] As indicated in the privilege of September 23, 1524 (see above, n. 3).

[14] Orth, "Geofroy Tory et l'enluminure", p. 40 and n. 11, observes that the privileges, granted only to finished products, not to projects still in the making, allow us to date the blocks with precision. She concludes that the interlaced initials of Henri de Navarre and Marguerite d'Angoulême (a5ᵛ) must have been added to the printer's stock after their marriage on January 24, 1527; but I believe the blocks might have been ready by September 5, 1526, the date of the privilege, which is only five months before the marriage.

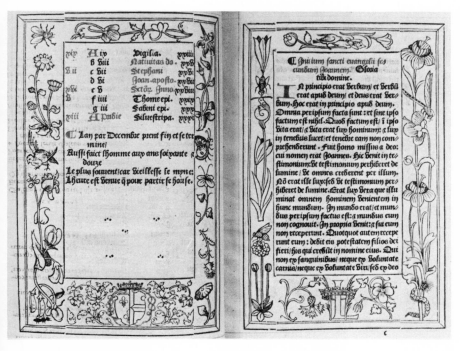

Geofroy Tory's edition of *Hore in laudem beatissime virginis Marie*
(Paris: by S. Du Bois, 1527). [b]8ᵛ and c1ʳ. *Houghton Library.*

the irises of a6ʳ, or the daffodils of a8ʳ (repeated on c1ʳ, see plate, above)
running the entire length of the border, their graceful rigidity surprisingly
reminiscent of an Art Deco motif. The elongated character of the borders
of the rectos is accentuated by the use which is made of the lateral space.
The designs, well-centered, are freestanding. If they touch the border-
rules, they do so as if by accident, without resting or weighing on them
in any way. Depicted are flowers, birds, and insects. Their rendering is
realistic and gracefully simple.

By contrast, the arabesques of the borders of the versos are formed
of deeper, shorter curves. The many subjects with which they are filled
seem to compete for attention. Flowers and foliage twist and turn, only
to be interrupted by birds, insects, and animals attempting a curve of
their own (see plate above). The whole width of the border is occupied,
and all this activity is barely contained by the border-rules. Animals rest
against the rules, flowers touch them, while tendrils attempt to escape

from them. The subjects themselves have a different feel from those of the left border, less straightforward, more removed from reality. The flowers are more stylized, the stems and foliage full of scroll-like curlicues. Symbolic subjects and animals, never to be found in the borders of the rectos, are common in those of the versos. Interspersed here and there among flowers and insects, are François I's Salamander, a phoenix on a pyre, a rooster, rabbits and squirrels, a lapdog and a greyhound, even a monkey drinking from a cup. Present in all this is a slight affectation, an attempt at being cute, of which the borders on the right are completely devoid.

In the lower borders, dedication motifs alluding to the Royal Family and Tory's *Pot cassé* device alternate with the usual birds, flowers and insects. Aside from being the most regularly set, the lower borders are also the most numerous and the most carefully designed, two characteristics they share with the lateral borders of the rectos.

By contrast, the upper borders are both stylistically and technically the weakest. The motifs are not badly designed but repetitive; the proportions, as mentioned earlier, are far from perfect. Like the lateral borders of the versos, the upper borders seem to have been prepared in haste. Another stylistic link between upper borders and the lateral borders of the versos is the presence (in the upper border of a7^r) of a little owl, which in its "cuteness" resembles the animals mentioned earlier.

Though the evidence presented by the upper and lower borders is tenuous, the marked differences between the lateral borders of the rectos and versos point to the work of two different artists, one of whom, that of the rectos, is superior to the other, more refined in his taste, more accomplished in his art. Could the "Master of the rectos" be Tory himself? Bernard, as we know, dismisses the possibility. The borders, he thinks, are not up to Tory's standards and they bear none of his usual devices or mottos. "Peut-être le dessin était-il de Perreal et la gravure d'un des artistes employés par Geofroy Tory, qui devait avoir dès lors un atelier monté, si l'on en juge par le grand nombre de pièces qu'il produisit a cette époque."[15] It is true that the privilege of September 5, 1526 only mentions Tory's "peines, labeurs, fraiz & despens quil luy a cõuenu porter et soustenir tãt a la cõposition dudit liure [*Champ fleury*], q̃ pour la taille desdites Histoires, Vignettes, Frises, Bordeures, Coronemẽs et Entrelas, pour faire imprimer Heures. . . ."[16] The privilege of

---

[15] Bernard, p. 161. [16] See above, n. 4.

September 23, 1524 is more explicit, however: "Nostre cher et bien amé maistre Geufroy [sic] Tory libraire demourant à Paris . . . ha faict et faict faire certaines histoires et vignettes a l'antique et pareillement unes autres a la moderne pour icelles faire imprimer et servir a plusieurs usages d'heures . . ."[17]

Whether the "faict" refers to the design, to the "taille", or to the preparation of the blocks only, remains a matter of conjecture. The possibility that Tory is in some sense the "Master of the rectos" is thus not completely excluded. For once, Bernard is too cautious, and I think, too severe.[18] Though somewhat inferior in execution, the Du Bois *Hore* does reflect the concerns and ideals found in other Tory publications. The style, it is true, differs. Here Tory draws his inspiration from the medieval manuscript and its tradition of illuminated borders depicting flowers, fruit, birds and insects. Very common in the early printed *Hours* of the latter part of the fifteenth century, this style of borders, still in vogue in the 1520's, was accompanied by a renewal of interest in illumination. Pollard suggests that the Du Bois designs might well have been intended for illumination.[19] As graceful in their realism as their medieval counterparts, the Du Bois designs belong nevertheless to the style of the Renaissance. The static, tightly set subjects have been freed in the long movements of the arabesques; the heavy cuts, shadings and *criblé* backgrounds replaced by clear cursory lines on white grounds. The concern for unity is ever present. Though the subjects of the illustrations are essentially the same as those of Tory's earlier *Horae,* they have been freshly reinterpreted in the style "à la moderne." The use of the gothic font was motivated by the same concern. Even Bernard concedes: "Il était difficile de pousser plus loin l'amour de l'harmonie artistique",[20] a love we know to be at the heart of the "révolution Torienne" and one of the essential characteristics of the style of the Renaissance.

Following the Du Bois *Hore,* Tory published yet two more Books of Hours, the *Horae* of 1529 and that of 1530–31, both in the style "à l'antique." Upon his death in the summer of 1533, Tory's stock passed

[17] See above, n. 3.

[18] Johnson, p. 46, and J. Megret, "Geoffroy Tory," *Arts et Métiers Graphiques,* V/28 (1932), 7–15, are also of this opinion.

[19] A. F. Pollard, "The Books of Hours of Geofroy Tory," *Bibliographica,* I (1895), 114–122.

[20] Bernard, p. 161.

into the hands of Olivier Mallard, a Parisian printer whom Perrette Le Hullin, Tory's widow, married in December of the same year. In 1541 and 1542, Mallard published two Books of Hours in the Tory manner. One of these, the 1542 *Horae,* contains free copies of the borders "à la moderne," reduced to a duodecimo format. The same blocks reappear in turn in the 1556 *Horae* published in Paris by Thielman Kerver the younger,[21] successor to Mallard's stock, and in the 1560 Hours for the use of Chartres printed by Charles L'Angelier. Bernard suggests that these borders originally belonged to a 1531 Tory edition as yet unlocated:

> A une époque qu'il ne m'est pas possible de fixer exactement, mais qui n'est pas antérieure au mois de septembre 1531, Tory imprima un autre livre dans le format in 8°, avec des encadrements composés de plantes, d'animaux, d'insectes, d'oiseaux, etc., . . . mais d'un dessin plus petit, naturellement. Je n'ai pas vu ce livre, mais son existence m'est démontrée par la publication d'un livre d'Heures, faite postérieurement par Olivier Mallard, avec les mêmes cadres et vignettes . . . . Quant à l'attribution que je fais de ces bois a Tory, elle ressort pour moi de la forme des cadres, copiés sur les heures de 1527 . . . J'ignore, ai-je dit, le titre du livre auquel Tory a fait servir ces bois pour la première fois; cependant, il me semble qu'on peut conclure de l'emploi qu'en fit Olivier Mallard lui-même . . . que ce fut un livre d'Heures.[22]

The gracelessness and awkward quality of the designs, their duodecimo format and poor execution are convincing evidence that the borders found in Mallard, Kerver and L'Angelier's *Horae* are not original Tory blocks. It does not exclude the possibility — though remote — of the existence of an intermediate 1531 Tory edition, which for some reason has not reached us.

The privilege granted the Du Bois *Hore* was valid for ten years from the date of publication. The *achevé d'imprimer* was dated October 22, 1527. In February 1538, four months after the expiration of the privilege, two of the original Du Bois *Hore* illustrations (the Coronation and Crucifixion) reappeared in Guillaume Petit's *La formation de lhomme*[23], printed by Mallard for Galliot du Pré. However, the blocks of the

---

[21]Mortimer, no. 313.   [22]Bernard, p. 168–169.   [23]Mortimer, no. 422.

borders "à la moderne," never used again during Tory's lifetime, have not been found in any of the works of his French successors.

2

In the "Prologuo" of his 1540 *Ho presto Joam das indias*, the Lisbon printer Luiz Rodrigues addresses himself to King João III in these terms:

> Apart from the Bishop of Lamego's encouraging me to do this, your Highness commanded me to print the work, saying that you would derive great satisfaction from it, which was a very great reward for me . . . And as, my Lord, ever since I have been yours, my desire has always been directed towards your service, to be fruitful in it: though my strength may fail me, the will never fails me, so I went to Paris to look for woodcuts, founts, craftmen, and other things proper to printing. These are not of less elegance and quality than those of Italy, France and Germany, where that art is most flourishing, as your Highness may see from the work I have set up in this city, and with no small satisfaction, for it seems to me that your Highness takes pleasure in this, as is shown by the favours you have granted me, and those which I hope you will grant me in the future.[24]

Rodrigues' account of his trip to Paris to acquire "estampas, caratules de letras, officiaes & outras cousas convenientes a impressam" is of particular interest, for even though the early book trade between France and Portugal is well-documented, it usually involves the marketing of French books in Portugal. In 1519, the Parisian bookseller Jean Petit asked a dealer from Rouen to help him recover debts owed him in Portugal. Jehan Perre of Paris dealt primarily with Spain but apparently found it profitable enough to open his own outlet in Coimbra. The Regnaults, who had a shop in Medina del Campo, also sold in Lisbon, in particular to Luiz Rodrigues, who, in 1539, bought from them 240 *livres tournois* worth of books. Portuguese dealers occasionally came to France to order or buy editions. Two such dealers, Alfonce Fernandes

---

[24] Quoted and translated in *King Manuel*, no. 42.

and Lazare Doncoigne got together and arranged the delivery from Paris to Lisbon "de la marchandise de livres, en lettre d'impression, relliez tant en latin, portugalays que autres langaiges jusques a la valeur de 400 ducatz dor."[25]

However, Rodrigues' trip to Paris was of different nature. He arrived in the French capital in late 1538 or early 1539, intent on buying typographical material. Bookseller to King João III for many years, Rodrigues decided to set up his own press. In the fall of 1539, he became one of the first Portuguese *imprimidores*. Before him, most printers in Portugal had been of foreign extraction. Their typographical stock — early gothic fonts and poorly assorted woodblocks of German and Italian origin — had been either brought over from their native land, copied, or acquired from their Spanish colleagues. In establishing his new press, Rodrigues intended to further the development of printing in Portugal and to raise its standards of "elegance and quality."

While buying his material in Paris, Rodrigues also hired a *compagnon imprimeur*, Raollet Duboys, to come to Lisbon for two years (1539–1541) and help get the press started.[26] The first fully dated book to come out of Rodrigues' press was the *Insino Christão approuado pella Sancta Inquisiçam* dated September 23, 1539.[27] Bibliographers[28] however are of the opinion that the *Regimento de como os contadores das comarcas hã de prouer sobre as capellas* is the first book to be printed by Rodrigues. One of the peculiarities of this book is its colophon, dated September 27, 1514. Actually, this edition, a faithful reproduction of the Lisbon, 1514 edition printed by João Pedro Bonhomini de Cremona, was probably printed in the summer of 1539 by Rodrigues, whose mark appears on the recto of numbered leaf lviii.

Five of the pages in the first two gatherings of the *Regimento* are surrounded by woodcut borders — not just any woodcut borders, but Tory's very own, the 1527 Du Bois borders "à la moderne," which

---

[25] All these examples are taken from Annie Parent, *Les métiers du livre à Paris au XVIᵉ siècle (1536–1560)*, Histoire et civilisation du livre, 6 (Geneva, 1974), p. 157.

[26] Parent, p. 157.

[27] A. J. Anselmo, *Bibliographia das obras impressas em Portugal no sécolo XVI* (Lisbon, 1926), no. 1004.

[28] *King Manuel*, no. 40; I. F. da Silva, *Diccionario bibliographico portugues*, 22 v. (Lisbon, 1858–1923), XVIII, 164; F. M. de Sousa Viterbo, *O movimento typográfico em Portugal no século XVI* (Coimbra, 1924), p. 255.

Rodrigues most probably acquired from Mallard himself.[29] The Tory borders found in the *Regimento* are all of the wide, lateral outer kind. With the exception of the recto of the 6th preliminary leaf, where we find unknown borders at top and bottom, Tory's borders frame all four sides. The *Regimento* is printed in folio; the average height of its pages is about 235 mm., a height which Tory's blocks could not accommodate. To remedy this situation, Rodrigues did not hesitate to mutilate one of Tory's blocks. He had the upper part of one of Tory's borders (b2[r]) cut into four little sections, each about 15 mm. high. Fitted at top or bottom of the regular borders, these small pieces enabled Rodrigues to "stretch" the lateral borders to size.

The cutting of the blocks to fit, a device used by all early printers with limited stocks, did not presage well for Rodrigues' aspirations to "quality and elegance" nor for the future of Tory's borders. It was therefore with some relief that I came across the title-page of André de Resende's *De uerborū coniugatione commentarius*, printed by Rodrigues in 1540. The title of the *De uerborū* (plate, p. 184) is printed within a small architectural frame surmounted by the arms of Portugal, flanked by two armillary spheres. The whole, in turn, is surrounded by Tory's borders, almost as intended for a recto, that is with an inner border on the left and an outer on the right. Two of the blocks (upper and lateral inner) are actually the same as those used on the Du Bois *Hore* title-page, yet in order to accommodate gracefully the width (ca. 55mm.) of the small architectural frame, the original width of Tory's borders needed to be slightly expanded. Two very small woodblocks (ca. 7mm. wide), specially cut for Rodrigues, were added to the left of the top border and to the right of the lower border. The two designs (a small bird and a flower) are well in keeping with the style of the original borders. Barely discernible, they increase the inside width of the frame (to ca. 76mm.) so that it accommodates the pedestal of the architectural frame (ca. 72mm.) and leaves ample room on each side of the posts.

The same year Rodrigues also used this title-page layout for Jorge Coelho's *De patientia christiana*, with a slight modification: the small flower addition is placed to the left instead of to the right of the lower

---

[29] Reproductions of title-pages or of leaves containing Tory's borders in the *Regimento* as well as in all other Portuguese works mentioned below can be found in *King Manuel*; a short-title list of the Portuguese works containing these borders, together with their references in *King Manuel*, is appended at the end of my essay.

Luiz Rodrigues' edition of A. de Resende's *De uerborū* (Lisbon, 1530).
Title-page. *Houghton Library.*

block. The proportions remain the same as in the *De uerborū*. The overall impression from both of these title-pages is one of ease and grace. This is not the case, however, of the *Lyuro das obras de Garcia de Resēde* printed by Rodrigues in 1545. The *Lyuro* is printed in folio; its title-page is large and striking: two heavy rectangular blocks, displaying an armillary sphere and the arms of Portugal, rest on a frame containing the title. The frame is made up of three of Tory's blocks, all mutilated to size: two outer borders (cut to ca. 112mm.) and an inner border (cut to ca. 150mm.) used sideways as a lower piece. The title, printed in two different typefaces, and the woodcut historiated initial add to the confusion. Here again, as in the *Regimento*, Tory's blocks have been misused to fit a format for which they were not intended. They were forced this time to coexist with blocks of a completely different nature and style.

As mentioned before, Luiz Rodrigues was "Livreiro del Rei", bookseller-publisher of the King long before he started his own press. In this capacity, he occasionally employed the printer Germão Galharde. Of French extraction (Germain Gaillard?), Galharde established his Lisbon press around 1519 and became "Impressor Regio" in 1530. Galharde was a prolific, if not a creative printer. His title-pages are often ornamented with poorly fitting, borrowed material: blocks from the stock of his colleagues and predecessors, Valentim Fernandes, João de Cremona, and Hermão de Campos. We know that Galharde also borrowed from Rodrigues, as the title of his 1540 *Regra z statutos da ordem de Santiago* (plate, p. 187) is ornamented with Tory's borders. The title is surrounded by four elements in a way which departs from Tory's intent. Upper and lower pieces are in their regular position, but instead of the usual inner and outer borders, outer borders have been used on both sides. The symmetry of the lateral borders creates a more balanced frame. The title, however, is not well-centered. It is thrown off to the right by the xylographic initial, a voluminous and archaic R of Germanic origin. The lower border, the crowned L of Louise de Savoie, is incongruous in the context of a book of rules of the Order of Santiago, though possibly Galharde meant it to compliment Dom Jorge de Lancastre, Duke of Coimbra, the Master of the Order at the time. If not totally successful, the title-page of the *Regra* is nevertheless pleasant. Of the blocks used by Galharde, the upper border is the only one which can be traced directly to Rodrigues.

Following the death of Rodrigues in the later part of 1545, the greatest part of his typographical stock moved to Coimbra, where we find it in the hands of João de Barreira and João Alvares. João de Barreira, probably of Spanish origin, is thought to have started his career in Lisbon as Rodrigues' apprentice. In 1542, he established himself in Coimbra with João Alvares as partner. Both soon held the title of "Impressores da Universidade." Their publications are filled with Rodrigues' blocks, including his device, the Griffin, which they adopted as their own. It is with no surprise then, that we find Tory's borders in works published under their joint or individual imprint.

The title-pages of two of their joint enterprises use almost the same set of Tory's borders: Gregorio Martins Caminha's *Tractado da forma dos libellos*, published in 1549 and Padre Gaspar Barzeo's *Copia de vna carta*, published ca. 1550.

The title-pages are organized as if they formed a verso of Tory's *Hore*, that is with an inner (narrow) border on the right and an outer (wide) border on the left. Among the four elements, only one, the outer border, can be traced directly to Rodrigues, as we first encountered it in his *Regimento*. In the interim, this block had been put to an unknown use and mutilated, as it is now missing upper and lower outer rules, giving both title-pages a rather ragged appearance. The title of the *Tractado* is long and fits very tightly within the borders; that of the *Copia de vna carta*, more airy and gracious, has the Griffin device at head.

Barreira and Alvares also printed individually, under their own imprints. Among Barreira's production, we find two very pleasant title-pages framed by Tory's borders: Leonor de Noronha's *Esta he a segunda parte da historia de nossa redenção*, Coimbra, 1554, and Ruy Gonçalves' *Dos priuilegios & praerogatiuas q̃ ho genero feminino tẽ por dereito comũ*, Lisbon or Coimbra, 1557. The title of each of these works is surrounded by four elements, but as in Galharde's *Regra*, lateral borders of the same size have been used on the right and the left. The *Historia* uses two outer (wide) borders, the *Dos priuilegios* two inner (narrow) borders,[30] resulting in well-balanced frames. Particularly gracious is the title-page of the *Dos Priuilegios* with its slender borders containing, well-centered between two verses of the Sapientia and the title proper, the armorial shield of Dona Catarina. Among the blocks used by Bar-

---

[30] Joined on the same title-page, as they could never have been in the Du Bois *Hore*, these two narrow borders best illustrate the presence of two artists at work on Tory's borders: the arabesque on the left inner border is sinuous, elongated, almost rectilinear; whereas that on the recto is formed of deep, short curves, punctuated by blank spaces.

Germão Galharde's edition of the *Regra* (Lisbon, 1540). Title-page.
Houghton Library.

reira, two (the outer and lower borders of the *Historia*) were already used in the work of Galharde; another (the lower border of the *Dos Priuilegios*) was used jointly with Alvares.

Alvares' innovations are not as successful as those of his associate. The title-page of his *Copia de vnas Cartas de algunos padres y hermanos dela compañia de Iesus*, Coimbra, 1555, is flanked by two outer borders. Upper and lower borders have been inverted for no apparent reason. At the top is a lower border (the Crowned Salamander of François I) and at the foot, an upper border used upside down. Though not devoid of charm, there is a somewhat shabby, unfinished feel to the title-page. Of these blocks only one, the upper border used at foot, has been used before, under Barreira's and Alvares' joint imprint.

Francisco Correa, a Coimbra printer who worked at the Colegio Real, also admired Tory's borders. The title-page of Sancho de No-ronha's *Tractado moral*, which Correa printed in 1549, is framed by two narrow borders copied from Tory's stock and modified. Both borders have been reduced to 146mm.: in the right border (a copy of Tory's inner border of d6^v), a long rose stem at the foot has simply been shortened; in the left border (a copy of the inner border of b6^r), a large leaf at the foot has been cut in half. Correa added some *criblé* work around the leaf to make it look as though it grew out of the ground; and he accentuated the outside rules of the lateral border. Instead of copying Tory's upper and lower borders, Correa used simple rules. With the Royal arms of Portugal and a well-centered title, the whole has a charming and polished look. Although presumably copied from Ro-drigues' stock, this is the first known appearance of the designs in Portugal since their initial use by Tory in 1527.

The copies made by Antonio de Mariz, however, can be traced to Tory borders in the stock of João de Barreira. Mariz, who later married Izabel João, João Alvares' daughter, first established his press in Coimbra in 1556. From 1562 to 1569, he was active in Braga, printing for the Archbishop Bartholomeu dos Martyres. Three of the works coming out of his Braga press have titles within "Tory style" borders. The first is the *Manvale secvndum Ordinẽ almae Bracarẽsis Ecclesiae*, printed in 1562. The border on the title-page (see plate, p. 189) is composed of the usual four elements. The two lateral borders are reversed copies of two of Tory's inner borders, that of a4^v and b1^r. The upper and lower borders are free copies with simple arabesques of flowers. Upper and lower borders are much wider (ca. 125mm.) than Tory's original pieces.

Antonio de Mariz' edition of the *Manvale* (Braga, 1562). Title-page.
Houghton Library.

The result is a roomier, elegant rectangular frame, spacious enough to accomodate a coat of arms, a couple of vignettes, or simply, a well-spaced title.

Mariz used the very same borders in two other Braga imprints: on the divisional title-page of Part II of Bartholomeu dos Martyres' *Catechismo*, 1564, and on the title-page of his 1567 edition of Gregorio Martins Caminha's *Tractado da forma dos Libellos*.

After being used by Coimbra printers over a period of nine years (1549–1557), Tory's borders reappeared in Lisbon in the latter part of the century. Probably brought back by Barreira or Alvares, who were also active in that city, they passed into the hands of Manuel João, who used them in his 1565 edition of *O primeiro [–terçeiro] liuro das Ordenações*. The book is printed in folio, and João's use of the border is reminiscent of Rodrigues' when dealing with the same format. Two outer borders (mutilated at foot to about 151mm.) form the pillars of a massive architectural frame. These pillars, which rest on a pedestal, below which appears the title, support a heavy triangular pediment. The inside frame is fully occupied by a woodcut of the Royal arms, with the Griffin crest flanked by an armillary sphere and the Cross of the Order of Christ. If Tory's borders are misused and overpowered by other blocks, the overall effect is nevertheless monumental, well in keeping with the content of the work. The left border can be traced back to Alvares, the right border, to Rodrigues' original stock.

The latest appearance of Tory's borders I am able to document[31] is in Antonio Ribeiro's 1575 edition of Jeronymo Osorio's *Epistola . . . ad Serenissimam Elisabetam Angliae Reginam* (plate, p. 191). The young Ribeiro, who was to become one of the major printers of the latter part of the century, had just set up his Lisbon press the year before. Like most beginners, he must have acquired his stock from various sources, Alvares, Barreira, or possibly Correa, with whom he was later associated.[32]

After Manuel João's ponderous title-page, Ribeiro's simple use of

[31] Based on the evidence to be found in *King Manuel*; a visit to the Biblioteca Nacional of Lisbon, the Biblioteca Geral of Coimbra, and the Braganza Palace, Villa Viçosa, where King Manuel's collection is now located, is planned to complete this study.

[32] Jointly, they printed the Almeirin, 1578 edition of *Allegações de direito por parte de D. Catarina de Bragança* (Anselmo, p. 267; V. A. Deslandes, *Documentos para a historia da typographia portugueza nos secolos XVI et XVII* (Lisbon, 1888), p. [102], n. 1).

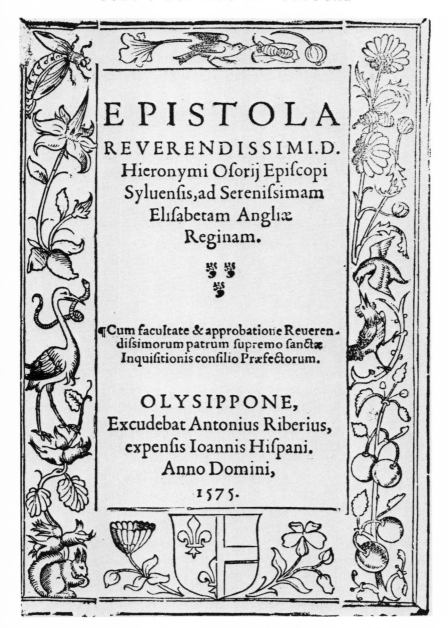

EPISTOLA

REVERENDISSIMI.D.
Hieronymi Oſorij Epiſcopi
Syluenſis, ad Sereniſsimam
Eliſabetam Angliæ
Reginam.

¶Cum facultate & approbatione Reueren-
diſsimorum patrum ſupremo ſanctæ
Inquiſitionis conſilio Præfectorum.

OLYSIPPONE,
Excudebat Antonius Riberius,
expenſis Ioannis Hiſpani.
Anno Domini,
1575.

Antonio Ribeiro's edition of J. Osorio's *Epistola* (Lisbon, 1575). Title-page.
University of Illinois, Urbana.

the borders in the *Epistola* is most welcome. The blocks (with the exception of an upper outer rule, which has apparently been mangled) are still fresh and graceful. Two outer borders have been placed on each side, while upper and lower borders are used in their proper positions. The lower border, an armorial shield of France and Savoy, may be somewhat out of place on the title-page of a letter to the Queen of England, but as we have seen on other occasions, this sort of consideration did not weigh much with Portuguese printers. Two of Ribeiro's blocks can be traced to earlier owners: the border on the right already encountered in Galharde's stock and the upper border found in Rodrigues' original stock.

With the *Epistola*, thirty-seven years of almost continuous use of Tory's borders come to an end. Intriguing, the extraordinary survival of the blocks also proves fruitful as it throws light on some important aspects of the trade of the period: origin of the typographic stock, associations between printers, attitudes toward the tools of the trade and aesthetic concerns.

As they set up their presses in the first part of the sixteenth century, early Portuguese printers acquired their typographic stock from their local or Spanish predecessors. The ornamental material handed them — original blocks or local copies — was mostly of German or Italian origin. French blocks were seldom to be found, even in the work of Germão Galharde. The Frenchman must have come to Portugal empty-handed, for he started out with material from Fernandes, Bonhomini and Campos. The fresh input of French material for which Rodrigues is responsible is thus a rare phenomenon, due no doubt to his commercial ties with France in his capacity of bookseller-publisher.

As such, and later as proprietor of a printing press, Rodrigues played a dominant role among the Lisbon printers of his time. His associations were numerous and far-reaching. His apprentice Barreira became in his own time the leading figure in Coimbra. Although Galharde had temporarily set up his press in that city in the 1530's, it was Barreira and his associate Alvares who, through their work and influence in the latter part of the century, turned Coimbra into a major printing center, second only to Lisbon.

The passage of Tory's blocks from hand to hand reveals a parsimonious attitude shared by all printers alike, French or Portuguese. With the press, the typographic stock constituted the printer's major asset. Expensive and difficult to acquire, the blocks were used, lent, traded or sold but rarely discarded, unless badly mangled or broken. Mutilation only occurred when necessity — a large format, or a special occasion, as in the case of Luiz Rodrigues or Manuel João — dictated it. Even then the unused portion was carefully kept and put to use, sometimes years later.

The ways the blocks were used, however, illustrate profound differences in the aesthetic ideals of Northern printers and of their Portuguese counterparts. Tory's borders, as we have seen, were the product of an already extremely refined trade, whose ideal of beauty and harmony dictated the agreement of content, typeface and illustrations. The three elements — liturgical text, gothic font and borders "à la moderne" — enhanced each other, contributing to the success of the Du Bois *Hore*.

No such goals animated the work of early Portuguese printers. Agreement of text and style of ornamentation was not one of their concerns: Tory's borders are used in a variety of contexts, at the head of official material, or ecclesiastic, devotional, educational or literary works. The aesthetic ideal of early Portuguese printers was simply one of functional beauty: a legible text with an attractive title-page. Ornamentation within the text was rare. The first page of a "Prologo", or a divisional title-page would occasionally be decorated, but never do we find the borders surrounding multiple pages of text, as originally intended.

The Tory title-pages in the work of our seven printers provide graphic evidence of the evolution of taste in Portugal between 1539 and 1575. Upon his return, Rodrigues either crudely mutilated the blocks for his own needs or used them as they were originally intended. It was with Galharde, but above all with the printers of Coimbra, Barreira and Correa, that the borders were freely and creatively adapted to their new title-page role. By replacing the inner and outer borders by two lateral borders of the same size, these printers obtained a well-balanced and roomy frame, ready to house title, vignettes or arms of the dedicatee. By widening the upper and lower pieces and reducing the height of the lower border, Mariz further departed from the by then obsolete medieval model. Monumental blocks were increasingly replaced by well-centered titles and imprints, tapered into two superimposed triangles as in the work of Ribeiro. Notwithstanding the badly-assorted fonts and the old French woodcut borders, the modern title-page was born, simple, functional, yet beautiful. Geofroy Tory could only have approved of it.

APPENDIX

Short Title List of Portuguese Works
Containing Tory's Borders "à la Moderne."

LUIZ RODRIGUES

1. Regimento de como os contadores das comarcas hã de prouer sobre as capellas. [Lisbon], 1514 [i.e. 1539?]
   Hofer collection. Typ 535.39.708F.
   King Manuel 40.
2. L. Andreae Resendii De uerborũ coniugatione commentarius. Lisbon, 1540.
   Hofer Collection. Typ 535.40.738 (A) & (B).
   King Manuel 43.
3. Georgii Coelii lvsitani De patientia christiana liber vnvs. [Lisbon], 1540.
   Houghton Library *PC5.C6506.540d.
   King Manuel 44.
4. Lyuro das obras de Garcia de Resẽde. [Lisbon], 1545.
   King Manuel 59.

GERMÃO GALHARDE

5. Regra z statutos da ordem de Santiago. Lisbon, 1540.
   Hofer Collection. Typ 535.40.656.
6. *King Manuel* 51 describes a reissue (?) of this work dated 1542 with almost identical t.-p.

JOÃO DE BARREIRA AND JOÃO ALVARES

7. Tractado da forma dos Libellos. E da forma das allegacoẽs iudiciaes . . . Feyto pelo licẽciado Gregorio Martĩz Caminha. Coimbra, 1549.
   King Manuel 67.
8. Copia de vna carta, que escriuio de la India el padre. M. Gaspar de la compañia de Iesus. [Coimbra, 1550?].
   King Manuel 71.

JOÃO DE BARREIRA

9. Esta he a segunda parte da historia de nossa redençaõ [de Leonor de Noronha]. Coimbra, 1554.
   King Manuel 294.

10. Dos priuilegios & praerogatiuas q̃ ho genero feminino tẽ por dereito comũ [de Ruy Gonçalves]. [Lisbon or Coimbra], 1557.
King Manuel 91.

JOÃO ALVARES

11. Copia de vnas Cartas de algunos padres y hermanos dela compañia de Iesus que escriuieron dela India, Iapon, y Brasil. [Coimbra], 1555.
King Manuel 87.

FRANCISCO CORREA

12. Tractado moral de louuores & perígos dalgũs estados seculares . . . Composto por Dom Sancho de Noronha. Coimbra, 1549.
King Manuel 66.

ANTONIO DE MARIZ

13. Manvale secvndvm Ordinẽ almae Bracarẽsis Ecclesiae. Braga, 1562. Hofer Collection. Typ 535.62.262.

14. Catechismo ou Doutrina Christaã & Praticas spirituaes. Ordenado por Dom Frey Bartholameu dos Martyres. Braga, 1564.
King Manuel 104.

15. Tractado da forma dos Libellos...Feyto pello Licenciado Gregorio Martiz Caminha. Braga, 1567.
King Manuel 345.

MANUEL JOÃO

16. O primeiro [–terçeiro] liuro das Ordenações. Lisbon, 1565.
King Manuel 111.

ANTONIO RIBEIRO

17. Epistola reverendissimi. D. Hieronymi Osorij . . . ad Serenissimam Elisabetam Angliae Reginam. Lisbon, 1575.
King Manuel 151.

A Catalogue of Ladies to be set up by AUCTION.

Catalogues will be diftributed by the Door-Keepers of each Meeting-Houfe in *London* and *Weftminfter*.

ADVERTISEMENT.

ON Monday *the twenty ninth of this Inftant* June, *will begin, and to be continued from Day to Day, to be fet up by Auction, or who bids moft, at the Dancing-School in* Freemans-Yard, Cornhill, *a Choice Collection of Ladies from fifteen to twenty five Years of Age, their Fortunes from one to ten thoufand Pounds, no part of the fame being in the Exchequer, or Chamber of* London, *They may be viewed by any Gentleman in* Lincolns-Inn-Gardens, *between the hours of five and nine on* Sunday next, *till all are gone off.*

All Gentlemen will be accepted who have clear Limbs and Members entire, upon due Examination.

The CATALOGUE.

		l.
1	ONE tall lufty Maiden Lady, aged 23 Years, worth	1000
2	One Young Widow who buried her Husband, a Grocer, 6 Months after Marriage	3520
3	One fuperfine neat fhapt Lady, not 15, Black	1600
4	A Young Widow with Child	3000
5	The eldeft Daughter of an Eminent Merchant	6000
6	A Vintners Widow, a fine Woman, without Children, having a Manfion Houfe in *Effex*	4000
7	A Merchants only Daughter near *Leaden-Hall-Street*	8000
8	Two Sifters lately come from the Country near the *May-Pole* in the *Strand*, each	2000
9	A Linnen-Drapers Daughter near *Cornhill*	2500
10	The only Daughter of a Merchant in *London*, whofe Grand-father left her 3000 *l.* befides a Fathers Blefling (a crofs old Gentleman)	3000
11	A pretty little young Lady at her own difpofal	5000
12	A Drugfters Daughter tall and Slender	2500
13	A Doctor of Phyficks Daughter near *Smithfield*	1800
14	A Lady without Father or Mother, whofe Fortune is aboard the *Streights* Fleet, if it efcape the *French*, worth (all Cuftoms paid)	10000
15	Three Sifters pretty Women, Knights Daughters, each	1200
16	A pretty young Lady unfkill'd in the Tricks of the Town	1100
17	A Sergeant at Law's Daughter, fo, fo	2500
18	A Proctors Daughter at the Commons, indifferent	7000
19	An Attornies Daughter in the City	2000
20	A Vintners Daughter not very Streight	4500
21	A Mercers three Daughters on *Ludgate-hill*, each	2000
22	A Mercers Daughter in *Pater-Nofter-Row*	1200
23	A Mercers Daughter in *Covent-Garden*, if Married to one of her Fathers Kidney	9000
24	An Upholfterers Daughter in *Stocks-Market*	1500
25	A Coffee-Mans Daughter near the *Exchange*	2500
26	A Worthy painful Teachers Daughter, at prefent oo. when her Father goes to Heaven	8000
27	A Brewers youngeft Daughter, whofe Fortune was gain'd fince the laft Act of Parl.	3500
28	A young Heirefs, a Country Lady, and a good Houfewife	1500
29	A pretty young Lady with moft excellent Qualifications	1100
30	Three Sifters, Daughters of an Eminent Scrivener	5000
31	The youngeft Daughter of a large fat Gentleman near *Lombard-ftreet*, (if Friends ftand by him) payable two Months after *Midfummer*	4000

There are feveral young Ladies very importunate to be in the CATALOGUE, *but their Fortunes not coming up to the Sum propos'd, 'twas deny'd: However, if this meet with Encouragement, they may hope to be in the next.*

52

[Richard Ames] *A Catalogue of Ladies* [1691]. 287×191mm. *Houghton Library.* (cropped at top)

196

Richard Ames (*d.* 1692): A Catalogue

HUGH AMORY

THAT RICHARD AMES occupies an entire column in vol. 2 of the *Cambridge Bibliography of English Literature*, whereas Mrs. Behn, Mrs. Radcliffe, nay, Robert Bage are scanted with a sprinkling of entries among the "Minor Fiction" has many motives: the superstitious reverence for poetry — or rather, verse — of the Victorians; the sheer abundance of Ames's anonymous *œuvre*, already conveniently identified in bibliographies shortly after his death; and the rarity and triviality of his pieces, which no doubt attracted editors like J. O. Halliwell-Phillipps as virtues in themselves. More important, perhaps, was the documentary interest of these ephemera, which are certainly prominent in the standard bibliographies of wine and economic literature; and no doubt they will be honored as well in the definitive *Bibliographia feminea et antifeminea* that our own age will eventually disgorge.

Wealth, wine, woman, and song, then, have stimulated such scholarship as we find, and not, apparently, the intrinsic merit of Ames's verse. The only reprintings of his poems since the eighteenth century have been limited, often facsimile productions aimed at connoisseurs, collectors, and librarians; he has never, I think, been anthologized, despite his prominence in the *CBEL*. If there is any consensus on Ames, I suppose it must be that his verse is too indifferent to merit a critical edition — for the contemporary editions are badly disfigured with misprints. I cannot, however, even if I would, challenge the general justice of this opinion. The present bibliographical essay, which is incomparably fuller than any of its predecessors, began when Jim Walsh initiated me into the art of cataloguing, and I suppose that his choice, at least, was largely determined by the poet's position in the alphabet. Harvard is fortunate in its holdings of these productions.

I must also confess that, besides his lack of any conspicuously redeeming literary value, my poet is nearly anonymous: *vox, praeterea nihil*. Our only source is *The Life and Errors* of that eccentric bookseller, John Dunton, who includes him among "the *Characters* of the Authors for whom I printed":

Mr. *Ames*, originally a *Coat-seller;* but had always some *Yammerings* [i.e. longings] *upon him after Learning* and the *Muses.* He has almost writ as many pretty, little Pleasant Poems as *Taylor* the *Water-Poet;* you might engage him upon what Project you pleas'd, if you'd but conceal him, for his *Principles* did never resist in such Cases.... *Wine and Women* were the great Bane of his Life and Happiness; he dy'd in an *Hospital*, but I hope he was truly penitent; for a little before his Decèase, he said to me, with a Deal of Concern. *Ah Mr. Dunton! with what another Face does the World appear, now I have Death in View!*[1]

Unfortunately, this tells us little that we do not already know from the poet's own mouth, and that little cannot be verified. There seems to be no trace of Ames among the records of the Drapers' or Mercers' companies; and his political principles, so far as we can tell, never wavered in the support of King William. He died in 1692, leaving behind a slew of palinodes supporting love, marriage, sobriety, and chastity.

His canon rests largely on two posthumous lists. The first and less important of these appeared in *The Bacchanalian Sessions*, and it is obviously a bookseller's production, giving accurate titles and prices for a group of properties that perhaps belonged to Edmond Richardson. But it is difficult to judge from seventeenth-century imprints: Randal Taylor and Richard Baldwin, who figure as the publishers of so many of them, are "trade publishers", who specialized in distributing pamphlets that belonged to other members of the trade.[2] John Dunton certainly advertised many of Ames's productions in his *Athenian Mercury*, and I have not seen other advertisements outside the *Term Catalogues;* but the only title he mentions in his *Life and Errors* is *The Double Descent*. The only entry in the Stationers' Register is for *Sylvia's Revenge*, to Joseph Streater. The evidence for the ownership of Ames's "copies" is thus confused; but it would probably be wrong to see him as a prototypical Israel Hackney, slaving away for John Dunton.

The second list, in the second edition of *The Folly of Love*, includes all the titles of the first, but it is an entirely independent and obviously amateur compilation. *The Long Vacation* and *The Female Fire-ships*,

---

[1] *The Life and Errors of John Dunton* (London, 1705), pp. 224, 247.

[2] Michael Treadwell, "London Trade Publishers 1675–1750," *The Library*, 6th ser., 4 (1982), [99]–134.

for example, appear under their subtitles, and the listing of both *The Character of a Bigotted Prince* and *Chuse Which You Will* may suggest, to some, that the compiler was unaware that these were different issues of the same text. These features guarantee at once the sincerity of the attributions and their uncertainty. Kurt Zimansky, who compiled the section on Ames in the *New CBEL*, was perhaps premature in concluding that "The Lent Keepers" is now lost; perhaps it is not dead, but sleepeth, and Wing knows it under a different name. Given the approximate citations of many titles in the list, I hope I have not forced the evidence in equating an "Elegy on the French fleet" with *The French King's Lamentation for the Loss of his Fleet*. Since there is some doubt whether the compiler saw all the pieces in his list or not, one might, perhaps, argue that an "Elegy on the French fleet" is simply *Britannia Victrix* under another name, and that the "Letter from Leghorn" is only *The Present State of England* (which is dated from Leghorn). Such doubts, though inevitable, cannot, however, serve as the basis for attribution, and I have followed Zimansky in assuming that all the titles in the list are mutually exclusive. In later editions of *The Folly of Love*, the bookseller redrew the list, eliminating amateur descriptions and inserting a number of pieces that are certainly not by Ames.

Neither list includes *The Double Descent*, the Sylvia poems, or the posthumous *Fatal Friendship*. In the first list, this should cause no surprise, since we may presume the bookseller who compiled it had no interest in other booksellers' productions; in the second list, they are rather more difficult to account for. The Sylvia poems, in particular, were among Ames's best-known and most often reprinted pieces: the *Athenian Mercury*, for example, can refer to him as "Silvia's bullying satirist"; and *The Search after Wit* exclaims, "Here's *Sylvia's Revenge*, Sir, and the *Follies of Love*: / Sure these you ne'er read, Sir, if no *Wit* you e'er saw there," in order to show what "Little *Dick*" is capable of. It is certainly strange, then, that the apparently knowledgeable compiler should omit these poems, but I cannot show that it was more than a simple oversight.

The present essay ascribes six pieces to Ames that have not previously been identified as his work, expanding the total of known titles by 25%. One of these, *The Circulation of Money Demonstrated*, is noteworthy as an early instance of the vogue for inanimate narration, best-known today from Charles Johnston's *Chrysal, or The Adventures of a Guinea* (1760–65). *The French King's Lamentation* is a conventional satire on the Jacobites' dismay following the battle of La Hogue. The King's opening words do little to alter the received opinion of Ames's skill in verse:

> Hence, hence, ye *Slaves*, do not my *Wrath* provoke,
> And of my *Loss at Sea* no longer *Croke*.

The remainder of these new pieces belong to a group of mock-catalogues, apparently written by a team, and represented in the list of *The Folly of Love* by a single entry for an "Auction of ladies." These in turn initiated a vogue for catalogues not only of ladies, but also of other minorities like Jacobites, bachelors, beaus, whores, and poets. The exact extent of Ames's part in this complex will probably always remain uncertain: we do not know the names of his partners, and it is even difficult to be sure where their enterprise ended and the imitations, replies, and spurious continuations of others began. Only three titles may be assigned to Ames and his partners with any assurance: the original *Catalogue of Ladies* and its sequel, the *Second Catalogue*, and, confirmed by the authority of the *Athenian Mercury*, the *Continuation* of the *Second Catalogue*, of July 6.

In its original conception, the *Catalogue* is impersonal, listing such "properties" as "An Attornies Daughter in the City" or "A Vintners Daughter not very Streight," which could hardly have reflected on known individuals (see plate, p. 196). Freeman's Yard, where the sale was supposed to take place, was well known for its auctions, though "the Dancing-School in *Freemans-Yard*" is bawdily suggestive, as is the note that the ladies "may be viewed by any Gentleman in *Lincolns-Inn-Gardens*" — a known haunt of prostitution. The first two catalogues are supposed to be "distributed by the Door-Keepers of each Meeting-House in London and Westminster" — probably with the innuendo (familiar from Swift's *Tale of a Tub*) that the religious enthusiasm of the Independents led to sexual license; their specialized term for a church (as the Presbyterians and Anglicans would have called it) is here generalized into a place of sexual congress. Despite these satiric and indeed fantastic overtones, the point of the *Catalogue* seems originally to have been a simple hoax, and is so interpreted in the Edinburgh reprint, which uses the same text for a new "sale" on September 24.

The conditions of the sale are to "who bids most", and we may recall that auctions to the highest bidder were still something of a novelty in the last quarter of the seventeenth century, for many Englishmen.[3] Indeed, a large number of these pieces may be found in a collection of catalogues of real and imaginary sales formed by John Bagford (1650– 1716), now in the British Library (Harl. 5947).[4] This novelty, of course, is part of the satirist's stock of grievances, his farrago: women, the series implies, are a mere drug on the market — we might compare Moll Flanders' rueful observation, that "the Market run very unhappily on the Mens side."[5] The ladies' fortunes, the *Catalogue* solemnly assures us (referring to recent economic crises) are "from one to ten thousand Pound, no part of the same being in the *Exchequer*, or Chamber of *London*." These fantasies (as so often in economics) are nearly indistinguishable from facts. There is an interesting parallel to the Catalogues of ladies in an issue of John Houghton's *A Collection for Improvement of Husbandry and Trade* for July 26, 1695: "A *Gentleman* about 30 Years of Age, that says He has a *Very Good Estate*, would willingly Match Himself to some *Good Young Gentlewoman*, that has a Fortune of 3 000*l.* or thereabout, and he will make *Settlement* to Content." Houghton prefixes a note to this advertisement: "I have undertaken to Advertize all sorts of things that are honorable; and what follows, is not otherwise, and I am well paid for it." Anything is barely possible, if you can only keep a straight face.

Like any hoax, however, it could not be enjoyed until it was discovered, and the laconic style of the original *Catalogue* soon dissolved into the free play of fantasy and outrageous embroidery, both in the genuine and the spurious continuations. The genuine *Continuation* of the *Second Catalogue*, for example, openly acknowledges the by-now obvious truth that it is distributed "by the booksellers of London and Westminster", but goes on to offer for sale, among less distinctive properties, "The Widdow of the Famous Dr. S---fold [i.e. Saffold]", a favorite

---

[3] The earliest English book auctions date from 1676; Pepys's description of a sale by the candle is, of course, the *locus classicus*, *The Diary*, ed. Robert Latham and William Matthews (Berkeley, Cal., 1970–   ), I, 284 (Nov. 5, 1660).

[4] See the *Catalogue and Indexes to the Title-pages of English Printed Books . . . in the . . . Bagford Collection*, comp. M. H. Wolf (London [1974]); since Wolf's descriptions are often idiosyncratic, I have added call nos. in citing this collection below.

[5] Daniel Defoe, *The Fortunes and Misfortunes of the Famous Moll Flanders*, ed. Edward Kelly (New York [1973]), p. 54.

butt of Ames. *An Out-cry of Poets*, if I read it rightly, offers for sale Thomas D'Urfey, Elkanah Settle, John Dunton, and Henry Neville Payne, among others, variously disguised, possibly including Ames himself under the name of "Mr. *Multum in Parvo*, a Gentleman of Low Stature but of High Learning." Rival auctioneers tried to perpetuate the fast-vanishing fabric of illusion, as in *A Catalogue of Batchelors*, which confers fictitious names like "Count *Canaile*" on "lots" that had already been more neutrally advertised in other catalogues. *An Account of the Auction* lewdly changes the conditions of bidding to a sale by the candle, and pretends that it has actually taken place. Eventually, the fiction degenerated into mere formal pretense: *A Catalogue of Jilts* is a straightforward libel on the *demi-monde*, thinly clothed in dashes.

In deference to received opinion, I have divided my catalogue between Ames's writings and his ana, but the distinction is somewhat artificial. Strikingly, many of these pieces appeared in series and the series themselves may be corporate productions. Tom Brown is certainly a very likely collaborator in Ames's auctions, and his own series of petititions of 1692–93 is an exact parallel. The cataloguing problem is less to work out the precise attribution than to lay bare the publishing connection or theme of pieces that are scattered far and wide in the alphabet. The short-title format, of course, was originally designed for a period when series played a relatively minor role, and it is poorly suited to their description: Wing's STC is thus always threatening to lapse from the glory of a catalogue into the condition of an inventory. The rarity of these pieces also militates against a perception of their connections, even in a more generous format like the pre–1956 National Union Catalogue: 13 titles, or about 20% of my entries, survive in unique copies, often owing to the omnivorous instinct of Narcissus Luttrell. The defects of Antonio Panizzi's rules are only too familiar to anyone who has seriously tried to find an anonymous piece in the British Library Catalogue; but once you have found it, they have the outstanding merit, denied to the National Union Catalogue, of separating and bringing together those snarls of replies, continuations, and imitations that are so typical of eighteenth-century literature — *ce vaste pays du pour et du contre*, as Fontenelle called it. The future of Ames studies, then, probably lies neither in departments of literature, nor in the National Union Catalogue and its supplements, or the *CBEL*, but in catalogues like David Foxon's, *souple et ondoyante*, whose example I follow at a distance. And it is ironically appropriate that the inventor of the auction-catalogue-as-a-literary-form (not to put too keen an edge upon it) should himself survive only in catalogues. In the same spirit and conscious of the same fate, I offer the following catalogue in tribute to the honorable, anonymous, and difficult enterprise that Jim Walsh has carried on for so many years.[6]

Catalogue

SHORT REFERENCES

Ashton: John Ashton, *Humour, Wit & Satire of the Seventeenth Century* (London, 1883).

1CBEL: *The Cambridge Bibliography of English Literature*, ed. F. W. Bateson (New York, 1941–57), v. 2.

2CBEL: *The New Cambridge Bibliography of English Literature*, ed. George Watson (Cambridge, 1969–77), v. 2.

Foxon: David F. Foxon, *English Verse 1701–1750* (London, New York, 1975).

HC, II: W. C. Hazlitt, *Second Series of Bibliographical Collections and Notes on Early English Literature* (London, 1882).

LBR: Narcissus Luttrell, *A Brief Historical Relation of State Affairs* (Oxford, 1857).

Macdonald: Hugh Macdonald, *John Dryden; a Bibliography* (Oxford, 1939).

Stonehill: Charles A. Stonehill, et al., *Anonyma and Pseudonyma* (London, 1926–27).

1Wing: Donald G. Wing, *Short-title Catalogue of Books Printed in England . . . 1641–1700* (New York, 1945–51).

[6] I completed work on this catalogue on a leave of absence from Houghton as Munby Fellow at the Cambridge University Library, with the assistance of a grant from the British Academy; I am most grateful to all three institutions for their generosity. The Wing Revision generously imparted information from its working records, and I am particularly indebted to Timothy Crist and Carolyn Nelson. Of the many librarians who helped me, I would especially like to thank Ms Jean Archibald of the British Library, who untiringly answered my queries, and Stephen Parks at Yale, who showed me his Luttrell file. I have also benefitted from the expert advice of my colleagues Roger Stoddard and Katharine Pantzer, who kindly vetted an earlier version of my catalogue.

2*Wing:* —— , —— , 2d ed., rev. & enl. (New York, 1972–   ).

Wing citations pose a number of problems that will not be entirely removed even when the Revision is complete: for one thing, the University Microfilm series refers only to *1Wing;* for another, the two editions differ in scope; and finally, though I have, through the kindness of the editors, secured provisional references for items "Not in *Wing*," these are necessarily subject to change. I have therefore adopted the following conventions:

An item entered under the same number in both editions is cited as "*1–2Wing*".

An item entered under a new number in 2*Wing* is cited with the old number added in curves, e.g. 2*Wing* X000 (Y000).

A bare citation of 2*Wing*, then, means that the item is not in the first edition (though the number may be); a bare citation of *1Wing* means that the item will probably be entered under this number in the forthcoming volumes of the Revision.

When the same item is entered under two different numbers, so that one is a ghost, they are connected by an equals sign, e.g. X000 = Y000.

When an entry has been deleted in 2*Wing*, the first edition is cited, with the reason for the deletion added in curves; when an item only appears in 2*Wing*, but should not, it is cited by its number followed by "(to be deleted)". When an item is in neither edition, it is cited as "Not in *Wing*", followed by the provisional reference in italics, if one has been assigned by the Revision, e.g. "Not in *Wing* (*X000*)".

DESCRIPTIVE CONVENTIONS

Title: titles are abbreviated without specific notice of ellipses at the beginning and end, except that the symbol ([), to be read "at head of title", prefaces material omitted at the beginning, and final punctuation is omitted when none is present at that point in the original. Drop-head or caption titles are preceded by the symbol [dh], except for broadsides and half-sheets.

Imprint: abbreviated and normalized, except that the name of the printer or publisher is given as it appears on the title-page or elsewhere in the piece. I have supplied the names of any concealed printers I was able to identify in square brackets, and noted the names of publishers in the Term Catalogues, when these differed from those in the imprint. The location of the imprint is not specifically noted: it may be assumed to be at the end of the text of broadsides, half-sheets, or pieces with drop-head titles.

Date: The day and month of publication, where known, are supplied in square brackets following the imprint, citing the following authorities in curves:

> *AM:* advertisements in the *Athenian Mercury.*
> *PB:* advertisements in the *Post-Boy.*
> *SR:* entries in the *Stationers' Register*, ed. Arber.
> *TC:* advertisements in the *Term Catalogues*, ed. Arber.
> Luttrell: Narcissus Luttrell's manuscript dates of publication (as they are generally supposed to be).

Format: I have used Foxon's 1° format for half-sheets that were printed on both sides, retaining Wing's conventional "bds." for those that were printed on one side only.

Collation: paginary collation follows the revised Anglo-American Cataloguing Rules (1941), except that integral advertisements are not ignored; blank leaves are only recorded in the register of signatures.

Location Symbols: for American Libraries, I use the symbols in the *pre–1956 National Union Catalogue;* for British libraries, the symbols in 2*Wing*. The following appear in neither authority:

> ICU(c): items from the John Crerar Library, Chicago, now in the Library of the University of Chicago.
> MR(c): the Earl of Crawford's collection of broadsides, formerly at Haigh Hall, later in Cambridge University Library, now in the John Rylands Library, Manchester.
> NZTu: The Turnbull Library, Wellington, N.Z.

Italicized locations mean that I have examined the copy or copies there; a superscript x following a location means that I have seen a microfilm or xerox of the copy. The number of copies and their points of interest and defects, if any, are reported following the location in curves, with call numbers if I thought these would be useful.

Since I have not collated copies word-for-word, there must be many textual variants that I have overlooked; I have not assigned separate reference numbers to different states, which are reported as though they were variant copies.

Section 1.
Authentic writings.

1. [——] An auction of whores. *London, for N. H, over against the Eagle and Child, in St. Martin le Grand* [Aug. 25, 1691 (Luttrell)]. bds.

Not in *Wing (A2974B).*
    Rather a prospectus for the "sale" than the catalogue itself; cf. no. 4.

MH

2. [——] The bacchanalian sessions. *London, for E. Hawkins, 1693* [May 20 (Luttrell)]. 4°: [A]–G²; 2p.l., 24p.

1–2Wing A2975.
    With poem, "To the memory of Mr. Richard Ames," & a list of his writings.

C, DT, EN, *L* (Luttrell copy: 643.k.2 (1.)), O; CLU-C, CSmH^x, CtY, MH.

3. [——] Britannia victrix. *London, for R. Taylor, 1692* [June 25 *(AM)*]. f°: A–D²; 1p.l., 14p.

2Wing A2975A (B4818).
    Advt. in *TC,* II, 412 "for H. Newman."

CT, L, O; *CtY, MH, NN.*

4. [——] A catalogue of jilts, cracks, prostitutes *London, for R. W. near Smithfield, 1691* [Aug. 28 (Luttrell)]. 1°: 2p.

2Wing C1340.
    Probably by Ames, if this is the "list" of particulars to be had "in all booksellers shops, and coffee-houses, for a penny a piece," advertised in no. 1.

ICN^x (Luttrell copy, priced 1^d).

5. [——] A catalogue of ladies to be set up by auction. [Numb. 1 ... [London, June 29, 1691]. bds.

Not in *Wing* (excluded as a numbered serial).
 Attr. to Ames in no. 22 under title: An auction of ladies.
 In this edition, there are five short rules between "Child" and "3000" in lot no. 4.
 To begin "the twenty ninth of this instant June."

L (Harl. 5947, f. 165); *CtY*, *MH* (cropped), *PPL*.

6. [——] ——. [London, July? 1691] bds.

Not in *Wing*.
 In this edition, there are four short rules between "Child" and "3000" in lot no. 4.
 Order of London editions arbitrarily assigned.

MR(c)

7. [——] ——. [Edinburgh? Sep. 24, 1691?] bds.

Not in *Wing*.
 To begin "the twenty fourth of this instant September"; at end (not in the other eds.): Thir [Scots for "These"] catalogues are to be had on the Exchange, a penny a piece.

EN (in tract volume of Scotch imprints).

8. [——] The character of a bigotted prince. *London, for Richard Baldwin, 1691* [Nov. *(TC)*]. 4°: [A]–G² (G2 advts.); 2p.l., 22p., 1l.

2Wing A2975AB (C1963).

AU, CT, L (–G2), O (–[A]1); CLU-C, *CSmH*, CtY, DFo, MH+.

9. [——] Chuse which you will. *London, for R. Stafford, 1692* [May *(TC)*]. 4°: [A]²(±) B-G² (G2 advts.); 2p.l., 22p., 1l.

2Wing A2975AD = A2975AC (C3925 *bis*).
 A reissue of no. 8, with cancel preliminaries.
 Advt. in *TC*, II, 404 (May) "for H[ugh]. N[ewman]." The copies listed with that imprint in *2Wing* A2975AC have imprint: for R. Stafford.

CT, *L*, *LVF*, O; InU.

10. [——] The circulation of money demonstrated [London, 1691?] bds.

Not in *Wing (A2975AE)*.
> Misdated 1640 in Kress Lib. *Supplement, 1473–1848* (1967) no. S679. Date inferred in part from word-usage: "rapparee"; "commode"; "circulation."

MH-B (imprint trimmed away).

11. [——] A continuation of a Catalogue of ladies . . . By E. Cl----r, auctioner [pseud.], that sold the young heiress in Q---- street. [Numb. 2 . . . [London, July 6, 1691] bds.

Not in *Wing* (excluded as a numbered serial).
> In continuation of *A second catalogue* (no. 36), to begin "the 6th of this instant July"; catalogues are "distributed by the booksellers of London and Westminster."
> Title attr. to "Silvia's bullying satirist" [i.e. R. Ames] in *AM*, July 7, 1691; doubtfully ascribed to Brown in B. Boyce, *Tom Brown* (1939), p. 110n, who may have assisted Ames.
> Repr. (slightly expurgated) in *Ashton*, pp. 150–152.

L (2 cops., incl. Harl. 5947, f. 166).

12. [——] A dialogue between Claret & Darby=ale. *London, for E. Richardson, 1692* [Nov. 24, 1691 (Luttrell)]. 4°: A–C²; 1p.l., 10p.

2*Wing* A2975B (W732).
> Also wrongly ascribed to Edward Ward.
> Advt. in *TC*, II, 384 as "sold by Richard Baldwin."

L (Luttrell copy: 164.m.6); CLU-C, *CSmH*ˣ, *CtY*, MH, TxU.

13. [——] The double descent. *London, for John Dunton, 1692* [May 7 (*AM*)]. 4°: A–G²; 28p. (pp. 13–20 misn. 15–22)

1–2Wing A2976.
> Attr. to Ames by Dunton, *Life & errors* (1705), p. 247; not listed in nos. 2 or 22.
> Sheets D–E, containing pp. 15–22 (i.e. 13–20) are set in larger type, possibly cancels.

A, CT; *CtY*.

14. [——] ———. *London, for D. Kean* [i.e. J. Dunton?], *1692*.

1–2Wing A2976A.

    Another issue, with variant imprint; "D. Kean" is not otherwise recorded in *Wing*, and may be a variant of "Don Kainophilus," one of Dunton's pseudonyms.

C, DT, *L*; ICN, *MH*.

15. [——] An elegy on the death of Dr. Thomas Saffold. *London, printed* [by R. Baldwin] *for A. Turner, 1691* [May 13 (Luttrell)] bds.

1–2Wing E370.

    J. W. Draper, *The funeral elegy* (1929), p. 197 records the Bodleian copy (Wood 429 (48)) with reading "Staffold", a mistranscription.

    Repr. (bowdlerized) in C. J. Thompson *The quacks of old London* (1928), pp. 45–47.

L, O; *MH* (Luttrell copy).

16. [——] An elegy on the death of that brave sea-commander . . . Reer-admiral Carter. *London, for Richard Baldwin*, MDXCCII [*sic:* June? 1692]. bds.

1–2Wing E385 (with misreading "Garter": the "C" is filed from a "G" in the original).

    Carter was buried June 2 (*LBR*, II, 472).

L.

17. [——] An elegy on the death of that learned, pious, and laborious minister . . . M.ʳ Richard Baxter *London, printed* [by G. Croom] *for Richard Baldwin, 1691* [Dec.]. bds.

1–2Wing E389.

    Attr. to Ames in no. 22 under title "Elegy on Mr. Baxter"; no other anon. elegy found.

    Baxter was buried Dec. 17 (*LBR*, II, 314).

L.

18. [——] A farther search after claret. *London, for E. Hawkins, 1691* [Mar.?] 4°: A–F² (F2ᵛ advt.); 2p.l., 19, [1]p.

1–2Wing A2977.

 The search after claret (no. 34) was published Feb. 24 & *A last search* (no. 28) Apr. 9.

 Facsim. of the Huth copy repr. in *The search after claret* (1912: 50 copies) with an introduction by A. S. Simon.

O; *CtY*, ICU (c), *MH*: in this state, stanza xxv has two lines & C2ᵛ has incorrect catchword "We".

DT, *HUTH*ˣ, *L*: in this state, stanza xxv has six lines & C2ᵛ has correct catchword "At".

19. [——] Fatal friendship. *London, for, and sold by Randal Taylor,*
1693 [Oct. 25, 1692 (Luttrell)]. 4°: A², B–D⁴, E² (E2 advt., C1 missigned "D"); 2p.l., 26p., 1l.

 1–2Wing A2978.

 "By the author of The search after claret"; not listed in no. 22 or no. 2.

 Advt. as "for R. Taylor . . . and Rich Southby" in no. 33, which adds that Ames wrote it "a little before his death."

A, C, L (2, incl. Luttrell copy: 164.n.79 (–E2)), O; *CSmH*ˣ, *CtY*, FU, ICN, *MH*.

20. [——] The female fire=ships: a satyr against whoring. *London, for*
E. Richardson, 1691 [May 1 (Luttrell)]. 4°: [A]–F²; 2p.l., 19p.

 1–2Wing A2979.

 Advt. in *TC*, II, 381 "for R. Taylor."

EN, L (Luttrell copy: 163.l.43), O; *CtY*, TxU; NZTu.

21. [——] The folly of love. A new satyr against woman. *London, for*
E. Hawkins, 1691 [Feb. *(TC)*]. 4°: A², B–D⁴, E²; 2p.l., 27p.

 1–2Wing A2980.

 Facsim. of the CLU-C copy repr. in *Satires on women* [*sic*], ed. Felicity A. Nussbaum (Augustan repr. soc. no. 180, 1976).

 The "old" satire is Robert Gould's *Love given o'er.*

L (2), O; *CLU-C*ˣ, *CtY*, NIC.

22. [——] ——. 2d ed., corr. *London, for E. Hawkins, 1693.* 4°:
A–G²; 2p.l., 24p.

1–2Wing A2981.
Adds "The batchelors lettany" and a list of writings "by the same author."

C, L, O; CtY, MH.

23. [——] ———. 4th ed. *London, for E. Hawkins, 1700* [Nov. 30 (Luttrell)]. 4°: A–G²; 2p.l., 24p.

1–2Wing A2982.
With list of poems to be had "of several booksellers in London," most of them by Ames.

L (Luttrell copy: 164.l.53), LVF.

24. [——] ———. 5th ed., corr. *London, for E. Hawkins, 1701.* 4°: A–G²; 2p.l., 24p.

Foxon A182.

The t.-p. is found in two states, with readings "batchelors"/ "bachelors" in subtitle: *L*; ICN, NN / CSmH, *ViUˣ*.

25. [——] The French king's lamentation for the loss of his fleet. *London, for R. Stafford, 1692* [June 1 (Luttrell)]. 1°: [2]p.

2Wing F2185D.
Attr. to Ames in no. 22 under title: Elegy on the French fleet.

ICNˣ.

26. [——] Islington-wells. *London, for E. Richardson, 1691* [Aug. 4 (Luttrell)]. 4°: [A]–F²; 2p.l., 19p.

1–2Wing A2983.
Repr. 1861 (30 copies), ed. J. O. Halliwell-Phillipps.

C, EN, L (2 incl. Luttrell copy: 162.l.29), LG, O; CLU-C, DFo, *ICNˣ, MH*; NZTu.

27. [——] The Jacobite conventicle. *London, for R. Stafford, 1692* [May *(TC)*]. 4°: [A]–G² (F1 missigned "E"); 2p.l., 22, [2]p.

1–2Wing A2984.

Advt. in *TC*, II, 403 "for H[ugh]. N[ewman]."

A satire on "Mr. Sh[ales]", the minister Sheild[s] alias Shales arrested Mar. 15 *LBR*, II, 386, 389; III, 20).

AU, C (with signature on F1 corrected by stamping), EN, *L*, O; *CtY*, DFo, IU, *MH*.

28. [——] The last search after claret   *London, for E. Hawkins, 1691* [Apr. 9 (Luttrell)]. 4°: [A]–D²; 2p.l., 11p.

1–2 Wing A2985.
    Signed: Satyrical Dick [pseud.].
    Dedicated to "the most ingenuous author of the Search after wit."
    Facsim. of the Huth copy repr. in *The search after claret* (1912: 50 copies) with an introduction by A. S. Simon.
    2CBEL records two 1691 editions or issues, apparently in error: all copies agree in the following test readings: p.l.2ᵛ, line 8 "accquainting"; p. 4, line 12 "tA old"; p. 8, line 2 "estem'd"; p. 9 — no catchword.

DT, *HUTH*ˣ, *L* (Luttrell copy: 164.m.5), *LUG*ˣ; *CtY* (–D2), ICU (c), *MH*.

29. [——] Lawyerus bootatus & spurratus: or, The long vacation. *London, for E. Richardson, 1691* [Nov. *(TC)*]. 4°: A–F²; 2p.l., 20p.

1–2 Wing A2986.
    "By a student of Lincoln's Inn"; dedication signed "P.Q." The records of Lincoln's Inn & the other Inns of Court do not mention Ames.

C, EN, *L*, LL, O; *CtY*, *MH*, PU-L, TxU; NZTu.

30. [——] [dh] A letter from Leghorn, March the twenty foureh [!], 169$\frac{0}{1}$. *London, for L. C. 1691.* 4°: A²; 4p.

1–2 Wing M95A.
    Signed "W.M."; continuation promised, but if published, not identified.
    Title and satiric allegory derive from *A letter from Leghorn* and its congeners "from aboard the Van-Herring," 1679–81.

*CSmH*ˣ.

31. [——] The pleasures of love and marriage. *London, for H[ugh]. N[ewman]., to be sold by R. Baldwin, 1691* [Apr. 2 (Luttrell)]. 4°:

[A]², B–D⁴, E² (E2 advt., D1 missigned "E"); 2p.l., 18(i.e. 26)p., 1l. (p. 26 misn. "18").

1–2Wing A2987 [misn. "2887" in *2Wing*].
Signed: Astrophel [pseud.]

DT, EN, *L* (Luttrell copy: 161.l.7), O; DFo, *MH*; NZTu.

32. [——] The present state of England. A vision. *London, for Randal Taylor, 1692* [Mar. 15 *(AM)*]. 4°: [A]², B–D⁴, E² ([A]1 blk.?); 1p.l., 28p.

1Wing P3262.
Also wrongly ascribed to Samuel Grascome.

C(−[A]1), E, EN, DT, *L*(−[A]1)+; CSmH, *CtY* (−[A]1), DFo, ICN, NN.

33. [——] The rake: or, The libertine's religion   *London, for R. Taylor, 1693* [Feb. *(TC)*]. 4°: A², B–C⁴, D–E²; 2p.l., 24p.

1–2Wing A2988.

C, GK, *L*, O; *CSmH*ˣ, *CtY*, ICN, *MH*, TxU+.

34. [——] The search after claret. *London, for E. Hawkins, 1691* [Feb. 24 (Luttrell)]. 4°: A–F²; 2p.l., 18p., 1l.

1–2Wing A2989.
Advt. in *TC*, II, 381 "for E. Richardson."

DT, *L* (Luttrell copy: 164.m.4), *LUG*ˣ, O; *CtY*, ICU (c), *MH*, TxU.

35. [——] ——. 2d ed. *London, for E. Hawkins, 1691*. 4°: A–F²; 2p.l., 18p., 1l.

1–2Wing A2990.
Sigs. E–F are reimposed from the 1st edition.
Facsim. of the Huth copy repr. in *The search after claret* (1912: 50 copies) with an introduction by A. S. Simon.

BQ, *HUTH*ˣ, LG; CSmH, *MH*.

36. [——] A second catalogue of ladies to be sold by auction. [Numb. ii . . . [London, July 6, 1691] bds.

Not in *Wing* (excluded as a numbered serial).
  To begin "the 6th. of this instant July."

Press variant in lot 16, "Herodin"/ "Heroine": *MR(c)*ˣ (cropped) /
*PL*ˣ.

37. [——] The siege and surrender of Mons. *London, for Richard
Baldwin, 1691* [Apr. 23]. 4°: [B]², C⁴, (c)², D–E⁴; 2p.l., 28p.

1–2Wing A2992.
  "Licensed, April 23. 1691"; a drama, apparently never staged.

EN, *L* (2), LG, OW; CSmH, *CtY*, DFo, ICU, *MB*+.

38. [——] Sylvia's complaint . . . Being the second part of Sylvia's
revenge. *London printed, and sold by Richard Baldwin, 1692* [June
13 (Luttrell)]. 4°: [A]², B–D⁴; 2p.l., 24p.

2Wing A2992A (S6333).
  Also wrongly attr. to Gould: cf. E. H. Sloane, *Robert Gould* (1940),
p. 126. Not listed in no. 22 or no. 2.
  "The emulation. A pindarique ode": pp. 21–24.

EN, *L* (Luttrell copy: 164.l.52), O; *CSmH*ˣ, MH.

39. [——] ——. 2d ed. *London, for Robert Battersby, 1697.*

2Wing A2992B (S6334).
  A reissue of no. 38, with cancel t.-p. ([A]1).

O.

40. [——] ——. 3d ed. *London, for Robert Battersby, 1698.* 4°: [A]²,
B–D⁴; 2p.l., 24p.

2Wing A2992C (S6334A).

CSmH, *ICN*ˣ.

41. [——] Sylvia's revenge. *London, printed by Joseph Streater, to be
sold by John Southby and most other booksellers, 1688* [May 22
(SR)]. 4°: [A]–D⁴ ([A]1 vert. title, "A satyr"; D4 advts.); 4p.l., 22p.,
1l.

2Wing A2992D (S6335).

"The epistle dedicatory" is signed "M.P.", supposed to be a woman; sometimes wrongly identified as Matthew Prior. Also wrongly attr. to Gould; cf. E. H. Sloane, *Robert Gould* (1940), p. 125.

Ent. to Joseph Streater in *SR*, May 22, 1688, where it is attr. to Ames; not listed in no. 2 or 22. *Macdonald*, p. 250 says the Luttrell copy is dated May 29.

A reply to Robert Gould's *Love given o'er*.

HC, II, 715, records D4 blank, probably a ghost of an imperfect copy.

EN, *L*, O, OC; DFo, CLU-C, *CtY*, MH (–[A]1), ICN+.

42. [——] ——. *London, for Samuel Clement, 1692.* 4°: [A]–C⁴, D² ([A]1 vert. title, "A satyr"); 4p.l., 19p. (p. 17 misn. "71").

2Wing A2992E (S6336).

L (–[A]1,2); CSmH^x, *CtY*, MH.

43. [——] ——. 2d ed. *London, for Robert Battersby, 1697.*

2Wing A2992F (S6337).
   A reissue of no. 42, with cancel t.-p. ([A]2).

O.

44. [——] ——. 3d ed. *London, for Robert Battersby, 1699.*

2Wing A2992G.
   A reissue of no. 42, with cancel t.-p.

A^x.

45. [——] ——. 11th ed., corr. *London, for Susanna Battersby, 1707* [Nov. 9, 1706 *(PB)*]. 4°: [A]–F² (F2^v advts.); 2p.l., 19, [1]p.

Foxon A183.

DLC, ICN^x.

46. [——] ——. 12th ed. *London, for Susanna Battersby, 1720.* 4°: [A]–F² (F2^v advt.); 2p.l., 19, [1]p.

Foxon A184.

L.

47. [Gould, Robert, 1660?–1709] Love given over . . . with Sylvia's revenge [by R. Ames]. *London, printed and sold by H. Hills, 1709.* 8°: A⁸, B⁴; 24p.
Foxon G230.

> The t.-p. is found in two states: as above (Bodleian G. Pamph. 1283 (5)), or with reading "with the Sylvia's" (Bodleian G. Pamph. 1283 (5*)). These are not distinguished in locations below.

O (2), LVF; CLU-C, DFo, IU, *MB*+.

48. [——] ——. *London, printed and sold by H. Hills, 1710.* 8°: A⁸, B⁴; 24p.
Foxon G231.

> Also issued by T. Warner with other remainders of Hills's stock in *A collection of the best English poetry*, 2 v. (1717). The make-up of this collection varies from copy to copy: cf. W. J. Cameron in *N & Q*, 203 (1958), 300–303.

L; CLU-C, *MB*, *MH*+.

Section 2.
Imitations, satires, replies, false or dubious attributions to Ames.

49. [——] Abstersae lacrymae. The poet buffoon'd *London printed, and sold by Randal Taylor, 1694* [Nov. *(TC)*]. 4°: B–D²; 1p.l., 10p. (pp. [1–2] misn. "7–8").

> *1–2Wing* A113.
> A reply to "a late doggrel satyr, against the famous lottery in Freemans-yard" (i.e., no. 56).
> Advt. *TC*, II, 525 'for H. Newman'.

C, EN, L, O; CtY, *MH*.

50. [——] An account of the auction concerning the ladys [Numb. 1 . . . [London, July 4, 1691 *(AM)*]. 1°: A¹; 2p.

> *2Wing* A237A (to be deleted as a numbered serial).
> A probably spurious continuation of no. 5.

*MR(c)*ˣ; *PPL*ˣ.

51. [———] By consent. Charecters of some young women belonging to the Changes, who are to be disposed of by way of auction. [London, July 14,? 1691) bds.

> 2 *Wing* B6349B (with misreading "Characters").
> To begin "July 41 [i.e. 14]".
> An imitation of no. 5.

ICN^x (Luttrell copy, dated July 16, 1691).

52. [———] A catalogue of batchelors . . . being Chapmen for the ladys [London, July 6, 1691 (Luttrell)] bds.

> 2 *Wing* C1279.
> A companion piece to nos. 5 & 59, which it paraphrases; doubtfully Ames's.

ICN^x.

53. [———] A catalogue of Jacobites [London] *for the booksellers of London and Westminster.* [June? 1692] 1°: [2]p.

> Not in *Wing (C1339A).*
> Refers to the battle of La Hogue & to "the late Jacobite humiliation conventicle" (cf. no. 27).
> An imitation of no. 5, included in the list of pieces in no. 23; possibly by Ames.

L (Harl. 5947, f. 164); *InU*^x

54. [———] [dh] A catalogue of ladies and other women [Numb. 2 . . . [London, Aug. 10, 1691]. 4°: π²; 4p.

> 1 *Wing* C1340 (deleted in 2 *Wing* as a numbered serial).
> To begin Aug. 10, 1691.
> An imitation of no. 5: the first number in this series has not been identified; a continuation for Sep. 5 is promised, but if published, has not been found.

L (Harl. 5947, f. 169), MR(c).

55. [———] A catalogue of the bowes, of the town [London, July 10, 1691 (Luttrell)] bds.

2*Wing* C1368A.
   To begin "the 14 of this instant July."

*ICN*ˣ.

56. [——] Diluvium lachrymarum. A review of the fortunate & unfortunate adventurers. *London printed, to be sold by Randal Taylor, 1694. 4°:* [A]–C²; 12p.

1–2Wing D1492.
   A satire on Thomas Neale's "Million" lottery of 1693, possibly inspired by no. 5; included in the list of pieces in no. 23, but it is too late to be by Ames.

DT, L; CSmH, CtY, DFo, *MH*, NjP.

57. [Gould, Robert, 1660?–1709] A satyrical epistle to the female author of a poem, call'd Silvia's revenge *London, for R. Bentley, 1691. 4°:* A–F²; 24p.

1–2Wing G1436.
   Also wrongly attr. to Ames in *Stonehill;* repr. in Gould's *Works* (1709) under title: The poetess.

L; *CSmH*ˣ, CtY, ICU, *MH*.

58. [——] The lost maiden=head, or, Silvia's farewell to love. A new satyr against man. *London, for H. Smith, 1691* [May *(TC)*]. 4°: A–F²; 2p.l., 19p.

1–2Wing L3081.
   A companion piece to no. 63.

O; *CLU-C*ˣ.

59. [——] Mercurius matrimonialis: or, Chapmen for the ladies [London, July 4, 1691 (Luttrell)] bds.

1–2Wing M1766A.
   A companion piece to no. 5 & 52; possibly by Ames.
   Repr. in *Ashton*, pp. 157–158.

L (Harl. 5947, f. 167), *MR (c)*ˣ; ICN (Luttrell copy), *MH*, *PPL*ˣ.

60. [——] An out-cry of poets; or, A catalogue of wits to be sold *London, for J. Harlow, 1691* [Aug. 4?] bds.

   1–2 Wing O596.
   To begin "next Tuesday"; refers to the *Athenian mercury* of July 26.

   MR (c), O; *MH*.

61. [——] [dh] The poet's new auction for city=ladies: or, Characters in effigies. *London, 1703.* 4°: π²; 4p.

   L (Harl. 5947, f. 171).

62. [——] [dh] A proposal of the poets to raise Their Majesties a sum of money. *London, for the assigns of Mr Jordan and Tubman* [pseuds.] *deceased* [1692?]. 4°: A²; 4p.

   1 Wing P3709.
   For a Glory office, an Epithalamium office, & an Elegy office, ironically ascribed (p. 4) to the "City poet" (i.e. Elkanah Settle). Also reissued as pt. 4 of *A collection of the several late petitions* (1693), in which pts. 1 & 5 are by Thomas Brown (cf. *The sessions of the poets* (1696)); probably by Brown, perhaps assisted by Ames.
   Refers to the war; Saffold's death.

   L (Harl. 5947, f. 173); CtY, IU, *MH*.

63. [——] The restor'd maiden=head. A new satyr against woman *Dondon* [!], *for H. Smith, 1691.* 4°: A–F²; 2p.l., 19p.

   1 Wing R1177.
   A companion piece to no. 58.

   CSmHˣ, CtY, IU, *MH*, TxU.

64. [——] [dh] A search after knavery, or, A visitation of the bakers. *London, for T. Pinch-gut in Thieving-lane* [pseud.], *1693* [Dec. 15 (Luttrell)]. 4°: π²; 4p. 1 illus.

   Not in *Wing (S2202A).*

   LVFˣ.

65. [——] A search after wit; or, A visitation of the authors. *London, for E. Hawkins, 1691* (Apr. 2 (Luttrell)). 4°: [A]–F²; 2p.l., 19p.

1–2Wing A2991.

    Attr. to Ames in *1–2CBEL* & *1–2Wing*; "presumeably *not* by Ames" (*Macdonald* 267); not listed in no. 2 or 22.

    A reply to no. 34; Ames replies in no. 28.

C, L (2 incl. Luttrell (annotated): 161.m.3), O; CtY, DFo, *MH*.

66. Vincent, Nathaniel, 1639?–1697. An elegy upon the death of that holy, reverend, and learned minister of Christ, Mʳ Richard Baxter. *London, for Thomas Parkhurst, 1691* [Dec.]. bds.

1Wing V406A.

    Title attr. to Ames in *1CBEL*; no anon. elegy on Baxter with this title found.

MH

The Transatlantic Printing History of Joseph Priestley's *Discourses Relating to the Evidences of Revealed Religion*, 1794–99

JOHN LANCASTER

T HE THREE VOLUMES of Priestley's *Discourses* have a complex printing and publishing history, which is reflected in the variety of issues and editions, not fully recorded in Crook's bibliography[1] or elsewhere. Not all of the details of that history are yet clear; even after the many remaining unseen widely scattered copies are examined, questions will probably remain unanswered.

But the direct comparison of a number of sets and single volumes side by side in the extensive Priestley collections at Harvard, Yale, the Library Company of Philadelphia, the British Library, Dr. Williams's Library, London, and the John Rylands Library, Manchester, as well as a number of individual copies elsewhere, enables the outlines of the work's history to be drawn with some certainty, and many of the details to be suggested with a degree of probability. The remaining questions can also be formulated more precisely.[2]

The work consists of a total of 32 discourses, of which the first 12 were delivered in Hackney in 1793–94, before Priestley's departure for the United States. The remainder were delivered in Philadelphia in 1796–97.

[1] Ronald E. Crook, *A Bibliography of Joseph Priestley 1733–1804* (London: The Library Association, 1966). Since Crook seldom examined more than one copy (usually one in Birmingham), it is not surprising that his listing contains major flaws.

[2] The research on which this note is based was begun in the course of cataloguing the extensive Priestley holdings of the Houghton Library, and continued during a number of trips made primarily on other business for the Amherst College Library. I am particularly grateful to Miss Marjorie Wynne and Mr. Ferenc Gyorgy at Yale, and to Mr. Hugh Amory at Harvard, for enabling me to examine in one place the copies scattered among several libraries at those institutions.

VOLUME 1 The Hackney talks were published in 1794 by Joseph Johnson in London (and reprinted the following year in Boston by William Spotswood) with the slightly variant title *Discourses on the Evidence of Revealed Religion,* and with no indication that the volume was to be considered the first of a set. The London edition was later reissued by Johnson with a cancel title-leaf identifying it as volume 1 of the set and changing the title to agree with that of the two later volumes. The cancel retained the 1794 imprint date, but was printed later, probably in 1799.

VOLUME 2 The first group of Philadelphia discourses, 13 in number, was delivered in 1796, and published there that year. The edition was divided between John Thompson, the printer, and Thomas Dobson. This volume was also reprinted for Johnson; the reprint edition, like the first, had originally no indication on the title-page that it was to be considered a second volume to the 1794 work. Later, probably in 1799, the reprint was furnished with a cancel title-leaf identifying it as volume 2 of the set. Sheets of the American edition still in Johnson's stock were apparently (only one copy encountered) also furnished with the cancel title-leaf.

Volume 2 is further complicated in that there are two different settings of about half the sheets of the American edition. The occurrence of any given setting of a sheet does not correlate with issue under Dobson's or Thompson's imprint; neither is it found exclusively with any one setting of any other sheet. No clue has yet been found to the reason for the resetting.

VOLUME 3 This volume contains the talks given in Philadelphia in 1797, and was published there in that year, this time printed by Dobson and issued only under his imprint. The American sheets were reissued by Johnson in London; he again reprinted the work as well. The title-pages for both the reissue and the new edition identify them as volume 3 and bear the date 1799. The cancel title-leaf is conjugate with a new contents leaf, as found in the new edition; clearly, an overrun of the title and contents of the reprint edition was printed and used to reissue the American sheets.

LONDON PUBLICATION The picture that emerges is one of Johnson, having published the first set of discourses, importing the American editions of the second and third, and reprinting when stock ran low. Then, probably in 1799,[3] when reprinting the third group, he treated the three volumes as a unit, furnishing the remaining copies of all volumes with cancel titles (the three title-pages that designate the volumes as a set are nearly identical in spacing, rules, and type-faces).

THE DISNEY COPY This picture is complicated by the existence of a set at the Houghton Library, Harvard,[4] which belonged to John Disney and contains evidence that is apparently self-contradictory. The set is uniformly bound, with Disney's monogram in gilt on the front covers, and his device on the rear covers.

The first volume is of the London edition and has the cancel title-leaf designating it "Vol. I."; that leaf is watermarked "98" (presumably indicating year of manufacture; many of the sheets of the London reprint edition of volume 3 are similarly watermarked). Disney's note on the front pastedown, however, reads: "April 8.th 1794. / [JD monogram] / from the author."

The second volume is of the reprint edition, with the cancel title-leaf identifying it as "Vol. II." It bears two notes by Disney: on the front paste-down, "Oct.[r] 18. 1796. [JD monogram]"; and on the recto of the first front free endpaper, "The American Edition, wth the English Title page." The spine is stamped "*1796 / AMERICA*" in one panel.

The third volume is of the American edition, with the London cancel title identifying it as "Vol. III." Disney's note on the front paste-down reads: "August 16. 1797 [JD monogram]". A spine panel reads, however, "*1799 / AMERICA*". The cancel title-leaf is immediately followed by the conjugate cancel contents leaf; the original contents leaf is present, bound following the preface.

The discrepancies between Disney's manuscript dates and the inferred title-page date in volume 1 and the printed title-page date in volume 3 can easily enough be explained by postulating either the insertion of the cancel titles at a later date or Disney's transcribing his dates (of publication?) into the volumes after binding. The latter suggestion is supported by the agreement of title-page date and spine date in vol. 3 as well as by the physical evidence (edge staining).

[3] Notices of the American editions of vol. 2 appear in the *Critical Review* for Jan. 1797 (XIX:47) and of vol. 3 in the issue for Oct. 1798 (XXIV:196–7); the second notice makes no mention of the Johnson three-volume set.

[4] Vol. 1: *EC75.P9338.794da; Vol. 2: *EC75.P9338.796dba; Vol. 3: *EC75.P9338.797da.

The Disney copy of volume 2 provides evidence indicating that the American sheets were reissued (as well as merely available for sale) in London. It is not of the American edition, and so could not have come to Disney direct from America; therefore he must have acquired it in London under the impression that he was receiving the American sheets. The copy does, however, also contain one contradiction for which no satisfactory explanation has been found: Disney must have received his copy with the cancel title; otherwise he would have known from the imprint that he did not have the American edition. But then how explain that date he notes on the paste-down, since the cancel title for volume 2 was certainly not printed so long before the cancel titles for volumes 1 and 3?

VOLUME I

1.1.a.   *First (London) edition, first issue. 1794.*

Discourses on the evidence of revealed religion. By Joseph Priestley . . .
London: Printed for J. Johnson, no. 72, St. Paul's church-yard. 1794.
    8°. A–Dd⁸ Ee² [Ff]⁴; xvi, 420, [8] p. $1–4 (except A1, Ee2) signed; A3 missigned A2.

Press figures:

A4ᵛ: 7	G8ᵛ: 8	L1ᵛ: 1	Q5ʳ: 1	U8ʳ: 1	Bb5ᵛ: 3
B5ʳ: 7	H8ʳ: 3	L2ᵛ: 8	Q7ᵛ: 5	X5ᵛ: 5	Bb7ʳ: 8
C7ᵛ: 3	H8ᵛ: 7	M2ᵛ: 1	R1ᵛ: 4	Y3ᵛ: 8	Cc2ʳ: 1
D7ʳ: 8	I5ʳ: 5	N8ᵛ: 1	R2ᵛ: 1	Z2ᵛ: 1	Cc5ʳ: 3
E7ʳ: 6	I5ᵛ: 7	O1ᵛ: 1	S5ʳ: 1	Z5ᵛ: 8	Dd8ʳ: 8
F8ᵛ: 1	K1ᵛ: 5	P7ʳ: 3	S7ᵛ: 4	Aa6ʳ: 3	Ee2ʳ: 5
G5ᵛ: 5	K5ʳ: 8	P8ʳ: 1	T8ʳ: 5	Aa6ᵛ: 8	

Contents: [i] t.–p. [ii] blank [iii]iv–vi Dedication, dated "Clapton, March 1794", to Rev. Thomas Belsham [vii]viii–xiii Preface [xiv] blank [xv]xvi Contents [1] 2–386 text, Discourses I–XII [387]388–411[412]413–420 Appendices I–IV [421–428] Catalogue of books by Priestley printed for Johnson [The catalogue is lacking in some copies.] Errata slip in some copies, ca. 7 × 7.5 cm., usually trimmed to ca. 4 × 5 cm. and mounted on p. xiii, xvi, or [421].

Copies seen: CtY (2), CtY–M, MH, PPL, PU; British Library, Dr. Williams's Library (2), John Rylands Library (3).

1.1.b. *First (London) edition, second issue.* 1794 [i.e. 1799?].

Discourses relating to the evidences of revealed religion. Vol. 1. Delivered at Hackney in 1793, 1794, by Joseph Priestley . . . London: Printed for J. Johnson, in St. Paul's church yard. 1794.
8°. A–Dd⁸ Ee² (±A1); xvi, 420 p.

Signing, press figures, contents (except for catalogue), and errata as in 1.1.a.

Copies seen: CtY–M, MH; British Library, Dr. Williams's Library.

1.2. *Second (Boston) edition.* 1795.

Discourses on the evidence of revealed religion. By Joseph Priestley . . . The second edition.
Boston: Printed and sold by William Spotswood, no. 55 Marlborough-Street. 1795.
12°. A–U–V–W–Y⁶; xii, 275, [1] p. $1–3 (except A1–2) signed.

Contents: [i] t.–p. [ii] blank [iii]iv–vi Dedication [vii]viii–xii Preface [1]2–275 text, Discourses I–XII [276] Contents
Evans 29353.
Note: omits the Appendices of the first edition, as well as the long quotation from Deuteronomy following Discourse VI.

Copies seen: CtY, CtY–M, MH, MH–AH.

VOLUME II

II.1.a1. *First (Philadelphia) edition, Dobson issue.* 1796.

Discourses relating to the evidences of revealed religion, delivered in the church of the Universalists, at Philadelphia, 1796. And published at the request of many of the hearers. By Joseph Priestley . . .
Philadelphia, Printed for T. Dobson, by John Thompson. 1796.
Copy right secured according to law.

8°. a⁸ b² [c]₁ B–K⁴ L–Ii⁸ [Kk]⁴ (±H3); xx, [2], 426 (i.e.
424), [8] p. $1–2 (except b, C–K: $1 only; a: $2 only) signed;
nos. 377–378 omitted in paging.

Contents: [i] t.–p. [ii] blank [iii]iv–vii Dedication to John Adams, dated
"Philadelphia, May, 1796" [viii] blank [ix]x–xx Preface [xxi] Contents
[xxii] Errata [1]2–376, 379–426 text, Discourses I–XIII (p. [26] blank;
first page of each discourse unnumbered, i.e. [27, 56, 86, 114, 146,
176, 201, 237, 269, 313, 356, 395]) [427–434] Advertisements for
Priestley's works
Evans 31050 (apparently a ghost; cf. Short-title Evans) may be an
erroneous entry for this issue.

Note: Gatherings B–K, O, T–U, Cc–Hh, and [Kk] are of the same
setting in all copies seen; gatherings a–b, [c]₁, and Ii exhibit changes
in setting (possibly indicating reimposition), but evidence of spacing
and broken types show them to be of the same setting in all copies
seen; gatherings L–N, P–S, and X–Bb are found in two settings. Points
of distinction are designated A and B in the list below for convenience
of reference; no priority is implied, nor is there any correlation between
sheets.

Ref.	*Point*	*Setting A*	*Setting B*
a2ʳ	"2" of signature mark	as tall as "a"	taller than "a"
b1ʳ	Last line begins	not copy	copy
[c]1ᵛ	Errata contain	13 items	21 items
L3ᵛ	First para., last line	'time.'	"ly long time."
M7ʳ	Last word & catchword	go-vernment	govern-ment
N3ᵛ	Last line begins	ly	pily
P3ᵛ	Font of quotation in ¶ 2	italic	roman
Q1ᵛ–2ʳ	Font of quotation	italic	roman
R2ʳ	Para. 2, last line	Christians.	tians.
S1ʳ	Para. 1, last line	*them all.*	*all.*
X2ᵛ	Last line	kind.	[ends] mankind.
Y5ʳ	Last line begins	Jarius,	Jairus,
Z1ᵛ	Last line	*eyes.*	*our eyes.*
Aa8ʳ	Line 5 ends	dif-	differ-
Bb4ᵛ	Para. 1, last line begins	reverse	customs

Copies seen: CtY, CtY–D, MA (2), MH, MH–AH, PHi, PP, PU.

II.1.a2. *First (Philadelphia) edition, Thompson issue.* 1796.

Discourses relating to the evidences of revealed religion, delivered in the church of the Universalists, at Philadelphia, 1796. And published at the request of many of the hearers. By Joseph Priestley . . .
Philadelphia, Printed by John Thompson. MDCCXCVI.

Collation, signing, and contents as in II.1.a.

Copies seen: CtY–M, MH, MH–AH, PPL (2).

II.1.b. *First (Philadelphia) edition, Johnson (London) reissue.* 1796 [i.e. 1799?]

Discourses relating to the evidences of revealed religion. Vol. II. Being the first delivered at Philadelphia in 1796, by Joseph Priestley . . .
Philadelphia printed. London: Reprinted for J. Johnson, in St. Paul's church-yard. 1796.
    8°. a^8 b^2 [c]1 B–K^4 L–Ii^8 (±a1, H3); xx, [2], 426 (i.e. 424) p.

Signing and contents (except for catalogue) same as in II.1.a1/a2.
Note: the title-page is of the same setting as II.2.b.

Copy seen: Dr. Williams's Library.

II.2.a. *Second (London) edition, first issue.* 1796.

Discourses relating to the evidences of revealed religion: delivered in Philadelphia, 1796; and published at the request of many of the hearers. By Joseph Priestley . . .
Philadelphia, printed. London: Re-printed for J. Johnson, in St. Paul's church yard. 1796.
    8°. a^4 A–Aa^8 Bb^4; xxii, [2], 375, [1] p. $1–4 (except a1, 3–4 and Bb3–4) signed.

Press figures:

a3^v: 1	D7^v: 8	H1^v: 7	M7^v: 8	Q7^v: 8	X2^v: 7
A2^v: 6	E2^v: 8	H8^v: 8	N2^v: 6	R4^v: 8	Y1^v: 8
B3^v: 8	F2^v: 8	I2^v: 8	O5^r: 8	S6^v: 8	Z8^r: 7
B6^v: 6	F6^r: 7	K7^r: 8	P7^v: 8	T2^v: 8	Aa7^r: 1
C8^v: 8	G7^r: 8	L8^r: 7	P8^v: 7	U3^v: 7	

Contents: [i] t.–p. [ii] blank [iii]iv–viii Dedication [ix]x–xxii Preface [xxiii] Contents [xxiv] blank [1]2–375 text, Discourses I–XIII [376] blank

Note: in some copies, A2 is a cancel (with no press figure); the cancel changes a direct attribution to Volney of the denial of Christ's existence (p. xii) into an inference.

Copies seen: CtY, MH–AH; British Library, Dr. Williams's Library (2), John Rylands Library, Warrington Public Library.

II.2.b. *Second (London) edition, second issue.* 1796 [i.e. 1799?]

Title as in II.1.b.

8°. a⁴ A–Aa⁸ Bb⁴ (±a1); xxii, [2], 375, [1] p.

Signing, press figures, and contents as in II.2.a.

Copies seen: CtY–M, MH; British Library, Birmingham Public Library.

VOLUME III

III.1.a. *First (Philadelphia) edition, first (Philadelphia) issue.* 1797.

Discourses relating to the evidences of revealed religion, delivered in Philadelphia. By Joseph Priestley . . . Vol. II. . . .
Philadelphia, Printed by Thomas Dobson, at the Stone-house n° 41, South-Second street. 1797.

8°. [a]² b⁴ B–Zz⁴ 3A–3O⁴ 3P²; xi, [1], 474, [2] p. $1–2 (except 3P2) signed; $1 has "VOL. II." flush left on signature line.

Press figures:

b1^v: 1	M4^v: 2	Y4^v: 1	Ii4^v: 4	Tt4^v: 1	3G4^v: 2
B4^v: 4	N4^v: 1	Z4^v: 1	Kk4^v: 2	Uu4^v: 1	3H4^v: 4
C4^v: 2	O4^v: 1	Aa4^v: 1	Ll4^v: 1	Xx4^v: 2	3I4^v: 1
D4^v: 1	P4^v: 1	Bb4^v: 1	Mm4^v: 4	Yy4^v: 4	3K4^v: 2
E4^v: 1	Q4^v: 4	Cc4^v: 4	Nn4^v: 1	3A4^v: 1	3L4^v: 1
F4^v: 1	R4^v: 1	Dd4^v: 1	Oo4^v: 1	3B4^v: 2	3M4^v: 1
G3^v: 4	S4^v: 2	Ee4^v: 4	Pp4^v: 1	3C4^v: 4	3N4^v: 2
H4^v: 4	T4^v: 4	Ff4^v: 1	Qq3^v: 2	3D4^v: 4	3O4^v: 4
I4^v: 4	U4^v: 4	Gg4^v: 1	Rr4^v: 2	3E4^v: 4	3P2^v: 1
K4^v: 4	X4^v: 1	Hh4^v: 1	Ss3^v: 1	3F4^v: 2	

Contents: [i] t.–p. [ii] blank [iii] Contents [iv] blank [v]vi–xi Preface, dated "Philadelphia, March 28, 1797" [xii] blank [1]2–468 text, Discourses I–VII (p. [242] blank; first page of each discourse or part unnumbered i.e. [25, 42, 136, 189, 243, 381, 420]) [469]470[471] 472–474 Appendices I–II [475–476] Catalogue of books sold by Dobson An errata slip is inserted or mounted in various places in some copies. Evans 32715.

Copies seen: CtY–M, MA, MH, MH–AH (3), PHi, PP, PPL, PU; British Library, Dr. Williams's Library, John Rylands Library, Warrington Public Library.

III.1.b. *First (Philadelphia) edition, second (London) issue.* 1799.

Discourses relating to the evidences of revealed religion. Vol. III. Being the second delivered at Philadelphia in 1797, by Joseph Priestley . . .
Philadelphia printed. London: Reprinted for J. Johnson, in St. Paul's church-yard. 1799.

Collation, signing, press figures, and contents as in III.1.a., but [a]² is a cancel gathering, identical with A1.6 of III.2. [a]2ᵛ/A6ᵛ is numbered "xii" and is found both preceding b1 and following b4 in this issue. 3P2 (Catalogue) lacking in one copy (cancelled?).

Copies seen: MH; Dr. Williams's Library.

III.2. *Second (London) edition.* 1799.

Title as III.1.b.
    8°. A⁶ B–Hh⁸; xii, 479, [1] p. $1–4 (except A1, 4) signed; $1 has "VOL. III." flush left on signature line (except U1, erroneously, "VOL. II.").

Press figures:

A2ᵛ: 1	F8ʳ: 8	N6ʳ: 3	S5ᵛ: 4	Bb1ᵛ: 6	Ff8ʳ: 3
B5ʳ: 8	G8ᵛ: 6	N8ᵛ: 8	T4ᵛ: 4	Cc6ʳ: 4	Gg2ᵛ: 6
B5ᵛ: 5	H7ᵛ: 4	O3ᵛ: 1	U6ʳ: 4	Dd1ᵛ: 7	Gg5ᵛ: 3
C3ᵛ: 7	I8ʳ: 5	P8ᵛ: 7	X7ᵛ: 4	Dd2ᵛ: 4	Hh5ᵛ: 6
D5ᵛ: 3	K6ᵛ: 8	Q6ʳ: 1	Y8ᵛ: 3	Ee3ᵛ: 6	
D8ᵛ: 5	L6ʳ: 4	R5ᵛ: 1	Z3ᵛ: 1	Ee5ʳ: 4	
E5ʳ: 1	M8ʳ: 5	S4ᵛ: 1	Aa8ᵛ: 4	Ff6ᵛ: 8	

Contents: [i] t.–p. [ii] blank [iii] iv–x Preface [xi] xii Contents [1] 2–469 text, Discourses I–VII (p. [242] blank) [470] blank 471–479 Appendices I–II [480] Errata

Copies seen: CtY–M; British Library, Birmingham Public Library, Dr. Williams's Library.

United States
Dramatic Copyrights, 1790–1830:
A Provisional Catalogue

ROGER E. STODDARD

Plays are often an unwonted burden to the scholar. It is not so much the classics of Shakespeare or Molière, attractive for generations to antiquarian booksellers, collectors, bibliographers, and editors, but plays in general, the national drama, the international literature of the playhouse, that defy easy manipulation. Whether Viennese or American, French or German, how very difficult it can be to identify and locate the play one needs to annotate a text or to complete a study of a theme, an author, or a theatre. Once found, how difficult it can be to date the printing, to say nothing of attempting to repeat the process by identifying and locating the source of that text in the literature of another country. One's path through the maze of theatrical pamphlet ephemera is often blocked by nonce collections or play series, those persistent and international sales devices of play publishers. Sometimes manuscript plays can be associated with particular actors or performances, but their authors may be irretrievable. Most plays are lost forever, never published, manuscripts gone.

Such hazards may dishearten a scholar, but they may be embraced as challenges by the librarian who knows that his special skills as collector and recorder can enrich the common sources of research, library collections and bibliography. No wonder that more than one member of the Houghton Library staff is a collector and bibliographer of plays or that Houghton collections, historically strong in Anglo-American dramatic literature, are expanding into Austria, Germany, France, Italy, Portugal, and Spain.

Certain collections may be growing, but dramatic bibliography remains so primitive that any list of plays is eagerly seized upon by scholars and bibliographers desperate for facts or even clues. Hoping that even this miserable collection of fragments may provide a lead or solve a puzzle, one librarian offers it to another as a slight but positive contribution to a subject of their mutual interest.

No play was printed in British North America until 1765, when Henry Miller of Philadelphia published by subscription *Juvenile Poems on Various Subjects. With The Prince of Parthia, a Tragedy. By the Late Mr. Thomas Godfrey, Junr. of Philadelphia.* By the end of the century over one hundred different publishers in twenty-one cities in ten states had published 255 editions of plays, most of them British and 190 of them published in the 1790s. The growing popularity of the professional stage opened up the market for printed plays and offered native authors a new and expanding field for their talent. When Congress passed a federal copyright act on May 31, 1790, native playwrights as well as composers and text-book makers were ready to avail themselves of that new protection for the fruits of their intellectual labor.

Any citizen or resident of the United States (as author) or his executor, administrator, or assign (as proprietor) could copyright a text, establishing his sole right to print and sell it for fourteen years, renewable for a second term, if he met three requirements. First, he must deposit a printed copy of the title-page in the clerk's office of the Federal court in the district where he lived. The clerk was required to enter all titles in a special register. There was a charge of sixty cents for each entry and for each copy under seal of the entry that the clerk supplied. Second, within two months the author or proprietor must publish the entry "for the space of four weeks" in a newspaper printed in the United States. Third, within six months of publication he must send a copy of the book to the Secretary of State, "to be preserved in his office." Not until 1803, by passage of a supplementary act on April 29, 1802 was he required to insert in his published book the copyright entry "at full length in the title-page or in the page immediately following." All these requirements remained in effect until 1831 when the duration of copyright and the handling of deposit copies were altered.

The effect of the legislation was to disperse not only the registration procedure but even the records, part of which were preserved in the Department of State, part in the Federal District courts, and part in the Patent Office, from which the majority have been transferred to the Rare Book Division at the Library of Congress. The surviving early records, then, are not uniform, some are misplaced, and some are lost. Never can there be a definitive list of early United States copyrights or early dramatic copyrights, because the records are defective. For that reason, the following list is drawn from entries in the surviving registers and supplemented from notices in printed plays. Several of the printed notices cannot be substantiated in the registers. Printers were not reliable reporters of copyright information, as the list amply demonstrates. It is quite possible that many a copyright notice, printed in a book with the best of intentions, was never formalized in the clerk's office of the local District court, thereby risking the $100 forfeit that could result from claiming a copyright not legally held.

Decentralization of courts, including licensing and registration, of theatres and performance, and of writing, including playwriting, is to be expected in the United States. It is not surprising to find that the statistics reflect the early activity of the Boston, New York City, Philadelphia, and Charleston theatres:

State (District)	Number of Copyrights
Connecticut	2
District of Columbia	2
Kentucky	1
Maine	1
Massachusetts	24
New York	61
North Carolina	2
Pennsylvania	28
South Carolina	16
Vermont	1
Virginia	6
Total	144

The practice of printing copyright notices in books, required by statute in 1803, was not uniformly applied for several years, as the list demonstrates. Some books both before and after 1803 were printed without their copyright notices, and as late as 1819 some books carried general statements, such as "Copy right secured," instead of the full entry required by law. Only eight plays out of the 125 that were printed — nineteen of the plays entered were not printed immediately — were deposited with the Secretary of State as required by law. Only a dozen out of some two hundred volumes of native verse copyrighted before 1821 were deposited, so it is possible that when the early copyrights are canvassed in detail, it will be found that the deposit requirement was generally disregarded in America, just as it was in England.

Few American plays were reprinted in this early period, and there is no evidence that any dramatic copyrights were renewed. The only copyright to be infringed was Erastus Brown's, for his verse drama, *The Trial of Cain the First Murderer, in Poetry, by Rule of Court, in which a Predestinarian, a Universalian, and an Arminian Argue as Attorneys at the Bar*. Printed for the author at Stockbridge in 1815 and 1823, it was pirated at Auburn, N.Y., in 1817, at Bridgeport, Conn., in 1819, at Woodstock, Vt., in 1823, at Haverhill, N.H., in 1824, at Boston in 1827, and at Taunton, Ma., in 1828. It circulated not as a stage play for production, however, but as a sectarian tract in colportage.

A puzzling aspect of early American copyright practice is the entering by American proprietors of works written by British playwrights. There was no reason for an American to acquire publication rights from a foreign author, since the absence of reciprocal agreements left all foreign works freely available to American publishers without authorization or royalty. Performance rights could not have been involved because they were not recognized in America until 1855. A few examples will suffice to show the persistence of this extra-legal application of the copyright law.

As early as Mar. 12, 1796, John Williamson, manager of the Federal Street Theatre in Boston, entered as proprietor but never published "Oscar & Malvina or The Hall of Fingal," a ballet pantomime from Ossian that had been performed at Covent Garden in 1791. Perhaps Williamson believed (erroneously) that he was laying claim to the performance rights in the United States. The New York printer Frederick Turner, perhaps believing it to be American, entered and published without the author's name Frederick Reynolds's "Out of Place; or, The Lake of Lausanne" (Mar. 28, 1808); David Longworth of New York knew better when he entered "The Forty Thieves . . . By R. B. Sheridan & Colman the Younger" on Dec. 15, 1808 and Reynolds's "The Bridal Ring" on Nov. 5, 1812, publishing both; perhaps Mathew Carey of Philadelphia mistook Charles Lamb's "Mr. H. or Beware a Bad Name" as an American play when he entered and published it without Lamb's name (May 6, 1813); and at the height of American enthusiasm for Charles Mathews, the New York publisher Edward Murden entered "Mathews at Home" on Dec. 19, 1822 and "A Christmas at Brighton" on the following day. The bibliography of English plays in the eighteenth and nineteenth centuries, already complicated by unauthorized American editions, will be confused by flawed American copyrights when the registers are published and indexed.

The following provisional list of American copyrights of American plays is a mere first essay that will be improved and extended when lost copyright registers are found, when duplicate registers are collated, when copyright notices are located in newspapers, and when copyright certificates are discovered. Inspired by one bibliographer, may it encourage yet another.

EXPLANATION OF THE CATALOGUE

This list of native plays combines entries from surviving copyright registers and copyright notices in printed plays. Copyrights are grouped by state and arranged chronologically. Titles of printed plays are transcribed from them. Printers and publishers are omitted from the imprints unless they help to explain the registrant's connection with the book. Titles of unpublished plays are quoted from the copyrights. Contents notes list plays that are not named in the titles of the volumes in which they were printed. The first line of copyright data relates to the printed text: perhaps no copy can be located, or it contains no copyright notice. Copyright notices printed in the plays are quoted if they are non-specific, e.g. "Copy-right secured according to law." Specific copyright notices are expressed by formula: year, month, day, registrant, and status (with "au." for author, and "prop." for proprietor). The second line relates to the copyright entry: perhaps no entry can be located, or the records may be lost. Otherwise the entry is provided in formula unless it confirms the printed notice in every detail. Receipt dates for deposit copies are taken from the State Department Register, sometimes confirmed by later entry in the Patent Office Register when the deposit copies were transferred. The abbreviation "dt" stands for "deposited title-page." From this early period only the Pennsylvania title-pages survive in representative numbers. Unlike the variant job-printed "dt's" of later years, most are copies of the published title-pages, but a few omit the imprint. Square brackets in original sources are represented by angle brackets in the transcriptions; here square brackets identify material supplied by the compiler.

Without funds granted by the William F. Milton Fellowship Committee and research leave granted by the Harvard College Library this study could not have been undertaken; the compiler remains thankful for their confidence and aid. To his Houghton Library colleague Virginia Leigh Smyers and to his Library of Congress colleague Peter VanWingen he is grateful for help in verifying and checking some of the copyright data.

Connecticut

No Connecticut copyright records before September 10, 1804 have been located; later records are at the Library of Congress.

D. Humphreys, The Yankey in England, a drama, in five acts . . . [New Haven? 1815?].

> No printed copyright notice.
>
> 1815 Sep. 30 no. 246 by Hezekiah Howe (prop.).

Memoir of Jonathan Leavitt, a member of the junior class in Yale College, who died at New-Haven the 10th of May, 1821, aged eighteen years and one month. By a sister . . . (New-Haven, 1822).

> Includes: "The mistaken lover. A dialogue."
>
> 1822 Jan. 31 by Sumner Lincoln (prop.); records confirm, no. 381.

District of Columbia

No District of Columbia copyright records before August 8, 1845 have been located.

'Timothy Taste,' The freaks of Columbia; or, The removal of the seat of government: a farce, accompanied by an interlude, called "The metamorphosis;" to which is added, The new prospect before us . . . (Washington City, 1808).

> "City of Washington, District of Columbia, to wit. Be it known, and remembered, that the editor for the author, hath secured, according to law, the copy right of this work . . . this fourth day of July, 1808. By the editor . . . ."; records lost.
>
> Note: the anomalous copyright statement may be part of the satire, suggesting that the title was never entered.

G. Watterston, The child of feeling. A comedy, in five acts . . . (George Town, by Joseph Milligan, 1809).

> 1809 May 2 by Joseph Milligan (prop.); records lost.

Kentucky

The compiler has relied on the transcript of Kentucky copyright records in J. W. Townsend, ed., *Supplemental Check List of Kentucky Imprints 1788–1820 Including the Initial Printing of the Original Kentucky Copyright Ledger, 1800–1854* (American Imprints Inventory, No. 38, 1942).

"W. G. Dryden, The tragedy of Beauchamp, or The noble heroine in five acts . . . ."
No copy located.
1830 Oct. 30 by William G. Dryden (au. & prop.).

Maine

The Maine copyright records are at the Library of Congress.

N. Deering, Carabasset; a tragedy [three dots] in five acts . . . (Portland, 1830).
1830 Jun. 10 by Nathaniel Deering (au.); records and dt confirm.

Massachusetts

The Massachusetts copyright records are at the Library of Congress.

M. (O.) Warren, Poems, dramatic and miscellaneous (Boston, 1790).
Includes: "The sack of Rome. A tragedy, in five acts" and "The ladies of Castile. A tragedy, In five acts."

No printed copyright notice.
1790 Oct. 23 by Mrs. M. Warren (au.).

J. D. Burk, Bunker-Hill; or The death of General Warren: an historic tragedy. In five acts (New-York, 1797).
"Copy right secured according to law."
1796 Nov. 21 by John Burk (au.).

[Mrs. Sarah Marriott], "The land we live in; or Death of Major Andre."
No copy located.
1797 Jan. 30 by Francis Marriott (prop.).

"W. H. Brown, West Point preserved or The treason of Arnold. An historical tragedy in five acts."
No copy located.
1797 Mar. 10 by Margaret Brown (prop.).

W. C. White, Orlando: or Parental persecution, a tragedy . . . (Boston, 1797).
> No printed copyright notice.
>
> 1797 Mar. 18 by William Charles White (au.).

C. Prentiss, A collection of fugitive essays, in prose and verse . . . (Leominster, 1797).
> Includes: "Haven, or The merited gallows. In three acts."
>
> "Published according to act of Congress."
>
> 1797 Jul. 22 by Charles Prentiss (au.).

C. Stearns, Dramatic dialogues for the use of schools . . . (Leominster, 1798).
> "Published according to act of Congress."
>
> 1797 Nov. 11 by Charles Stearns (au.).

[J. (S.) Murray], The gleaner. A miscellaneous production . . . By Constantia (Boston, Feb. 1798). 3v.
> Includes: "Virtue triumphant" and "The traveller returned."
>
> "Published according to act of Congress."
>
> 1798 Mar. 22 by Judith Sargent Murray (au.).

"Peter Oliver, The adopted son. A comedy in five acts."
> No copy located.
>
> 1798 May 21 by Peter Oliver (au.).

T. P. Lathy, Reparation; or, The school for libertines. A dramatic piece in three acts . . . (Boston, 1800).
> No printed copyright notice.
>
> 1800 Jul. 22 by Thomas Pike Lathy (au.).

J. Croswell, A new world planted; or, The adventures of the forefathers of New-England; who landed in Plymouth, December 22, 1620. An historical drama — in five acts . . . (Boston, 1802).
> No printed copyright notice.
>
> 1803 Jun. 9 by Joseph Croswell (au.).

"M. C. Groves, The feast of the pilgrims; or The imigration [!] to Boston. A play, in five acts."
> No copy located.
>
> 1805 Sep. 5 by Matthew C. Groves (au.).

J. D. Turnbull, Rudolph, or The robbers of Calabria; a melo drame, in three acts . . . (Boston, 1807).
> "Copy right secured according to law."

1807 Apr. 20 by John D. Turnbull (au.).

J. D. Turnbull, The wood daemon, or, The clock has struck! A grand, romantic, cabalistic, melo drama, in three acts . . . (Boston, 1808).
1808 Mar. 31 by John D. Turnbull (au.); records confirm.

W. C. White, The clergyman's daughter; a tragedy, in five acts . . . (Boston, 1810).
1809 Oct. 5 by William Charles White (au.).
1810 Oct. 4 by William Charles White (au.).

W. C. White, The poor lodger; a comedy, in five acts . . . (Boston, 1811).
1810 Jan. 12 by William Charles White (au.).
1811 Feb. 16 by William C. White (au.).

J. Ellison, The American captive, or Siege of Tripoli. A drama in five acts . . . (Boston, 1812).
1811 Dec. 10 by James Ellison (au.).
1811 Dec. 19 by James Ellison (au.).

A. Eustaphiève, Reflections . . . To which is added a tragedy in five acts, entitled Alexis, the Czarevitz (Boston, 1812).
1811 Dec. 26 by Alexis Eustaphieve (au.); records confirm.

E. Brown, The trial of Cain, the first murderer, in poetry, by rule of court . . . (Stockbridge, 1815).
1815 Dec. 22 by Erastus Brown (au.); records confirm.

J. Neal, Otho: a tragedy, in five acts . . . (Boston, by West, Richardson and Lord, 1819).
1819 Nov. 13 by West, Richardson & Lord (prop.); records confirm.

The night-watch; or, Pirate's den: a melo-drama, in two acts[.] By a gentleman of Boston . . . (Boston, 1820).
"(Copyright secured.)"; no entry found.

[L. M. F. Child], Evenings in New England. Intended for juvenile amusement and instruction. By an American lady . . . (Boston, by Cummings, Hilliard & Co., 1824).
Includes: "General Lee. A drama" and "The triumphal arch. A drama."
1824 Dec. 10 by Cummings, Hilliard & Co. (prop.); records confirm.

Wilhelmina: a legendary, dramatic tale (Boston, by Cummings, Hilliard, and Company, 1826).
1826 May 29 by Cummings, Hilliard & Co. (prop.); records confirm.

[H. J. Finn et al.], Whimwhams, by four of us (Boston, by S. G. Goodrich, 1828).

Includes: "The woolen nightcap! or The mysterious flour sack!!"
1827 Dec. 19 by S. G. Goodrich (prop.); records confirm.

New York

The New York copyright records are at the Library of Congress.

D. Humphreys, The miscellaneous works (New-York, Hodge, Allen, and Campbell, 1790).
> Includes: "The widow of Malabar; or, The tyranny of custom. A tragedy. Imitated from the French of Le Mierre."
>
> "With copy-right according to law."
>
> 1792 Jan. 10 by Robert Hodge, Thomas Allen, and Samuel Campbell (prop.).

M. V. (B.) Faugeres, Belisarius: a tragedy . . . (New-York, 1795).
> No printed copyright notice.
>
> 1795 Jun. 26 by Peter V. Faugeres (prop.).

W. Dunlap, The archers, or Mountaineers of Switzerland; an opera, in three acts . . . (New-York, 1796).
> "⟨Copy right secured.⟩"
>
> 1796 Apr. 12 by William Dunlap (au.).

W. Milns, Songs, &c. in The comet: or He would be a philosopher. A comedy in five acts . . . The music by J. Hewitt (New-York, 1797).
> "(Copy-right secured according to act of Congress.)"
>
> 1797 Jan. 30 by William Milns (au.).

E. H. Smith, Edwin and Angelina; or The banditti. An opera, in three acts (New-York, 1797).
> "Copy-right secured according to law."
>
> 1797 Feb. 24 by Elihu Hubbard Smith (au.).
>
> 1797 May 23 deposit copy received per State Dept. Reg.
>
> No entry found in Patent Off. Reg.

J. Torrey, Superstition on his last legs, a poetical tragicomedy . . . in three scenes . . . (America, 1797).
> "Printed for the author, who has secured the coppy [!] right agreeably to act of Congress."
>
> Perhaps Torrey was relying on his author's entry, 7 Jul. 1796, for "Scriptural and alegorical [!] poems on the downfall of superstition," an unlocated book that may never have been printed.

W. Dunlap, Andre; a tragedy, in five acts . . . (New-York, 1798).
> "Copy right secured."
> 1798 Apr. 6 by William Dunlap (au.).

W. Milns, All in a bustle: or The new house. A comic prelude written for the opening of the new theatre in New-York . . . (New-York, 1798).
> "⟨Copy-right secured.)"; no entry found.

W. Dunlap, The German theatre.
> Three numbers, translations from Kotzebue, were published (New-York, 1800): The wild-goose chace, The virgin of the sun, and Pizarro in Peru.
>
> No printed copyright notice.
> 1800 Mar. 17 by William Dunlap (translator and author).

J. Minshull, A comic opera, entitled Rural felicity . . . (New-York, 1801).
> "Copy-right secured according to law."
> 1801 Apr. 29 by John Minshull (au.).

Select translations and imitations from the French of Marmontel and Gresset. By an officer of the army; who fought for America, under Gen. Wolfe, at the taking of Quebec . . . (New-York, 1801).
> Includes: "Sidney; or The self-murderer reclaimed: a tragi-comedy. From the French of Gresset."
>
> "Copy-right secured."; no entry found.

W. Winstanley, The hypocrite unmasked: a comedy, in five acts . . . (New-York, 1801).
> "Copy-right secured according to law."; no entry found.

W. Dunlap, Abaellino, the great bandit. Translated from the German, and adapted to the New-York Theatre . . . (New=York, by D. Longworth, 1802).
> "Copy-right secured."
> 1802 Nov. 4 by David Longworth (prop.).

W. Dunlap, Ribbemont, or The feudal baron, a tragedy in five acts . . . (New-York, by D. Longworth, 1803).
> "Copy-right secured."
> 1803 Mar. 17 by David Longworth (prop.).

J. Minshull, A comedy, entitled The sprightly widow, with The frolics of youth; or A speedy way of uniting the sexes, by honorable marriage . . . (New-York, 1803).
> "Copy-right secured according to law."
> 1803 Mar. 26 by John Minshull (au.).

C. Smith, The beautiful unknown, a dramatic history. Translated from the German of Augustus von Kotzebue (New York, by Burnton and Darling, 1803).
>No printed copyright notice.
>1803 Nov. 28 by Thomas H. Burnton and William Darling (prop.).

[L. C. Caigniez], The voice of nature, a drama in three acts. Translated and altered from a French melo-drame, called, The judgment of Solomon. By William Dunlap . . . (New=York, 1803).
>"Copy-right secured."; no entry found.

J. Minshull, He stoops to conquer, or The virgin wife triumphant; a comedy in three acts . . . (New-York, 1804).
>"Copy right secured according to law."
>1804 Oct. 25 by John Minshull (au.).

W. Dunlap, The wife of two husbands. A drama, in five acts . . . (New-York, 1804).
>"(Copy right secured.)"; no entry found.

J. Minshull, The merry dames, or The humourist's triumph over the poet in petticoats, and the gallant exploits of the knight of the comb. A comedy in three acts . . . (New-York, 1804).
>"(Copy-right secured.)"
>1805 Aug. 22 by John Minshull (au.).

[J. H. Payne], Julia, or The wanderer; a comedy, in five acts. As performed at the New-York Theatre. From the prompt-book — by permission (New-York, by D. Longworth, 1806).
>1806 Mar. 13 by David Longworth (prop.); records confirm.

W. Dunlap, The dramatic works . . . In ten volumes. Vol. I. The father of an only child. Leicester. Fontainville Abbey. Darby's return. (Philadelphia, 1806).
>1806 Jul. 7 by William Dunlap (au.); records confirm.

The Mercuriad, or Spanish practice of physic. A tragi-comedy, in five acts, in prose: being a burlesque on the excessive use, and an exposition of the malignant effects of mercury . . . By a friend to mankind . . . (Lansingburgh, 1807).
>"(Copy-right secured according to law.)"
>1807 Jun. 4 by David F Launy (prop.).

L. Beach, Jonathan Postfree, or The honest Yankee. A musical farce, in three acts . . . (New-York, by David Longworth, 1807).
>1806 Dec. 23 by David Longworth (prop.).

1807 Dec. 24 by David Longworth (prop.).

The juvenile theatre: containing the best dramatic productions of the celebrated Madam [!] de Genlis. Translated from the French by a friend to youth . . . (New-York, 1807).

"Copy-right secured."; no entry found.

C. Breck, The trust. A comedy. In five acts . . . (New-York, by D. Longworth, 1808).

1808 Jan. 5 by David Longworth (prop.); records confirm.

C. Breck, The fox chase. A comedy. In five acts . . . (New-York, by D. Longworth, 1808).

1808 Jan. 23 by David Longworth (prop.); records confirm.

A. B. Lindsley, Love and friendship; or, Yankee notions: a comedy, in three acts . . . (New-York, by D. Longworth, 1809).

No printed copyright notice.

1808 Apr. 15 by William Turner (prop.).

I. Cody, A tragedy, founded on the history of Joseph and his brethren, as recorded in sacred scripture. In five acts . . . (Schenectady, 1808).

"Published according to act of Congress."

1808 Sep. 27 by Isaac Cody (au.).

J. C. F. v. Schiller, The robbers: a tragedy, in five acts . . . A new edition, revised and corrected from the various translations (New-York, by David Longworth, 1808).

"Compiled from the various translations of Monk Lewis, &c. by a gentleman of New-York," according to Longworth's 1808, 1816 & 1818 catalogues.

1808 Nov. 18 by David Longworth (prop.); records confirm.

M. M. Noah, The fortress of Sorrento: a petit historical drama, in two acts (New-York, by D. Longworth, 1808).

1808 Dec. 4 by David Longworth (prop.).

1808 Dec. 5 by David Longworth (prop.).

W. Dunlap, The Italian father: a comedy, in five acts . . . (New-York, by D. Longworth, May — 1810).

1810 Apr. 30 by David Longworth (prop.); records confirm.

[C. N. Baldwin], Rinaldo Rinaldini; or, The great banditti [!]. A tragedy, in five acts. By an American, and a citizen of New-York (New-York, 1810).

"Copy right secured, according to law."

1810 Jun. 13 by Charles N. Baldwin (au.).

W. Dunlap, Yankee chronology; or, Huzza for the constitution! A musical interlude, in one act. To which are added, the patriotic songs of The freedom of the seas, and Yankee tars . . . (New-York, by D. Longworth, Dec. — 1812).

>1812 Dec. 9 by D. Longworth (prop.); records confirm.

[J. N. Barker], How to try a lover. A comedy. In three acts . . . (New-York, by David Longworth, 1817).

>1817 Feb. 11 by David Longworth (prop.); no entry found.

"J. D. Turnbull, Waldemar or The German exiles. A melo drama. In two acts . . . As performed with unbounded applause at the new theatre, in Montreal, Lower Canada several nights in November 1818. New scenery by Mr Milbourne [or Melbourne]. Music by P. Smith Esq."

>No copy located.
>1819 Feb. 26 So. Dis. by David Longworth (prop.).

[Mr. Mead], Wall-Street; or, Ten minutes before three; a farce, in three acts . . . (New-York, 1819).

>"Copy-right secured according to law."
>1819 Apr. 7 So. Dis. by William Holmes (prop.).

[V. Taylor], Things as they will be; or, All barkers are not biters. A farce, in three acts . . . By Who d'ye think? (New-York, 1819).

>1818 Jul. 12 So. Dis. by Vermilye Taylor (prop.).
>1819 Jul. 12 So. Dis. by Vermilye Taylor (prop.).

J. A. Hillhouse, Percy's masque, a drama, in five acts . . . (New-York, by C. S. Van Winkle, 1820).

>1820 Jun. 7 So. Dis. by C. S. Van Winkle (prop.).
>1820 Jun. 3 So. Dis. by C. S. Van Winkle (prop.).

Mary of Scotland, or The heir of Avenel. A drama, in three acts. Founded on the popular novel of "The abbot," . . . (New=York, by Henry I. Megarey, 1821).

>1821 May 23 So. Dis. by Henry I. Megarey (prop.); records confirm.

S. B. H. Judah, Odofriede; the outcast; a dramatic poem . . . (New-York, by Wiley and Halsted, 1822).

>1821 Dec. 20 So. Dis. by Samuel B. H. Judah (au.); records confirm.
>1822 Jun. 15 deposit copy received per State Dept. Reg.; no entry found in Patent Off. Reg.

[C. S. Talbot], Paddy's trip to America: or, The husband with three wives. A farce, in two acts (New=York, March, 1822).

1822 Mar. 11 So. Dis. by Charles Talbot (prop.); no entry found.

S. Woodworth, The deed of gift. A comic opera, in three acts . . . (New-York, by C. N. Baldwin, 1822).

    1822 Mar. 19 So. Dis. by Charles N. Baldwin (prop.); records confirm.

S. B. H. Judah, The rose of Arragon; or, The vigil of St. Mark: a melo=drama, in two acts . . . (New-York, by S. King, 1822).

    1822 May 7 So. Dis. by Solomon King (prop.).

    1822 May 9 So. Dis. by Solomon King (prop.).

S. B. H. Judah, A tale of Lexington: a national comedy, founded on the opening of the revolution. In three acts . . . (New York, by H. Sage's Book and Music Store, 1823).

    1823 Apr. 7 So. Dis. by George E. Sage (prop.).

    1823 Apr. 6 So. Dis. by George E. Sage (prop.).

S. Woodworth, La Fayette, or The castle of Olmutz. A drama, in three acts . . . (New-York, 1824).

    1824 Jul. 17 So. Dis. by Samuel Woodworth (au.); records confirm.

M. Hawkins, The saw-mill: or A Yankee trick. A comic opera, in two acts . . . (New-York, 1824).

    1824 Dec. 16 So. Dis. by Micah Hawkins (au.); no entry found.

J. A. Hillhouse, Hadad, a dramatic poem . . . (New-York, f. E. Bliss & E. White, 1825).

    1825 Mar. 17 So. Dis. by E. Bliss & E. White (prop.); records confirm.

    1825 Apr. 25 deposit copy received per State Dept. Reg.

S. Woodworth, The widow's son, or, Which is the traitor. A melo-drama, in three acts . . . (New-York, 1825).

    1825 Mar. 29 So. Dis. by Samuel Woodworth (au.); no entry found.

S. Woodworth, The forest rose, or American farmers. A pastoral opera, in two acts . . . Music, by John Davies, Esq. (New-York, 1825).

    1825 Sep. 24 So. Dis. by Samuel Woodworth (prop.).

    1825 Oct. 3 So. Dis. by Samuel Woodworth (au.).

J. H. Payne, Richelieu: a domestic tragedy, founded on fact. ⟨Accepted for performance at the Theatre Royal, Covent Garden, London; before it was altered by order of the Lord Chamberlain, and produced under a new name.⟩ In five acts . . . Now first printed from the author's manuscript (New-York, 1826).

    1826 May 27 So. Dis. by C. S. Van Winkle (prop.); records confirm.

E. de Jouy, Sylla, a tragedy, in five acts . . . Translated from the French, by a citizen of New-York (New York, by Clayton & Van Norden, 1826).
> Note: translation in prose.
> 1826 Aug. 31 So. Dis. by Clayton and Van Norden (prop.); records confirm.

E. de Jouy, Sylla, a tragedy. In five acts . . . Translated from the French, and adapted for representation at the Chatham Theatre, by a citizen of New-York (New-York, by E. M. Murden, 1827).
> Note: translation in verse.
> 1827 Jan. 15 So. Dis. by C. S. Van Winkle (prop.); records confirm.
> 1827 Jan. 30 deposit copy received per State Dept. Reg.
> The deposit copy at the Library of Congress, the only identifiable deposit copy of a dramatic work to survive from this period, is stitched, unbound, and docketed: "Recd 30 Jan: 1827."
> 1827 deposit copy received per Patent Off. Reg.

C. S. Talbot, Captain Morgan, or The conspiracy unveiled. A farce in two acts . . . (Rochester, 1827).
> 1827 Mar. 16 No. Dis. by C. S. Talbot (prop.).
> 1827 Mar. 16 No. Dis. by Edwin Scrantom [!] per records, Scranton per dt.

"L. V. Ferry, Charlotte Temple, or, Love, vice and treachery. The incidents selected from the novel of that name, by Mrs. Rowson, and other information obtained in New York, from persons acquainted with the facts. Originally written by L. V. Ferry, Esq. Revised, with additions, by J. D. Turnbull, artist of the Chatham Theatre . . . ."
> No copy located.
> 1828 Jan. 3 So. Dis. by L. V. Ferry (au.).

"A. C. G. de Pixerecourt, Charles the Bold: or The dirge of Nancy. A historic melo-drama, in three acts, and in prose. Intended for grand theatric representation. Translated from the French by a young gentleman of this city . . . The music composed by Mr. Alexandre, and the decorations arranged by Messrs. Allaux . . . ."
> No copy located.
> 1828 Mar. 21 So. Dis. by Francis Ferry Junior (prop.).

"The buried alive, or, Put to the test. A comedy in three acts."
> No copy located.
> 1828 Aug. 27 So. Dis. by William Foster (prop.).

"The inquisition or The Jew in Spain — a melo-drama in two acts — ."
> No copy located.

1828 Aug. 27 So. Dis. by William Foster (prop.).

"J. H. Hackett, Jonathan in England. A comedy in five acts. As altered from Colman Jr's comedy of Who wants a Guinea?"
> Not published until 1860 or 1861 (Spencer's Boston Theatre, 200).
> 1829 Jul. 17 So. Dis. by James H. Hackett (au.).

[L. L. Daponte], "Almachilde: or The Lombards, a tragedy in five acts . . . ."
> No copy located.
> 1829 Sep. 7 So. Dis. by George L. Hannuken [?] (prop.).

[J. H. Kennicott], Irma; or, The prediction. A tragedy. In five acts . . . (New=York, by E. B. Clayton, 1830).
> 1830 Oct. 20 So. Dis. by E. B. Clayton (prop.); no entry found.

North Carolina

The North Carolina copyright records, described as being at the National Archives and beginning March 4, 1796, cannot be located.

E. Hall, Nolens volens, or The biter bit. A comedy in five acts . . . (Newbern, 1809).
> "Copy right secured."; records not located.

J. H. Jung-Stilling, Scenes in the world of spirits . . . Translated from the third original edition . . . (New-Market [Va., 1815?]).
> 1815 Jan. 13 by Gottlieb Shober ("proprietor and author in the English language"); records not located.

Pennsylvania

The Pennsylvania copyright records are at the Library of Congress.

[R. Tyler], The contrast, a comedy; in five acts: written by a citizen of the United States . . . (Philadelphia, 1790).
> "Published (under an assignment of the copy-right) by Thomas Wignell."
> 1790 Jun. 15 no. 2 by Thomas Wignell (prop.) per records; sig. [A], including title-page, docketed: "the property of Thomas Wignell. Entered 15th June, '90."

S. (H.) Rowson, Slaves in Algiers; or, A struggle for freedom: a play, interspersed with songs, in three acts . . . (Philadelphia, 1794).
> "Copy-right secured according to law."
> 1794 Dec. 23 no. 80 by Susannah Rowson (au.) per records and dt.

[J. Murdock], The triumphs of love; or, Happy reconciliation. A comedy. In four acts. Written by an American, and a citizen of Philadelphia . . . (Philadelphia, September 10, 1795).

> "Registered agreeable to law."
> 1795 Sep. 19 no. 111 by John Murdock (au.) per records and dt.

'A. Barton,' The disappointment, or, The force of credulity. A new comic-opera. In three acts . . . Second edition, revised and corrected, with large additions by the author . . . (Philadelphia, f. and s. by Francis Shallus, 1796).

> "Copy right secured according to act of Congress."
> 1796 May 23 no. 137 by Francis Shallus (prop.) per records and dt.

J. N. Barker, The Indian princess; or, La belle sauvage. An operatic melo-drame. In three acts . . . (Philadelphia, by T. & G. Palmer, f. G. E. Blake, 1808).

> 1808 May 30 by George E. Blake (prop.); records and dt confirm, no. 214.
> 1808 Jun. 25 no. 222 by George E. Blake (prop.) per records, adding: "The music by John Bray."

J. N. Barker, Tears and smiles. A comedy. In five acts . . . (Philadelphia, by T. & G. Palmer, f. G. E. Blake, 1808).

> 1808 Jun. 13 by George E. Blake (prop.).
> 1808 Jun. 14 no. 220 by George E. Blake (prop.) per records and dt.

[J. P. Puglia], "The embargo; a comedy in three acts. Written by me, author of &c. &c. &c. &c. &c."

> No printed copy located; MS. at Harvard.
> 1808 Oct. 27 no. 243 by James Ph. Puglia (prop.) per records and dt.

[J. P. Puglia], "The double disappointment; or, A touch at modern times. A comedy in three acts. Written by me, author of &c. &c. &c. &c. &c."

> No printed copy located; MS. at Harvard ("The complete disappointment [etc.]").
> 1808 Oct. 27 no. 244 by James Ph. Puglia (prop.) per records and dt.

[J. Hutton], The orphan of Prague. A new drama. In five acts . . . (Philadelphia, 1808).

> No printed copyright notice.
> 1808 Nov. 7 no. 247 by Nathaniel Hutton Junior (prop.) per records and dt.

M. J. O'Conway, The knights templars, a historical tragedy . . . Translated from the original of M. Raynouard . . . (Philadelphia, 1809).

> 1809 Feb. 16 by Matthias James O'Conway (prop.).

1809 Jan. 6 no. 260 by Matthias James O'Conway (prop.) per records and dt.

Records and dt confirm printed notice, no. 268, adding to the original entry "To which is prefixed an interesting history . . . of that illustrious order."

J. Hutton, The school for prodigals: a comedy. In five acts . . . (Philadelphia, 1809).

"Entered according to law."

1809 Mar. 8 no. 273 by Joseph Hutton (au.) per records and dt.

J. Bray, The tooth-ache; or, Mistakes of a morning. A petite comedy, in one act. A free translation from the French . . . (Philadelphia, by M. Carey, April, 1814).

1814 Apr. 1 by Mathew Carey (prop.); no entry found.

[J. N. Barker], "A new historical melo-drama, in two acts, called The armorer's escape, or, Three years at Nootka Sound. Founded on the interesting narrative of John R. Jewitt . . . ."

No copy located.

1817 Mar. 21 no. 864 by John R. Jewitt (au.) per records and dt.

F. (W.) d'Arusmont, Altorf, a tragedy . . . (Philadelphia, by M. Carey & Son, 1819).

1819 May 20 E. Dis. by Mathew Carey and Son (prop.); records and dt confirm, no. 1086.

The magician, and "the holy alliance," or "the spirit of the book." A melo drama, a hundred acts in one . . . Translated from the original Greek ms. of Reynaldo de Moscheto . . . By Tobias S. Alltruth . . . [Philadelphia? 1820?].

No printed copyright notice.

1820 Nov. 21 E. Dis. no. 1187 by David Hanna (prop.) per records and dt.

M. C. Clarke, The benevolent lawyers, or, Villainy detected. A comedy, in five acts . . . (Philadelphia, 1823).

1823 Feb. 20 E. Dis. by Mary Clarke (au.); records and dt confirm, no. 1375.

"F. Megia, Riego, or, Spain enslaved. A tragedy, in five acts . . . Translated from the Spanish, by Chauncey Bulkley, Esq. . . . ."

No copy located.

1824 Jun. 16 E. Dis. no. 1480 by Felix Megia (au.) per records and dt.

The witch of New England; a romance (Philadelphia, by H. C. Carey & I. Lea, 1824).

Includes: "The lover. A dramatic fragment."

1824 Jul. 26 E. Dis. by H. C. Carey & I. Lea (prop.); records and dt confirm, no. 1491.

W. Lee, La Fayette; or, The fortress of Olmutz. A melo drama. In three acts. Founded on events in the life of General La Fayette . . . (Philadelphia, by Thomas Town [etc.], 1824).

1823 Sep. 1 by Thomas Town (prop.); no entry found.

F. Megia, Pizarro, ó los Peruanos. Tragedia en 5 actos . . . (Filadelfia, 1824).

1824 Dec. 29 E. Dis. by Felix Megia (au.); records and dt confirm, no. 1536.

F. Megia, Lafayette en Monte Vernon, en 17 de Octubre 1824. Drama en 2 actos . . . (Filadelfia, 1825).

1825 Jan. 18 E. Dis. by Felix Megia (au.); records and dt confirm, no. 1540.

F. Megia, Lafayette in Mount Vernon. A drama in two acts . . . Translated from the Spanish for the author by Chauncey Bulkley, Esq. . . . (Philadelphia, 1825).

1825 Jan. 18 E. Dis. by Felix Megia (au.); no entry found for this translation; apparently Megia relied on the copyright of the Spanish original.

F. Megia, Eliezer y Nephtaly, poema en quatro cantos . . . puesto en verso espagnol por Felix Megia . . . (Filadelfia, 1826).

Includes: "Guillermo Tell, ó La Suiza libre. Tragedia en 5 actos . . . ."

1826 Mar. 9 E. Dis. by Felix Megia (au.); records and dt confirm, no. 1643.

Lopez and Wemyss' edition. The acting American Theatre . . . (Philadelphia, 1826–27).

A play series in 16 numbers, including two plays by the American author J. N. Barker: no. 3, The tragedy of superstition, 1826, and no. 5, Marmion, 1826.

1826 Apr. 3 E. Dis. by Matthias Lopez and Francis C. Wemyss (prop.); records and dt confirm, no. 1650.

1826 Jun. 22 deposit copies of nos. 1–3 received per State Dept. Reg.

1826 Nov. 4 deposit copies of nos. 4–7 received per State Dept. Reg.

n. d. deposit copy of J. N. Barker's Marmion [no. 5] received per Patent Off. Reg.

Note: no. 1, Wild oats by the English playwright John O'Keeffe was entered separately on 1 Mar. 1826 no. 1641 by Matthias Lopez and Francis C. Wemyss (prop.) per records and dt.

[J. A. Stone], Tancred; or The siege of Antioch. A drama, in three acts . . . (Philadelphia, f. prop., 1827).
>   1827 Apr. 20 E. Dis. by John P. Milnor (prop.); records and dt confirm, no. 1782.
>   1827 Apr. 28 deposit copy received per State Dept. Reg.

J. McHenry, The usurper, an historical tragedy, in five acts . . . (Philadelphia, 1829).
>   1829 Mar. 24 E. Dis. by Neal & Mackenzie (prop.); records and dt confirm, no. 2019.

G. W. Featherstonaugh, The death of Ugolino. A tragedy . . . (Philadelphia, by Carey and Lea, 1830).
>   1830 May 7 E. Dis. by Carey and Lea (prop.); records confirm, no. 2179.

D. P. Brown, Sertorius: or, The Roman patriot. A tragedy . . . (Philadelphia, by E. L. Carey & A. Hart, 1830).
>   1830 Aug. 31 E. Dis. by David Paul Brown (au.); records and dt confirm, no. 2244.
>   *Note:* another issue (Mifflin & Parry, 1830) bears no copyright notice.

South Carolina

The early South Carolina copyright records are at the University of South Carolina, Columbia, S. C. The compiler has relied on the transcript provided in W. S. Kable, "South Carolina District Copyrights: 1794–1820," *Proof*, 1 (1971), 180–98, and on a report of the later records by Mrs. Eleanor M. Richardson.

J. Beete, The man of the times: or, A scarcity of cash. A farce . . . (Charleston, 1797).
>   "⟨Copy-right secured according to law.⟩"
>   1797 May 6 by John Beete (au.), no. 8.

J. B. Williamson, Preservation; or, The hovel of the rocks: a play, in five acts: interspersed with part of Lillo's drama, in three acts, called "Fatal curiosity." . . . (Charleston, 1800).
>   "⟨Copy-right secured according to law.⟩"
>   1800 Mar. 25 by John B. Williamson (au.), no. 13.

J. Workman, Liberty in Louisiana; a comedy . . . The second edition, with additions and corrections (Charleston, 1804).

1804 Apr. 2 by James Workman (au.); records confirm without specifying registrant's status, no. 19.

Flareau, The ocean spectre, an entire new grand melo drame: in five acts . . . Translated from the French . . . [Charleston? 1804?].
"Copy right secured according to law."
1804 Apr. 12 by David Cromwell, no. 20.

W. Ioor, Independence; or Which do you like best, the peer, or the farmer? A comedy, in five acts (founded on the novel of "The independent,") . . . (Charleston, 1803).
"Copy-right secured according to law."
1805 Apr. 25 by William Ioor, no. 25.

J. B. White, Foscari, or, The Venetian exile; a tragedy, in five acts . . . (Charleston, 1806).
"⟨Entered according to act of Congress.⟩"
1806 Feb. 19 by John B. White, no. 29.

J. B. White, The mysteries of the castle, or The victim of revenge. A drama, in five acts . . . (Charleston, 1807).
"⟨Entered, according to act of Congress.⟩"
1807 Mar. 17 by John B. White, no. 32.

W. Ioor, The battle of the Eutaw Springs, and evacuation of Charleston, or The glorious 14th of December, 1782. A national drama, in five acts . . . (Charleston, 1807).
"⟨Entered according to act of Congress.⟩"; no entry found.

[Sarah (Pogson) Smith], The female enthusiast: a tragedy, in five acts. By a lady (Charleston, by J. Hoff, 1807).
"Entered according to act of Congress."
1807 Jul. 28 by John Hoff (prop.), no. 33.

J. B. White, Modern honor: a tragedy, in five acts . . . (Charleston, 1812).
"⟨Entered according to act of Congress.⟩"
1812 Apr. 16 by John B. White (au.), no. 57.

E. C. Holland, The corsair. A melo-drama, in four acts. Collected and arranged for the stage from Lord Byron's poem . . . (Charleston, 1818).
"⟨Copy-right secured.⟩"
1818 Jan. 16 by Edwin C. Holland (au. and prop.), no. 92.

[Sarah (Pogson) Smith], Essays, religious, moral, dramatic & poetical . . . By a lady (Charleston, 1818).

Includes: "The young Carolinians; or, Americans in Algiers. A play in five acts," "A tyrant's victims, a tragedy, in five acts," and "The orphans, a play, in five acts."

"Coppy [!] right secured according to law."

1818 Oct. 28 by Miss Pogson (au. and prop.), no. 97.

W. Crafts, The sea serpent; or, Gloucester hoax. A dramatic jeu d'esprit, in three acts . . . (Charleston, by A. E. Miller, 1819).

"Copy-right secured according to law."

1819 Jan. 19 by Archibald E. Miller (prop.), no. 100.

J. B. White, The triumph of liberty, or Louisiana preserved[.] A national drama, in five acts . . . (Charleston, 1819).

"⟨Copy right secured.⟩"

1819 Apr. 3 by John Blake White (prop. and au.), no. 102.

"Henry Goldsmith, Aurilla or A rival's vengeance. (A pathetic melo drama/ in two acts. Interspersed with music, chorusses &c. &c".

No copy located.

1824 May 14 by Henry Goldsmith (prop.), no. 161.

O. Cromwell, The soldier's wreath, or The battle ground of New Orleans, and other poems . . . (Charleston, 1828).

Includes: "Kosciusko, or The fall of Warsaw. A play in verse."

1828 Feb. 13 by Oliver Cromwell (au. and prop.); records confirm, no. 201.

Vermont

The early Vermont copyright records are at the Federal Records Center, Waltham, Massachusetts.

A. Selden, Effusions of the heart, containing a number of original poetical pieces, on various subjects . . . (Bennington, 1820).

Includes: "Naomi, a sacred drama, in five scenes," "Lady Jane Gray and Lord Guilford Dudley. A dramatic poem," and "The Irish exiles in America, a drama in five scenes."

1819 Nov. 20 by Almira Selden (au.); records confirm.

Virginia

A bundle of title-leaves, the only evidence of the registration of early Virginia copyrights, was published by J. H. Whitty, "A Record of Virginia Copyright Entries (1790–1844)," as a supplement to the *Seventh*

Annual Report of the Library Board of the Virginia State Library 1909–1910 (Richmond, 1911), [1]–52.

W. Munford, Poems, and compositions in prose (Richmond, 1798).
  Includes: "Almoran and Hamet, a tragedy founded on an eastern tale . . . ."
  1798 Oct. 29 by William Munford (au.); dt, docketed Oct. 9, 1798, suggests entry.

D. Darling, Beaux without belles, or, Ladies we can do without you. A musical farce . . . (Charlottesville, 1820).
  1820 Sep. 20 by David Darling (au. and prop.); dt, docketed Sep. 20, 1820, suggests entry.

"J. Hutton, The duel, or A week after wedlock. A petit comedy. Drawn from the French of Le Panneau, and adapted to the English stage . . . As cast at the theatre, Petersburg. Petersburg, 1820."
  No copy located.
  1820 Nov. 9 by Thos. P. Camm per dt.

J. Doddridge, Logan. The last of the race of Shikellemus chief of the Cayuga nation. A dramatic piece . . . (Buffaloe Creek: Brooke County, Va., 1823).
  "Copyright secured."; unconfirmed.

[J. C. Price], The ignis fatuus; or, A voice from the clouds . . . Comprising The climax of iniquity, an opera; The Quinciad, and other poems . . . (Richmond, 1827).
  1827 May 31 E. Dis. by James Cave Price (prop.); dt confirms.
  1827 Jul. 2 deposit copy received per State Dept. Reg.

"Nar[ ]-Mattah; or, The Wept of the Wish-Ton-Wish. A tragedy in five acts, by a Virginian. Written from Cooper's celebrated novel of the Wept of the Wish-ton-Wish. Richmond: R. H. Elton(?) publisher, 1830."
  No copy located.
  1830 Oct. 22 by E. H. Elton (?) (prop.) per dt.

Index

ESSAYS
IN HONOR
OF
JAMES
EDWARD
WALSH